D0733447

The Practice of Counselling

The Practice of Counselling in Primary Care

Edited by
Robert Bor and Damian McCann

JURO COLLEGE LIBRARY
Main Campus Midtown

WITHDRAWN

SAGE Publications
London · Thousand Oaks · New Delhi

MT

Editorial Selection and Introduction © Robert Bor and
Damian McCann 1999
Chapter 1 © Carole Trowbridge 1999
Chapter 2 © John Davy 1999
Chapter 3 © Susan Hopkins and Mary O'Callaghan 1999
Chapters 4 and 12 © Gilly Pembroke 1999
Chapter 5 © Teresa Schaefer, Jenny Chesshyre and Susan
Kendal 1999
Chapters 6 and 7 © Carole Waskett 1999
Chapters 8 and 9 © Christine Parrott 1999
Chapter 10 © Sheila Gill 1999
Chapter 11 © Jo Sexton 1999
Chapter 13 © Damian McCann 1999
Chapter 14 © Peter du Plessis and Robert Bor 1999

First published 1999

All rights reserved. No part of this publication may be
reproduced, stored in a retrieval system, transmitted or
utilized in any form or by any means, electronic,
mechanical, photocopying, recording or otherwise, without
permission in writing from the Publishers.

 SAGE Publications Ltd
6 Bonhill Street
London EC2A 4PU

SAGE Publications Inc.
2455 Teller Road
Thousand Oaks, California 91320

SAGE Publications India Pvt Ltd
32, M-Block Market
Greater Kailash - I
New Delhi 110 048

British Library Cataloguing in Publication data

A catalogue record for this book is
available from the British Library

ISBN 0 7619 5879 7
     0 7619 5880 0 (pbk)

Library of Congress catalog record available

Typeset by Type Study, Scarborough, North Yorkshire
Printed in Great Britain by Biddles Ltd, Guildford, Surrey

07- 0'-02

CONTENTS

CONTRIBUTORS

Robert Bor is Professor of Psychology at City University, London. He is a Chartered Clinical, Counselling and Health Psychologist and a UKCP Registered Family Therapist. He received specialist training in family therapy at the Tavistock Clinic, London and is a member of the Tavistock Society of Psychotherapists. He is also a BAC Accredited Counsellor. He works in a GP practice in North London and is extensively involved in counsellor training and research. He has a special interest in working collaboratively with GPs and other health care providers when facing challenging clinical situations. He has published several books on health care counselling and numerous papers on this topic. He is a member of the Institute of Family Therapy, London, American Family Therapy Academy, American Association for Marital and Family Therapy and is also a Churchill Fellow.

Jenny Chesshyre works as a counsellor in primary care, at a counselling centre and in private practice. She is also an affiliate counsellor with various Employee Assistance Programmes, including the Organization Stress Service at the Institute of Family Therapy. Her main interest is in counselling individuals and couples in health care settings.

John Davy is a Chartered Counselling, Educational and Health Psychologist, and an Associate Fellow of the British Psychological Society. He uses systemic, narrative and solution-focused approaches to therapy, and is also a qualified person-centred counsellor. His current interests include the application of competency-orientated therapies and consultation in medical settings including palliative care, and supervision across professional boundaries. John works part-time in the NHS, and is researching towards a Doctorate in Counselling Psychology at City University in London.

Peter du Plessis is Professional Head of Psychology and a consultant clinical psychologist at the Lewisham and Guy's NHS Mental Health

Trust. He has considerable experience in setting up and developing new mental health services and primary care counselling services. He is involved in the training of clinical and counselling psychologists and serves as an honorary lecturer at the City University and as faculty member of CBT Psychotherapy Training at the United Medical and Dental School of Guy's and St Thomas's. His special interest is the development of models of high standards of professional psychological practice.

Sheila Gill is a BAC Accredited Counsellor, UKRC Registered Independent Counsellor and experienced systemic therapist and trainer. She works in a student counselling service. Her expertise is in applying systemic and constructivist ideas to working with individuals, couples and families and within organizations.

Susan Hopkins is a psychodynamic counsellor in private practice in North London, working predominantly with patients referred by general practitioners. She has a Post-Graduate Diploma in Counselling in Primary Care from City University, London and is currently studying for the MSc in Counselling Psychology at City University. Before training as a counsellor, she worked in medical publishing, and as a practice manager in a primary care practice. She assists in the editing of the *Journal of the Balint Society*. Her particular interests include Balint-group work, psycho-somatic medicine and analytical psychology in which she is also undertaking further clinical training.

Susan Kendal trained as a social worker, working within a local authority setting. She is a BAC accredited counsellor and BPS Chartered Counselling Psychologist, with an MSc in Occupational Psychology from the University of Hertfordshire and an MSc in Counselling Psychology and Post-Graduate Diploma in Counselling in Primary Care from City University. Her research and special interests are occupational stress, adoption and birthmother issues and infertility. She works as a counsellor at the London School of Economics Student Health Centre and at a GP practice in North London.

Damian McCann is a qualified systemic practitioner, supervisor and trainer. He is a UKCP registered Systemic Psychotherapist and is also a member of the Association of Family & Systemic Therapy. He is currently employed as Principal Family Therapist at the Department of Child and Adolescent Psychiatry, Edgware Community Hospital and is visiting lecturer at City University, Birkbeck College and the Institute of Family Therapy, London. He has supervised a wide range of counsellors and trainees working in primary care and is interested in the development of supervision in these settings. In addition, he is the co-ordinator of the Lesbian and Gay Family Service based at the Institute of Family Therapy, London, and is completing his PhD at Birkbeck College, London.

Mary O'Callaghan works as a practice counsellor at the Dulwich Medical Centre and the Lordship Lane practice in South East London. She also works as an affiliate counsellor for a number of Employee Assistance Programmes and in private practice in Dulwich. Her special interest is in analytic psychology, in which she is undertaking an MA.

Christine Parrott is a BPS Chartered Counselling Psychologist. Originally from the United States, Christine earned a Bachelor of Arts at Dartmouth College in Hanover, New Hampshire. After moving to Britain in 1992, she earned her Masters and Post-Masters Degree in Counselling Psychology at City University, London. She also has a Diploma in Applied Hypnosis from University of London. Christine now works as a counselling psychologist, devoting much of her time to writing. Her special interests include the development of increased public awareness in psychology, the impact of values and ethics on the counselling process and the evolution of behaviour and emotions in people.

Gilly Pembroke is a self-employed counsellor who originally trained with Relate and Metanoia. She holds a Post-Graduate Diploma in Primary Healthcare and is BAC accredited. She has been attached to a GP practice in Twyford, Hampshire for the past eight years – a post which she created and developed, and also runs a small private practice. Drawing on psychodynamic, person-centred and systems approaches, she works with a wide range of problems encountered in a health care setting. This not only includes individual psychotherapy, but also work with adolescents, couples and families. An in-depth audit of her first five years' work at the surgery was recently undertaken. Her particular interests include depression and eating disorders. Gilly is married with three children.

Teresa Schaefer trained as a social worker and has specialized in special needs and bereavement in both local authorities and at Great Ormond Street Hospital. She also has experience in bereavement counselling in the USA. She has a Diploma in Adult Counselling from Birkbeck College and a Post-Graduate Diploma in Primary Health Care Counselling from City University. Previously a counsellor in a GP surgery in West London, she now works as a counsellor at the London School of Economics Student Health Centre. She is BAC accredited.

Jo Sexton has a Post-Graduate Diploma in Counselling in Primary Care and is a counsellor working in a general practice setting. She was originally trained to work psychodynamically but now prefers a more integrative approach. Her main interest is in combining the medical and psychological models in order to find the most effective help for people in distress.

Carole Trowbridge is a practice counsellor with a busy surgery in South East London. She holds a Post-Graduate Diploma in Counselling in Primary Health Care which she obtained at City University, and is currently studying for an MSc in Therapeutic Counselling with the University of Greenwich. She is a member of both the British Association for Counselling and its Counselling in Medical Settings Division. Her particular interest is in the application of eclectic and integrative approaches to counselling in medical settings.

Carole Waskett has been an accredited counsellor in several general practices over the past ten years. She also runs a varied private practice which includes therapy, employee assistance work and supervision, spiced up occasionally by teaching, training and writing.

With a psychodynamic background, she has been greatly influenced by systemic theory, and especially by her training in solution-focused brief therapy. She tries to live up to the principles of respect and collaboration with colleagues, supervisees and clients. She still finds helping people change stimulating and enjoyable.

FOREWORD

Graham Curtis Jenkins

Counsellors are now working in many thousands of General Practices in the United Kingdom and Northern Ireland. The growth in their numbers has been rapid, organic and for the most part unplanned.

Over the past ten years, increasing numbers of counsellors working in primary healthcare have been auditing and evaluating their work. A small number have developed an entirely new therapeutic service as part of primary healthcare. Counsellors often describe how they have had to learn to discard many of their cherished beliefs about long- versus short-term working, as well as attitudes to counsellor confidentiality, and have had to learn the often difficult lessons of how to work in a private practice free environment alongside other members of the Primary Care Team.

Learning how to develop a collaborative working model, integrating their work into that of the rest of the primary care team and making working links with NHS professionals working in traditional mental health services in the NHS have also exercised the minds and pens of these counsellors and others observing their work. The contributors to this book have described this process very well.

Here, for the first time is a book that brings together the collective experience of a group of primary care counsellors who describe in a practical, down-to-earth way what it is really like working in primary care. They write of the lessons they have learned and the wisdom they have gained from continuously reflecting on their day to day work. There is much of value in this book, not just for counsellors who think they might want to work in primary care, but also for counsellors with many years of experience of primary care counselling. The lonely life-style of many primary care counsellors, which often cuts them off from sharing in the experience of their counsellor colleagues, will become that much richer and informed by heeding the hard won lessons described so well in this book.

General Practitioners, mental health professionals and even academic counselling researchers, particularly if informed by a traditional, 'psychiatric' world view, can learn a lot from this book. Researchers coming fresh to counselling research from a traditional, mental health background will see why it is so difficult to carry out research based on a randomized control trials model: the number of variables that can affect service delivery and outcomes, and the non 'mental health' outcomes that are so valued by clients and GPs alike and which only become apparent as we learn how the interpretation of the bio-psychosocial model of health and illness, by patient and doctor, can so influence an outcome. I believe that the new health professional – the primary care counsellor – has now well and truly arrived and this book is a celebration of this.

I commend this book to all who wish to understand their role and further develop their skills as counsellors in primary care and to tell the wider audience in the National Health Service of their achievements.

INTRODUCTION

Robert Bor and Damian McCann

Over the past decade there has been enormous growth in professional counselling services, and in particular in primary health care settings. This is partly because of a renewed emphasis on the provision of health care outside of hospital settings, as well as a general increase in demand for counselling services. The growth of a primary care counselling specialty, however, has been met with mixed enthusiasm. Some have welcomed the addition of a counsellor to their team and patients in many settings have responded positively to both the service and to the therapy provided. On the other hand, there have been complaints about the lack of training of some primary care counsellors while others have compared the efficacy of counselling with prescriptions for psycho-active medication and have found results that do not put counselling in a positive light. Developments in this field over the past decade have been rapid but haphazard.

The idea for this book arose from trainees and colleagues with whom we have worked who suggested a text that went beyond the everyday skills of the generic counsellor and addressed primary care counselling issues at the level of the practising professional. The metaphor of a 'map' is a fitting one for this book because our aim is to offer guidance rather than to be prescriptive. The main emphasis is on the 'practice' of primary care counselling rather than on its background and history. Until the mid-1990s there was no provision for specialist training in the UK for counsellors working in primary care settings, in spite of the fact that people with serious psychopathology and complex medical and social problems are referred for assessment and treatment. The overall aim of this book is to address the unique and specific issues which coun-sellors face in the primary care setting and it is not intended to be a text-book for those without some formal training in this area.

All practitioners and trainee counsellors confront a number of impor-tant and challenging issues in primary care settings. These issues reflect the current developmental trajectory of the specialism of primary care counselling. They include among others (a) the need to collaborate with other professional carers while maintaining patient confidentiality; (b) attending to the patient's psychological problems and needs, whilst avoiding a mind–body split; (c) reconciling the need to sometimes give information and to be directive to patients, while honouring the basic tenets of psychotherapy and counselling in which empathy, reflection and non-directiveness are emphasized; (d) adapting models of psychotherapeutic practice to the workload demands of primary care settings; (e) providing counselling for a wide range of patients and problems, while relying increasingly on evidence based practice; (f) maximizing therapeutic contact and interventions in an era of diminishing resources; and (g) contending with issues relating to gender, sexuality, ethnicity and power, in both health care settings and the counselling room.

Our own experience as practitioners, supervisors and trainers has taught us that to seek to develop counselling skills without an understanding of the complex dynamics of health care teams and management skills is potentially self-defeating and could even inadvertently put the counsellor on a collision course with whom he or she most closely works. Given the scrutiny that primary care counsellors have come under, advanced practitioner skills and approaches of the kinds that we have attempted to address in this text should be of keen interest to counsellors at the forefront of modern practice.

One of the strengths of the counselling profession has been the availability of a wide range of therapeutic approaches to trainees. However, these have sometimes been applied inflexibly by practitioners, with the result that some patients have not been able to benefit from some of the more contemporary approaches to psychotherapy. The challenge for practitioners is to offer safe and effective therapies in a time-limited framework and to do so collaboratively both with the patient's family and support system, as well as with other professional colleagues. We recognize that a wide range of approaches to counselling and psychotherapy have been successfully used within this framework. This text, however, focuses primarily on the application of systemic, cognitive behavioural and psychodynamic approaches as applied and adapted by each of the contributors. This is not to suggest that these are the only approaches that can, or indeed should, be used. Rather, this reflects our background training and successful experience using these complementary frameworks. We hope that readers who are interested in using other therapeutic approaches will be able to use and adapt the skills and ideas presented in this book in their own settings and practice.

Although we recognize that primary health care counselling is a specialty, we readily accept that the career structure and indeed employment conditions of many practitioners are both unclear and unsatisfactory. For this reason, part of the book addresses basic career issues. This may be superfluous to the needs of some practitioners, although it is likely that most readers will have some interest in organizational issues. Each chapter addresses the concept of collaboration. While this may seem repetitive, this is not without justification. A well-trained and experienced practitioner is hardly likely to thrive, let alone survive, if he or she ignores the dynamics of the wider system and team within which they are required to work. In addition to an understanding of their context, counsellors also need to acquire skills for working with patients who have medical problems, patients' families and carers, as well as consultation skills to other professionals. Some of these are covered in this book though readers are referred to a recent specialist publication for a more detailed description of these skills (Bor et al., 1998).

The contributors offer a range of ideas which will be of interest to practitioners in the field as well as those in training.

Carole Trowbridge, in Chapter 1, introduces the reader to the specific issues relevant to setting up a primary care based counselling service. She reminds readers that if there is a good fit between what the practice needs and the counsellor can provide, then the scene is set for an invaluable addition to the health care team.

In Chapter 2, John Davy outlines the biopsychosocial model of health care. He offers guidelines to support the development of collaborative practice in primary care and suggests that holistic care is best managed through interdisciplinary rather than multidisciplinary approaches.

Chapter 3 continues the theme of collaboration. Susan Hopkins and Mary O'Callaghan explore the intrapersonal and interpersonal processes associated with the doctor/patient/counsellor relationship in the context of the primary health care team. They examine the conscious and unconscious processes at work within the relationship between these three separate but overlapping systems and suggest ways of managing these in practice.

Gilly Pembroke, in Chapter 4, is interested in helping the counsellor establish firm personal boundaries as a basis for appropriate and effective counselling. She addresses a central tension for most counsellors which is inherent in general practice settings, namely that of establishing one's autonomy at the same time as being part of a team. She suggests ways of educating and including other members of the health care team in the counsellor's work and also tackles the issue of managing one's colleagues in distress.

In Chapter 5, Teresa Schaefer, Jenny Chesshyre and Susan Kendal explore the referral process. They view referrals as the nodal point of primary health care counselling since they unite doctor, patient and counsellor in a dynamic relationship concerning a request for treatment. The authors offer advice to counsellors with a range of referral situations and outline a valuable framework for introducing a referral system.

Carole Waskett, in Chapter 6, tackles the thorny issue of patient flow. She explores the meaning of patient absences, particularly in relation to waiting lists, and suggests a number of strategies for dealing with the throughput of work.

Chapter 7 addresses the limits of confidentiality with regard to teamwork. Carole Waskett draws attention to clinical dilemmas, such as working with violent partnerships where the issue of confidentiality has to be carefully considered in order to ensure ethical and effective practice.

Chapters 8 and 9 offer the reader an overview of the theoretical concepts underpinning brief therapy and their clinical applications. Christine Parrott argues that long-term therapeutic approaches are simply ill-equipped to deal with the pressures of general practice and suggests that brief therapeutic approaches are thus a practical and ethical necessity. She outlines the philosophy of doing therapy briefly and in Chapter 9, using a brief therapeutic framework, plots the progress of therapy from the point of referral through to termination. The overriding philosophy of such an approach is that it recognizes the power of the patient and the value of time as a resource and therapeutic tool.

Sheila Gill, in Chapter 10, continues the theme of empowerment by addressing the position that assigns competence to the patient. The central tenet of her thinking is that the whole of the patient's life becomes relevant to the counsellor and not just the presenting problem. She discusses factors that promote as well as inhibit patient competence. She further suggests that viewing patients as competent and resourceful has many implications both ethically and in terms of the efficient provision of psychological care within a health care setting.

In Chapter 11, Jo Sexton addresses the importance of the relationship between counselling and medication. She points out that although it is not the counsellor's responsibility directly to advise the patient about medication, she will, nevertheless, be better placed to understand the effect of medication and related problems, such as treatment compliance, if she seeks to learn more about prescribed drugs. To that end, she explains the function of the central nervous system and provides a very useful checklist of psychotropic medications. In the final section of her chapter, she examines the application and possible interactive effects of psychotropic medication and counselling.

Chapter 12 is concerned with the training of primary care counsellors. Gilly Pembroke outlines the essential components of a training course designed to equip the counsellor to qualify and practise in this challenging field of work. She raises important questions concerning levels of competence both in the personal and professional domain. She also highlights the need for qualified counsellors to be resourceful in selecting appropriate packages for continued personal growth and professional development that are commensurate with counselling in primary health care.

Chapter 13 examines the contribution supervision makes to counsellors working in primary health care settings. Damian McCann focuses his attention towards developing effective and ethical supervisory practices. Three contrasting supervisory models are used to highlight considerations relevant to practice. He emphasizes the importance of counsellors being clear about their supervisory needs and explores a number of tensions and dilemmas inherent in the supervisory relationship.

Peter du Plessis and Robert Bor, in Chapter 14, emphasize the importance of evaluation in primary health care counselling. They point out that counsellors are now routinely asked to justify counselling in terms of cost and outcome. They explore factors that may deter counsellors from evaluating their practice, but also provide some compelling reasons for why counsellors need to become more involved in this important aspect of their work.

One of the pitfalls of an edited text is that the content can seem disjointed and patchy in quality. We have been fortunate in being able to work with dedicated contributors, all of whom are experienced and creative practitioners. Without exception, each has managed to produce material within tight deadlines while balancing this with the demands placed on them by their own families and professional practice. Furthermore, all the contributors willingly gave up time to meet as a group on several occasions in order to share ideas and experiences and to reflect critically on their own development and practice. We are enormously grateful to them for this. We are also grateful to Dr Graham Curtis Jenkins, Director of the Counselling in Primary Care Trust, who has been a tremendous source of support for this project as well as the development of the specialism in general.

There are many contemporary examples of innovative, creative and effective practice in primary care settings, and some counsellors are at the forefront of these. Moves towards evidence based practice have certainly revitalized the practice of counselling and no practitioner can afford to avoid this trend. However, counsellors need to be proactive and to take greater responsibility for making their practice contextually relevant in every aspect. A first step to doing this is the process of networking with other colleagues, something which hitherto has not been a main priority. In addition, continuing professional development can also assist and therefore needs to receive greater emphasis. Because of the extent and rate of change which we have become accustomed to in the health service, no professional can expect to practice in isolation of developments within the provision of health care generally. Counselling, like other professions, has often adopted a somewhat passive relationship to change and this will need addressing if we are to secure our role in the multidisciplinary primary care team of the future. Counsellors will be judged both on their work with their patients as well as their ability to convince their colleagues and employers of the benefits they bring to this setting.

A final note to readers. We use the term patient rather than client because of the health care settings in which we work. This is not meant to imply that the person is necessarily medically ill, nor an acknowledgement of the dominance of medical terminology. In addition, we often use the personal pronoun 'she' when referring to the counsellor, and 'he' when referring to the doctor or patient. This does not reflect any bias on the part of the contributors; they are merely convenient pronouns that aid clarity of meaning.

Wherever possible, we have asked contributors to illustrate their ideas through their clinical work. In order to preserve the confidential nature of this material however, many details have been changed i.e. name, gender, family composition, nature of problem and so on, so that specific cases could not be recognized.

Reference

Bor, R., Miller, R., Latz, M. and Salt, H. (1998) *Counselling in Health Care Settings*. London: Cassell.

CHAPTER 1

SETTING UP A COUNSELLING SERVICE

Carole Trowbridge

Despite the rise in both the profile and the credibility of counselling in primary health care, and the increased use of counsellors in general practice, there is as yet no clearly defined role for counsellors in the National Health Service, and no definitive framework for setting up a new service. This chapter sets out to clarify the specific issues that need to be addressed when developing a primary care based counselling service. The information is presented from the point of view of the prospective counsellor, but can equally be used by GPs, practice managers or health care providers who may intend to employ a counsellor as part of the primary care team.

It is assumed that the term 'counsellor' in this instance refers to someone who has a professional level qualification which permits them to practise, who is a member of (and ideally accredited by) one of the national counselling bodies (for example, BAC, or UKCP) and works in accordance with their code of ethics, and who has an appropriate depth of training and experience. The entry point for trainee counsellors, or those with little experience, would be to work under the supervision of an existing practice counsellor, and as such they would not be in the position of setting up a new service.

The chapter is divided into three sections: Getting Started; The Counselling Service in Context; and Setting up the Service. The content within these sections is grouped under a number of subheadings, which should enable you to search quickly for the relevant information.

1 Getting started

This section is primarily for those people who are considering setting up a counselling service in a general practice and who have not previously worked as a counsellor in this context.

Am I right for this setting?

By its very nature, a general practice lends itself to generalist rather than specialist counsellors, so for those wanting to work with a broad range of problems and life issues this is an ideal setting. However, some self-exploration before embarking on this route is valuable in clarifying your main reasons for wanting to work in a GP practice. Here are some questions you might like to ponder on when considering whether this is the right setting for you.

- Do you already have some experience of working in the NHS, or do you know somebody else who does (another counsellor, for example)?
- Have you been influenced by your own (or others') experiences as a patient in the system?
- How do you envisage your role within the primary health care team?
- Do your skills suit this setting? There needs to be a good fit between the counsellor's experience and the needs of the practice (Corney and Jenkins, 1993).
- Are you able to meet the requirement for brief, focused work?
- How flexible are you in terms of dealing with a broad range of pre-senting problems – anything from depression and anxiety, to diffi-cult relationship problems (perhaps including couples work), to major health issues, life-threatening illness and physical disability?
- Have you considered the broad cross-section of individual differ-ences you are likely to encounter – age, religion, culture, social status?
- How able are you to manage your own stress levels, especially in the face of mounting waiting lists and limited numbers of sessions, along with pressure from referrers and patients?
- Do you have the skills required for managing priorities, time, forms and paperwork, interactions with a range of professionals, net-working with other services, negotiating for rooms and funding, regular audit procedures?
- What are your expectations in terms of payment and employment status?

Do some background research and find out as much as you can about your chosen setting. Talk to other counsellors already working in the NHS, or identify someone such as a mental health coordinator for the local health authority and talk to them. Read available literature and guidelines (see references at the end of this chapter). If, having con-sidered the pros and cons, you then decide that this is definitely the setting for you, the next step is to find an appropriate surgery or health centre.

Which practice?

Working locally means less travel time and can be helpful if you have family or other work commitments, but *too* local and you run the risk of bumping into your patients in the supermarket, or being referred people that you know (or friends and relatives of people you know) which can lead to complex confidentiality issues. A balance needs to be struck between being close enough to be convenient and manageable, and far enough away to prevent encountering your patients on a day-to-day basis. Avoid the surgery which you attend as a patient yourself as it will inevitably create difficulties if your GP is both a professional colleague (or your boss) and your own doctor.

The following guidelines may help:

- Choose the area and the practices you are interested in, and find out which are in need of a counselling service.
- Determine whether they are looking for agency counsellors, NHS-employed, or self-employed.
- Find out whether the practice itself will be making the decisions or some central coordinator.
- Establish whether they currently provide (or have experience of) any form of counselling service.
- Check whether funding is available.

Many of these questions can be answered by the relevant local commissioning body or by a mental health coordinator, *before* you approach the practice. Local colleges can also be a useful source of information, since they often negotiate placements for counselling trainees and may well be aware of local counselling practice and policies. For instance, in some areas counsellors are only accepted through an agency which acts as an overseeing body, ensuring consistency of ethical standards, skills and professional indemnity. If this is the case, you may need to contact the agency rather than a specific practice. The more research you do before approaching the practice, the better prepared and more professional you will appear.

Can I meet the needs of the organization?

Working for any organization requires a clear understanding of its needs and expectations, so the question to ask is 'What does the NHS want from its counsellors, and specifically from me?' Indeed, do the GPs and other members of staff fully understand what a counsellor actually *does*, and how the role fits into this multidisciplinary context? Clarity of role is essential in order to avoid confusion and rivalry between colleagues. Explore and address the following:

- What is it that has attracted the practice to the idea of having an in-house counsellor at this point in time – do they in fact *need* a counsellor?
- How does the practice currently deal with patients' psychological problems?
- Is there a recognized need in the patient population (local or national) which is not being met by existing services?
- Has funding become available and prompted interest?
- What does the practice hope to gain from providing a counselling service? For example, they may be aiming to reduce the amount of prescribed psychotropic medication, or the number of 'boomerang' patients, or GP stress levels.

These questions are important, because evaluation of the effectiveness of the service you provide will be focused towards whichever is the primary motivation of the purchaser. Be clear about their main objectives, and decide whether you are the right person to help meet those objectives.

Benefits to patients in a general practice setting

The GP surgery or health centre is an accepted and well-recognized part of any community and it therefore has a number of advantages as a setting for counselling. A knowledge of these benefits is of value to you as a counsellor when making your proposal.

- **Credibility** – primary health care is generally well respected, and therefore engenders a certain level of trust and credibility.
- **Familiarity** – the GP surgery or health centre is somewhere people know.
- **Location** – it is usually not too far for patients to travel.
- **Normalizing** – virtually everyone goes there at some time or other (unlike specialist services, clinics, or counselling centres).
- **Non-stigmatizing** – it is not a specialist mental health service provider, so does not carry the same stigma.
- **Anonymity** – if the person wishes to keep their attendance for counselling a secret from friends or family, they can always say that they have a doctor's appointment. (Simple 'desk-front' techniques can also help preserve anonymity, for example suggesting that patients ask for you by name rather than saying 'I'm here to see the counsellor'.)

- **Cost** – the service is generally free and therefore accessible to people with limited income.

What am I offering and what do I want?

Decide why you are right for this setting, what particular skills and experience you will bring to it, and your own needs and expectations. What are you hoping for in terms of employment status, hours, payment, and what is the minimum you are prepared to accept? When you approach the practice, you may well be asked direct questions such as 'What are your charges?', in which case a good knowledge of local and national pay scales for counsellors in this setting is essential so that you do not over- or under-sell yourself. In terms of hours per week, this is usually governed by the availability of funding, but there are also some guidelines about this. The British Association for Counselling (BAC) recommends that counsellors should spend no more than two-thirds of their employed time (or a maximum of 20 hours) in contact with patients (Ball, 1995). The Counselling in Primary Care Trust suggests that a practice of around 9,000 patients would need the equivalent of a full-time counselling service ($35^1/_2$ hours per week) in order to fully meet its needs (Curtis Jenkins, 1993). Think about what *you* would consider to be acceptable in relation to the size of the practice, how you work and your availability.

Next, you need to decide how to sell yourself and your services. You might target your approach by focusing on the benefits to GPs as well as to patients. You could consider providing your services on a voluntary basis for a few months, so that you can demonstrate your worth, or you may want to negotiate for a specific employment package. A bit of self-marketing is also important in order to most effectively 'sell' your skills, experience and professionalism, but be honest and do not overdo it. The rule is to be clear in your own mind about what you are offering and what you expect in return *before* making your approach.

Whom to approach

Assuming that you find yourself in a position to make direct contact with the practice, then the practice manager (if there is one) is a good starting point. They manage the business and organizational issues of the practice, as well as the interface between the various health providers (GPs, nurses, health visitors, etc.) and therefore have a central and co-ordinating role. Some practices do not have a practice manager, in which case you would probably need to approach the senior partner instead.

Put yourself in the shoes of the person you intend to contact. Consider their needs, views and possible limitations, and then tailor your marketing strategy accordingly. It is unrealistic to expect that any practice will go out of its way to accommodate a counsellor. This does not necessarily reflect a lack of interest, but the fact that in some areas supply simply outstrips demand, and a practice may receive many calls and letters from prospective counsellors. Poor marketing on the part of counsellors themselves, coupled with some scepticism about their value, probably results in the majority of enquiries getting no further than the nearest bin, so it is essential to be aware of potential barriers and find ways to overcome them.

First contact

There are three obvious routes for initial contact: telephone, letter, or in person. However, this is not a good environment for cold calling because of the 'busy-ness' of a health centre, so it is generally best to avoid the latter. Managers are inevitably stretched, so it is more respectful of their time not to arrive unannounced. Remember that this is an organization in which brevity is a way of life, so you need an approach which respects that fact. As a courtesy, a brief telephone call or letter to introduce yourself and make your request is preferable, but keep it short and to the point. Time your approach to catch the person when they are likely to be at their least busy and most receptive to your proposal. You may need to negotiate with the receptionists (custodians of the GPs' time) in order to do that. Be clear about what you are offering and what you are asking for. If your purpose is to arrange a meeting, or to give a short presentation, then make that clear. Be courteous at all times and to all staff; first impressions count and these are shared rapidly between colleagues!

Checklist for offering your services

1   Identify who is the most appropriate person to speak to or write to, and decide which method is preferable. If it is to be telephone contact, find out the best time to call.
2   Outline your proposal as concisely as possible, including what you have to offer, a summary of your experience, your reasons for approaching this particular surgery, and the potential benefits of a counselling service. If your first contact is by telephone, follow this up in writing.
3   Acknowledge that the practice manager (or GP) may want to present

your proposal at the next practice meeting. This not only demonstrates your knowledge of (and respect for) organizational procedures, but also establishes a time-frame for something to happen. You can then offer either to attend the meeting and present your ideas in person, or to send additional information (for example, a detailed CV).

4   Arrange a follow-up phone call for a day or two after the meeting has taken place (preferably agreeing a date and time). Suggest that you will call the practice as this demonstrates your proactivity and avoids your needs being ignored or forgotten. Unless the practice has been actively searching for a counsellor, you are not likely to be at the top of their priority list, so it is in your own interest to retain the initiative.

5   With luck, you will be invited to discuss your proposal more fully. If you have not already done so, this is when you need to provide a detailed CV summarizing your specific expertise, therapeutic approach and relevant qualifications. You should also outline your supervisory arrangements and professional indemnity cover.

6   At a practice meeting, you may meet the practice manager, one or two of the GPs, a nurse or nurse practitioner, and possibly a community psychiatric nurse. Practice meetings are often held in between surgery times or during a lunch-break, so they tend to be very brief – this means that preparation is essential. Take along good quality handouts of the most relevant information, and outline your proposal clearly and briefly, maintaining a warm but professional manner. State who you are, what you are proposing, benefits to both the practice and the patients (including any information which might back that up, such as a summary of some relevant research), and how you envisage the service working.

7   Having presented your outline proposal, invite questions. You might have people in the room who are sceptical, or enthusiastic, but you will almost certainly find your ideas being challenged and tested, and rightly so. Anticipate and address any reservations, and respond to the need for evidence-based practice. Be honest, and aim to be neither confrontational nor overly defensive.

8   If all goes well, and the practice accepts your proposal, you can now begin planning what the service will look like.

2 The counselling service in context

This section examines the context in which the counselling service is set up. It focuses on organizational style and culture, as well as the needs and expectations of the practice, the counsellor and the patients.

Practice profile – know your environment

Just as every workplace is different, so every general practice or health centre has its own character, culture and social context. It is into this existing system that the new counselling service will be placed, so a good understanding of it is essential when deciding what that service will look like and how it will fit in.

Joining a general practice is a bit like meeting someone else's family for the first time. We become aware of certain rules, procedures and a style of interaction which characterize this system. We get a 'feel' for the atmosphere of the place, noticing what it looks like – the layout of the waiting room, how soft the chairs are, how noisy it is, what the reception area is like, and the faces of both patients and staff. We quickly form impressions about how relaxed or stressed it is, whether it is friendly and welcoming or cold and uninviting, and even the social class of the patient population. This initial snapshot tells us something about the environment in which we will be working.

Just as with all the practical issues (space, room layouts, patient list-size), it is important to begin to understand the culture, politics and values which underpin this 'family' of medical professionals. The ways in which different staff interact with one another, and with you, can be a valuable insight into how they interact with their patients. For instance, is the atmosphere one of empowerment and mutual respect, or of helplessness and mutual disregard? Do people come 'to get a pre-scription' or to seek help in solving their medical and emotional problems? Are the GPs very traditional and cautious of change, or are they progressive and up-beat in their outlook? What are their views on complementary therapies, and specifically on counselling?

A practice manager is often a good reflection of the organizational and interactional style of the place, for example calm and approachable, or stressed and best avoided. Look for evidence of networking between colleagues (doctors, nursing staff, health visitors, receptionists), or whether they see themselves as independent and unrelated groups who happen to share the same premises. This provides clues as to how your role as counsellor might be perceived, and whether you are likely to become an integrated member of the primary health care team, or just another separate service provider. Get to know the practice and its staff, so that the service you set up is compatible both with your own ideals and with the realities of the setting.

These issues are more important than they may at first appear, because the rules and culture of the setting have an impact both on you personally and on the people you will be working with. Below are two examples of real experiences. The first highlights the potential impact of the working environment, the second illustrates the uniqueness of social rules and acceptance rituals.

A colleague working for several months in a general practice was intrigued and surprised by the number of times patients commented that they would only see *one* of the two GPs, and felt it would be disloyal to see the other. It was only as a result of careful probing that she discovered that not only did the GPs share an intense mutual dislike, but that they also refused to speak to one another except about professional matters. Inadvertently perhaps, it seems that the patients had been affected by the issues going on around them.

Another colleague said that she had never really felt 'part of the team' until, after several years of working in the same health centre, she found that she had been added to the 'tea-towel rota'. Such was the significance of this in-house ritual (being allowed to take a turn in washing the dirty linen!) that it was only at this point that she felt she had 'served her apprenticeship' and finally been accepted into the family.

Service requirements – practice needs and expectations

In a business sense, the NHS and the practice itself are your primary clients, since they are buying a professional service from you. It is essential to understand not only what their needs are, but also their expectations in terms of how those needs will be met and what the service will look like. Here are some questions which might help to elicit these points.

- Why do they want this service, and why now?
- How do they view the counsellor's role?
- What patient issues do they hope to refer to you?
- What range of people do they anticipate you seeing – individuals, couples, children, families?
- What outcomes are they hoping for (fewer psychiatric referrals, a reduction in the prescribing of psychotropic drugs, reduced GP stress, qualitative effectiveness feedback, quantitative feedback)?
- Will your skills be used solely for the benefit of patients, or also for the staff?
- How many people do they hope to refer per month?
- How many sessions will they want each week, and how many for each patient?
- Will there be any flexibility in the number of sessions, so that patients requiring only one or two can be off-set against those with longer-term needs?
- What expectations do they have regarding your availability out-of-hours?
- How much paperwork, audit and evaluation is required of you?

If these issues are not clarified, there may well be a mis-match between the needs of the practice and your ability to meet them. Better to discover this early on, than to find yourself in a situation for which you are unsuited or unskilled.

Counsellor needs and expectations

Whilst some of the questions from the previous sections also apply here, there are some additional issues for prospective practice counsellors to consider in order to ensure an optimum fit between the business needs and their own personal and professional needs.

- Will this practice meet *your* needs, both as a counsellor and as an individual?
- What will your employment status be (part-time, self-employed, or employed by the practice) and to what extent will you be considered part of the team?
- How much funding is available, and for how long?
- Who will actually be making the referrals – GPs only, or other members of staff? What do you expect referrers to know or to do?
- Where does your responsibility for patients begin and end?
- What other mental health services are available in the area? You may well need to refer someone on, so it is important to know about the availability of specialist services and voluntary organizations, for example is there a local CRUSE and a local RELATE, and how will you work with them?
- What support do you need (administrative, professional, emotional) from other members of staff?
- What expectations do you have for your own professional develop-ment and working practice? Are you hoping for additional training? Would you like to consider working with groups? Do you anticipate opportunities for work shadowing and learning about other roles within primary health care?
- What are your limits – what are you *not* prepared to do?

Patient needs and expectations

In focusing on the needs of the practice and the counsellor, it is impor-tant not to overlook the needs and expectations of the patients them-selves. When an individual consults their GP, there is an expectation that the doctor will be able to help in some way and 'make it better'.

The person enters a system in which the medical model predominates, where people have symptoms, and symptoms have causes which can be treated or cured. The relationship is one in which the GP is seen as the possessor of specialist knowledge which is imparted to the patient. The counsellor working in a general practice setting therefore needs to be aware of the possible carry-over of this expectation into the counselling relationship, and consider how to manage it. Carefully devised referral criteria and procedures will help both the counsellor and the GP to ensure that patients' individual needs are met, and that they have realistic expectations of the counselling process.

3 Setting up the service

This section focuses on the practicalities of setting up a general practice counselling service. It covers a range of issues from process to paperwork. It is not exhaustive, so it is best to use it as a starting point and customize it for your own purposes.

Job outline

First, clarify and agree your role and professional status as a counsellor in this setting. If there is a local policy on counselling, make sure that you have a copy and know what is expected of you before you sign a contract. There will be guidelines on level of skill and training required (for example, BAC accreditation), on audit and evaluation, and even on preferred therapeutic approaches. Refer to BAC and Counselling in Primary Care Trust guidelines on counselling in medical settings, and other relevant publications. Consider whether you will be self-employed and contracted in, employed by the practice, or employed by (for example) a counselling agency.

   In order to agree your working hours and payment, it is helpful to have some idea of both local and national rates for primary health care counsellors and to consider this in the light of available funding. If administration time and supervision costs are covered, you may find that the rate offered is slightly lower than if pay is on the basis of contact time alone. The number of hours you work per week may be limited by funding arrangements, by the needs of the practice, or by your own preference. Whichever is the case, be clear about how many hours you will provide, which days and times, and how they will be divided between client contact and administration time. Remember also to agree a policy on payment for DNAs ('did not attend') and late cancellations, as this can make a significant difference. If you intend to offer any out-of-hours work, consider issues such as insurance cover, lock-up procedures, keys and alarms.

Having negotiated the terms of your agreement, it is advisable to summarize them in a formal contract, including such things as provision for unexpected absence (such as illness), holiday agreements, duration and renewal of contract, and period of notice required.

As a practising counsellor, you are legally responsible for your own ethical practice, whatever the setting. In the same way that a GP is medically accountable for the care of their patients, so the counsellor is professionally accountable for their own work and conduct. Professional indemnity insurance provides essential cover in the event of legal proceedings against you, but check any grey areas such as personal injury cover and out-of-hours working. Remember that you are also accountable to the organization for which you provide the service, so you need to be aware of and abide by both in-house policy and the terms of your contract.

Medical context

An NHS practice is a multidisciplinary working environment and reporting structures and organizational issues can be confusing, so it is a good idea to find someone who is willing to give you an overview. A working knowledge of the most commonly used jargon and doctors' short-hand can be useful, as some of it may appear in referral notes. You do not need to become a medical expert, but it also helps to be familiar with the names and effects of the most commonly used psychotropic drugs (see Chapter 11) since at least some of the people who consult you will have been prescribed them.

Patients' medical notes are fundamental to the continuity of medical care. Find out how they are used, who has access to them, who can write in them, and all requirements with respect to confidentiality, loss or damage.

In the broader context, you will undoubtedly be networking with existing mental health services. Ask for (or draw up) a list of contacts and organizations, and familiarize yourself with their referral criteria and procedures. Include information about both NHS and voluntary services (such as CRUSE, RELATE, Samaritans), self-help or local support groups, and private counsellors in the area.

Fitting in to the practice

Working in a general practice means fitting in with its culture, procedures and those who work there. In an environment where people spend hours at a time shut away in consulting rooms (you included), it can be difficult to get to know other members of staff, especially if you are only there for part of the week. This is an area in which it pays to be proactive. Find out who's who in the practice, and how people like to be addressed. Some GPs prefer to be very informal and will want you to use their first name only, whilst others are called Dr . . . by absolutely everyone, even colleagues. Tell people how *you* would like to be addressed, both directly and when being referred to with patients. Ask about daily routines, what goes where, which meetings need to be attended, social activities, break times (if they exist), administrative support and so on. Get invited to practice and team meetings when appropriate, and talk informally to the practice manager, GPs and other staff about practice issues. Receptionists fulfil a vital front-line role within a general practice. They are the interface between the customers and the providers and can be invaluable allies in this setting, so get to know them and what they do. You can be fairly certain that poor relationships with the team will cause your stress levels to rise and your work satisfaction to plummet.

As with all other mental health providers, counsellors lie somewhere along a continuum of mental health care, and professional relationships should ideally be collaborative rather than competitive. To avoid confusion, be clear about the distinction between the role of counsellor and the community psychiatric nurse. CPNs have specific mental health training and are employed to work with a defined range of issues, but there are occasions when their skills and yours may overlap. It is therefore essential that referral criteria and role boundaries are discussed and agreed.

Practical requirements

On the face of it, counsellors have very few practical requirements, but the very fact that our needs are modest means that they can be easily underestimated or overlooked. In private practice and dedicated counselling organizations it is relatively easy to establish a good counselling environment, but in a busy general practice space and equipment are often at a premium. You need to negotiate for a quiet room (ideally one which is dedicated to your use only) which will be free from interruption, comfortable chairs for both your patients and yourself (remember, you will be sitting for long periods of time), a supply of tissues, a clock and a telephone (which can be barred to calls when you are working). In addition, you will need a lockable filing cabinet and a collection point (a tray or a pigeon-hole) for correspondence and referrals.

You may wish to use leaflets and handouts, standard letters, referral forms, appointment cards and feedback sheets. At the very least, you will need a diary, note paper, envelopes, stamps and the occasional use of a photocopier. To avoid awkwardness or embarrassment, agree in advance how these will be supplied and paid for.

Referral from GP to counsellor

When setting up a new counselling service, it is essential to establish appropriate referral criteria and procedures, and these are covered in more detail in Chapter 5. Consider what will be a manageable referral rate, or it can be all too easy for demand to outstrip supply. However, do not be fooled into thinking that referral rates will be the same for all GPs, as this is rarely the case. This may reflect differences in their view of counselling, or their own counselling skills, or even of the choices patients make about which GP they go to with their emotional problems. If you have a waiting list, it is worth devising a standard acknowledgement letter to send to patients. This lets them know that you have received the referral, and also gives them a rough idea of how long they are likely to have to wait. You may also want to devise standard referral forms for the GPs, to ensure consistency of information and format.

Managing patient contact

There are some advantages to managing bookings and patient contact yourself. For instance, patients are not always available during the day and reception staff may not be in a position to make calls after hours. First contact is also an opportunity to introduce yourself to the patient and establish the beginnings of a therapeutic relationship. However, there are also advantages to leaving the administrative procedures to reception staff (as outlined in Chapter 6), so it is wise to consider the pros and cons of both options before deciding which to adopt.

Printed appointment cards can serve several useful purposes: to confirm a booking, to ensure that people have correct information, and as a reminder for forgetful patients. Add your name, contact number and a note about cancellation procedures for extra clarity.

Agree appropriate procedures with reception staff for patients arriving for a counselling appointment. Decide where they will wait, how you will know they have arrived, who will call them and how. If possible, use a room which does not face straight out onto the waiting area to minimize noise and help preserve patient anonymity, and ensure that reception staff know where you are working. Use a prominent notice to fend off interruptions during sessions, and bar the phone if possible. Unless you have your own room, some interruptions may be unavoidable (for example, if a piece of medical equipment is needed urgently), so consider how these should be managed. Be clear about session boundaries, such as start and finish times, and work consistently.

Agree a policy on how much patient information is required by whom, and for what purpose. As a general rule, session notes are for the sole use of the counsellor, and a minimum of information is required for entry into the patient's medical notes. A simple card can be used for this, showing start and finish dates for counselling, with a brief summary of reason for referral and outcome. Some GPs like to see this on completion, so that they know when a patient has finished working with you. The format of the records you keep will also be influenced by monitoring and audit requirements, and it is worthwhile designing referral forms and record cards so that information is captured in the most useful way.

Some practices have high DNA rates, which may affect counselling attendance (the fact that the service is free may also be significant). Aim to minimize this by emphasizing the importance of regular attendance and agreeing cancellation requirements. Out of respect to people on the waiting list, you may want to consider penalties (such as withdrawal from counselling following two consecutive failed appointments), but think carefully about the implications of this and how it might be managed.

Professional and personal boundaries

As a practising counsellor, you will need to work in accordance with a code of ethics which clearly outlines your professional responsibilities. Practical issues to consider are storage of patient counselling notes and who has access to them, what will be recorded for audit and evaluation purposes, and what level of discussion between counsellor and other staff is appropriate. Decide also whether it is appropriate for counselling notes and paperwork to be taken home. Professional indemnity insurance is essential, as is adequate and effective supervision. It is helpful to provide a copy of your insurance certificate and code of ethics (for example, BAC or UKCP) to the practice manager (or appropriate GP) so that these can be stored in your personal file.

Occasionally, people may ask about private counselling in preference to being on a waiting list. If you consider taking these people on yourself, think carefully about the implications as it could appear to be an un-ethical source of private patients and income. In general, it is probably best to refer these cases on to an alternative counsellor. Consider also whether you will accept requests for subsequent private counselling with any of your patients, and if so how to manage this ethically. For example, you might encourage a gap between finishing short-term NHS counselling and requesting more in-depth private work.

Hopefully, you will not find yourself in a situation where your personal safety is compromised, but it is wise to be cautious. Be aware of in-house alarm procedures (including panic buttons if installed), or consider using a personal alarm. Minimize risk by always ensuring that someone knows which room you are working in and what your session times are. Alert someone in the practice if you have any concerns about your personal safety with a particular patient.

Think very carefully about how much you will allow your work to spill over into your private life. If you are unable to contact a patient during working hours (as is often the case), are you willing to telephone them from home? Unless you work full-time at the surgery, patients will occasionally ask how to contact you between sessions should the need arise. Although it may be tempting to give your home phone number to certain patients, consider the implications carefully. How appropriate is it for someone to call you in your own time, especially if you do not have a separate business number? What will you do if a patient phones when you are in the middle of a dinner party, or in bed? In general, it may be better to suggest that they leave a message for you at the surgery. If it is urgent, the surgery can then call and let you know. As a safeguard, you could also arrange to phone in and check for messages on certain days.

Conclusion

Working as a counsellor in primary health care is a challenging and rewarding experience, but it can stand and fall by how well the service is initially set up. If there is a good fit between what the practice needs and the counsellor can provide, then the scene is set for an invaluable addition to the health care team. The value and effectiveness of the counselling service will be greatly enhanced by having good working practices in place to support the process. This means working closely with the practice manager and GPs in order to identify exactly what that service will cover and the procedures needed to underpin it. Collaborative practice is essential and your ability to develop appropriate relationships with professional colleagues is as important as with your patients. Take care to demonstrate and emphasize this when you first approach a practice and when setting up a practice-based counselling service.

Key points

- Think carefully about whether you are right for this setting, both from a personal and a professional point of view.
- Identify local requirements and target your approach accordingly.
- Negotiate a contract which is appropriate to the service you are to provide, and consider local and national policy regarding terms of employment.
- Get to know the practice – its culture, patient population and staff.
- Consider all practical details required to establish an ethical and professional counselling service.

References

Ball, V. (1995) *Guidelines for the Employment of Counsellors in General Practice*. Rugby: BAC Counselling in Medical Settings Division.

Corney, R. and Jenkins, R. (eds) (1993) *Counselling in General Practice*. London: Routledge.

Curtis Jenkins, G. (1993) *Information Booklet*. Staines: Counselling in Primary Care Trust.

Additional recommended reading

Breese, J. (1994) *Counselling in a General Practice Setting*. London: Central Book Publishing.

Corney, R. (1997) 'A counsellor in every general practice?', *European Journal of Psychotherapy, Counselling and Health*, 1(1): 5–20.

Curtis Jenkins, G., Bond, T. and Burton, M.V. (1995) *Supplement No.1*. Staines: Counselling in Primary Care Trust.

Curtis Jenkins, G. and Henderson, P. (1996) *Supplement No.2*. Staines: Counselling in Primary Care Trust.

Dryden, W., Charles-Edwards, D. and Woolfe, R. (eds) (1989) *Handbook of Counselling in Britain*. London: Routledge.

McLeod, J. (1993) *An Introduction to Counselling*. Buckingham: Open University Press.

Smith, A., Irving, J. and Brown, P. (1989) 'Counselling in the medical context', in W. Dryden, D. Charles-Edwards and R. Woolfe (eds), *Handbook of Counselling in Britain*. London: Routledge.

CHAPTER 2

A BIOPSYCHOSOCIAL APPROACH TO COUNSELLING IN PRIMARY CARE

John Davy

This chapter starts by contrasting the traditional biomedical approach to health care with a biopsychosocial model which recognizes that there are complex interactions between biological, psychological and social factors and contexts. Consequently, interdisciplinary collaboration between professionals will often be more effective than a multidisciplinary approach where each team member works in relative isolation. The chapter offers some guidelines to support the development of collaborative practice in primary care.

The development of biomedicine

In the early history of Western medicine, pioneers such as Hippocrates wrote about health and illness in terms of a complex interdependence between the body of the patient, their lifestyle, moods and spiritual practices, and their environment. Treatments were often framed in terms of restoring balance within the system, including the patient's relationship with the environment, the family and the gods. In contemporary language, there was a holistic approach to medical care.

Medical historians suggest that a biomedical approach, focusing on the investigation and management of the patient's body and biological disease processes, took root from the Renaissance onwards. This was fuelled by philosophical developments positing epistemological and ontological distinctions between mind and body (Cartesian dualism), the production of knowledge about the body from dissection, increasing availability of translated works from Arabic scholars and rediscovered classical Greek texts, and shifting power balances between civic and religious authorities. In effect, medical practitioners increasingly specialized in the care and study of the individualized patient's body, leaving the care of the soul to the Church and social welfare to the state's sovereign power (see East, 1995 for an overview of counselling in the context of medicine's historical development).

Positivist scientific methodology flourished, demonstrating its worth in the study and control of inanimate objects and forces. This developing paradigm of reducing complex phenomena to smaller parts, examining and then further reducing these, was taken up by medicine in the study of the body as a collection of organs whose structure and function could be examined separately. The reductionist approach to illness created and required a medical view of the patient as an object (or collection of objects) of study rather than a subject. An extreme version of this biomedical stance can still be heard when some medical staff discuss 'the appendix in bed 12', or 'the breast cancer coming in tomorrow'.

Western medical practice has claimed considerable success in the management of acute and infectious diseases and traumatic injuries over the past century. This has supported the credibility of reductionist scientific method as the dominant medical paradigm. Consequently, counsellors entering practice in modern medical settings sometimes find themselves struggling to mesh with the medical culture, given the emphasis in most therapeutic trainings on interpersonal relationships and intrapsychic processes, feelings, thoughts and meanings.

The development of biopsychosocial health care

It has become increasingly apparent during the second half of the twentieth century that biomedical models of care have their limits. Biomedicine has not solved the problems of the chronically ill and the disabled, or those with enduring and severe 'mental illness'. In some instances biomedicine has actually created new problems. Some families now face agonizing decisions about genetic testing and abortions, or infertility treatments and adoption, with few socially validated maps to guide them. Cancer patients and their families may face a bewildering variety of treatment options of unclear benefit to quality or length of life, perhaps leading into the uncertainties and tensions of three or four recurrences, in contrast to a clear expectation of death after the first recurrence.

Such factors have revived a view that many good GPs have always held, that effective health care requires emotional support, attention to relationships, helping families to construct meaning out of an illness experience, and mobilizing supportive networks beyond the medical practice, including the family. This has contributed to the recent trend for employing counsellors in primary care.

Counselling can be seen as an 'add-on' to an established biomedical system. This chapter contrasts such *multi*disciplinary practice with a more integrative and *inter*disciplinary approach, which recognizes that there are complex interactions between biological, psychological and social factors, requiring collaboration between health care professionals. This is often termed a 'biopsychosocial' approach, following a clarion call for a shift in the medical paradigm made by George Engel in 1977. (Engel is a prolific writer who has continued to develop the model and published extensively on this. The journal of collaborative family health care, *Families, Systems and Health* 14:4 (Winter 1996), contains several articles on and by Engel, and a list of his publications between 1942 and 1996.) The biopsychosocial model is based on general systems theory, stressing the need to understand symptoms and treatments in their biological, psychological and social contexts, including the combined family/professional health care system (see, for example, McDaniel et al., 1992).

Multidisciplinary practice

In a *multidisciplinary* approach to health care, each team member is viewed as having particular expertise in a certain kind of problem. In this model, effective team work requires an assessment of the problem type, leading to allocation of the work to the specialist in that area (see Figure 2.1).

Figure 2.1   A multidisciplinary model of health care

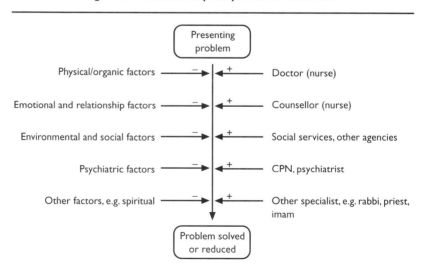

The multidisciplinary approach can seem attractive, since it appears to acknowledge each professional's expertise and separate identity. It offers a simple framework requiring relatively little collaboration beyond agreement and implementation of referral criteria and processes, combined with knowledge of, and access to, a range of specialist services inside and outside the GP practice.

This approach fits well with a biomedical approach to problem-solving which analyses the component parts of a system to find which is faulty, then directs treatment to mend this. This is probably a highly appropriate model of service delivery for some very straightforward problems, when combined with clear descriptions of the skills and expertise of the various providers and common agreement on referral criteria. This model of service delivery is based on a reductionist assumption that each aspect of a patient's life functions independently of others, and can be supported in like manner. However, in practice many presenting problems in primary care are complex, severe and/or chronic, and may involve a variety of interacting factors.

There is a risk that an 'add-on' counselling service which is not well integrated with other health care input will further contribute to a fragmentation of patient care and a continuation of the existing mind–body split in the traditional medical model. Just as, historically, medicine and the Church tacitly agreed to focus on separate aspects of the human condition (body vs. soul), an unwary counsellor in primary care can become 'the one who deals with the psychological/emotional/family stuff', while others work with 'the physical/real illnesses'.

A multidisciplinary approach based on separate specialties 'treating' within their area of expertise may lead to counsellors receiving 'dustbin' referrals where other practice members have encountered a problem they do not know how to solve (Example 1) or which they find distressing.

Example 1

Brian was referred to the counsellor by his GP because of persistent chest pains without apparent physical cause despite a number of tests. Brian accepted the GP's view that there was nothing wrong with his heart, and only visited the GP infrequently. He wanted to be free of the pains, but was puzzled about the rationale for seeing a counsellor. Brian seemed to be coping well with life in general. The counsellor and Brian spent three rather frustrating sessions together without finding a clear therapeutic focus before discontinuing. The GP seemed unsurprised, commenting only 'Well, I didn't think it would help but anything's worth a go, eh?' The counsellor resolved to be more wary of future referrals made on the basis that since 'nothing physical can be found, it must be psychological'. Brian's overall care remained unchanged and his chest pains persisted.

Professionals may sometimes try (consciously or not) to manage a difficulty within their own area of expertise by reframing it as a problem within the remit of a different professional's specialty and referring on. When this kind of referral is queried or refused, the referrer may become hostile, since their judgement is called into question and they are potentially faced with the same situation they have attempted to avoid with no new resources or strategies to manage it.

Counsellors are not highly placed in the medical hierarchy. Although an assertive counsellor can decline inappropriate referrals, in the long run the counsellor's position will be compromised if they are seen as uncooperative and say 'no' too many times.

A multidisciplinary approach may also lead to tensions and competition between the counsellor and those other team members (for example, nurse, receptionist, some GPs) who also see their role as providing psychosocial support, and may feel their 'territory' is under threat. This is a particularly severe risk for counsellors establishing a new service in a GP practice, since the new service constitutes an implicit or explicit attempt to improve the previous psychosocial support.

The multidisciplinary approach to health care is biopsychosocial only in the limited sense that the team as a whole includes practitioners who focus on 'bio-' factors, and those who focus more on '-psychosocial' issues. However, most patients will only meet one or a few members of the team, so the expertise contributing to each patient's overall care plan may vary considerably. Where a case appears to involve many different influences, the patient may end up 'doing the rounds' of several different professionals so that each can 'do their bit'. This can create further problems as the patient has to repeat their story many times, or finds themself in limbo with each professional assuming that others are taking the lead in the case. Still worse, a patient who finds that each consultation with a professional in the practice leads to a further referral may begin to feel that their problem is too severe or overwhelming for the practice to contain. In short, there can be a fragmentation of care, and patients may feel that they are slipping between the cracks.

Interdisciplinary practice

A simple multidisciplinary model such as that shown in Figure 2.1 depends on an assumption that different kinds of factors (organic, emotional, spiritual etc.) make separate contributions to the overall problem/solution development, which add together in a straightforward manner. This may lead to poor or no progress where presenting problems involve a complex interaction between factors traditionally

seen as the territory of different professionals. It may be helpful for counsellors to distinguish conceptually between 'disease', 'illness' and 'sickness'. Following Kleinman (1988) and Rolland (1994):

- **Disease** is the biological/physical description or understanding of
  a patient's condition. This is the traditional realm of biomedical
  expertise.
- **Illness** is the human (individual and family) experience of symptoms and suffering, including perceptions, beliefs, responses and
  adaptations. Whereas disease is something located in one person
  and their body, illness refers to the experiences of partners, family,
  friends and colleagues as well as the ill person, though the experience of each will vary.
- **Sickness** represents the meanings associated with particular diseases or physical issues by wider sociocultural forces, including
  political, economic and religious/moral discourses. Core social
  beliefs about the meaning of conditions such as AIDS, lung cancer,
  obesity, dementias, the menopause and impotence will shape and
  constrain the belief systems of families and professionals working
  with such conditions.

The interactions between biological, psychological and social factors
may be reciprocal and complex rather than simply additive (Figure 2.2).
The biopsychosocial approach emphasizes the *intersection* between
disease processes and developmental/life cycle themes for the individual and family (Figure 2.3).

The course of a disease (and treatment) can be likened to a wind
blowing across the life-path of the patient and family, blowing them off
the course which they had previously anticipated and planned for.
Severe and chronic illness may create wide divergences, pushing
families ever further into uncharted waters (Figure 2.4).

The experience of illness will vary with the life cycle stage it affects
(Example 2).

Example 2

A diagnosis of breast cancer in a young woman of 20 still living with her
parents may be experienced very differently from the same diagnosis with
a 66-year-old widow whose parents have already died. The young woman
may be faced with sterilization due to chemotherapy without previously
having contemplated motherhood, mutilating treatments and related anxieties about body image, and might be forced into greater reliance on her
parents at a time when she had previously been planning to set up home
on her own. The older woman might face similar mutilating treatments

Figure 2.2 Interactions between sickness, illness and disease

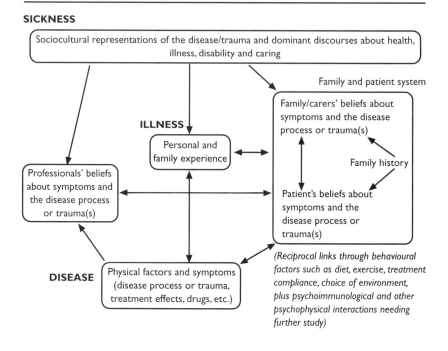

SICKNESS

Sociocultural representations of the disease/trauma and dominant discourses about health, illness, disability and caring

Family and patient system

Family/carers' beliefs about symptoms and the disease process or trauma(s)

ILLNESS

Personal and family experience

Family history

Professionals' beliefs about symptoms and the disease process or trauma(s)

Patient's beliefs about symptoms and the disease process or trauma(s)

DISEASE Physical factors and symptoms (disease process or trauma, treatment effects, drugs, etc.)

(Reciprocal links through behavioural factors such as diet, exercise, treatment compliance, choice of environment, plus psychoimmunological and other psychophysical interactions needing further study)

Figure 2.3 The interaction of disease and life cycle

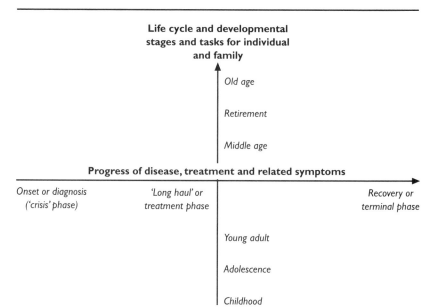

Life cycle and developmental stages and tasks for individual and family

Old age

Retirement

Middle age

Progress of disease, treatment and related symptoms

Onset or diagnosis ('crisis' phase)

'Long haul' or treatment phase

Recovery or terminal phase

Young adult

Adolescence

Childhood

Figure 2.4   The loss of an anticipated future

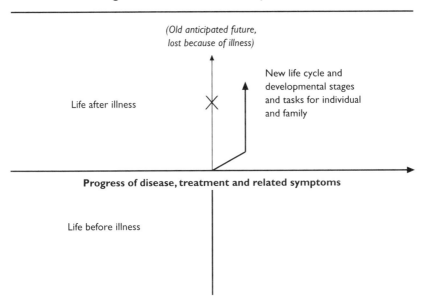

(Old anticipated future, lost because of illness)

Life after illness

New life cycle and developmental stages and tasks for individual and family

Progress of disease, treatment and related symptoms

Life before illness

and body image concerns but without the same levels of support and understanding from others in an ageist society (for example, not being offered equivalent reconstructive surgery). Her social and practical support options might be quite different without healthy parents to care for her, and she might instead be more reliant on her own children, social services or a network of retired friends in variable health.

Similarly, the experience of illness will vary with the nature and stage of the specific disease. The phases of 'onset/diagnosis', 'long haul/ treatment' and 'recovery/terminal' shown in Figure 2.3 will vary in their distinctness and significance in different illnesses. Some diseases may have a clear or acute initial onset (for example, heart attack), while others may be more insidious or mystifying (Alzheimer's, for example). Some conditions will tend to follow a relatively well-defined course for progression (as in Alzheimer's) or recovery (a broken leg), some will be relatively static (such as blindness), while others may have a relatively unpredictable or intermittent pattern of expression or progression (multiple sclerosis, brittle asthma or schizophrenia, for example). Some diseases or disabilities will be readily apparent to others (blindness), whilst others may be more concealed (diabetes), possibly leading to less discrimination, but perhaps also to less understanding and practical support. Illnesses will vary in the degree to which they are incapacitating, and similarly will vary in the expected outcome – from non-fatal through life-threatening to clearly fatal (see Rolland, 1994 for a more extended discussion of these themes in his chapter on 'The psychosocial typology of illness').

Conditions that are hard to predict by the patient or others, and that vary considerably over time, are likely to cause more disruption than conditions that can be anticipated and planned for. It is easier to make compensatory adjustments to a ship's steering when there is a moderate but steady cross-wind than when periods of calm are interspersed with typhoons, or when a succession of gales blow in random directions. Planning a journey tends to be easier when the distance to the destination is known (that is, when the duration of illness is known, whether ending in recovery or death), compared to a voyage of uncertain duration (a position facing many cancer patients prior to any recurrence).

The role of the counsellor in a health care setting can be compared to that of an assistant navigator, helping patients and families revise plans for lives thrown off course. Diseases and disabilities may be likened to difficult weather conditions, following patterns specific to the condition but with effects dependent on the point of its intersection with the life journey and a family's resources at that stage. In this metaphor, a variety of other professionals may help navigate and keep the ship in good shape for a difficult journey, with doctors playing a crucial role in weather forecasting.

Aims of biopsychosocially oriented counselling

Counselling should aim to help patients, carers and professionals:

- make some sense out of the illness experience in relation to the rest of the patient/carer(s)' lives and develop more capacity to predict and plan ahead;
- develop clearer boundaries between the illness experience and the rest of the patient and family's lives;
- develop a broader conceptualization of the location of the problem;
- reach agreement on meaningful and realistic goals;
- identify what is helpful;
- identify what is unhelpful.

Making sense of the illness experience

Patients need to construct some sense out of the illness experience in relation to the rest of their lives and develop more capacity to predict and plan ahead, both in relation to the illness and other life cycle or developmental tasks which might otherwise be 'left on hold' if the illness experience becomes too overwhelming. This requires attention to individual and intergenerational belief systems (Wright et al., 1996) and the family life cycle (Carter and McGoldrick, 1989).

Example 3

The counsellor working with Susan, the 20-year-old woman with breast cancer in Example 2, spent time with her plotting out on a large piece of paper a 'time-line' of her twenties 'as they might have been if this lurgy [her word] hadn't come on the scene'. Susan, an art student, illustrated the time-line with small cartoons rather than text, depicting events including 'I move out to a little flat of my own with a cat', 'I spend a Christmas on my own at long last', 'My girlfriend moves in with me and I come out to my friends', and in the second half of her might-have-been twenties, 'I come out to my parents', and 'I become rich and famous'. She drew 'a fork in the road' to show 'the path I'm on now', plotting out a bleak picture of a very dependent woman watched all the time by her parents. Over several sessions Susan and the counsellor mapped out several other forks in the road ahead, representing both choices she might make (such as whether to come out as a lesbian to her parents now, to make it possible for her girlfriend to visit her at home openly), and possible turns her illness might take. Some paths were very detailed, while Susan left some paths blank at this time, commenting for instance 'that's too bleak down there, I think it's just a dead end'. This process helped Susan rehearse some potentially difficult conversations with her family, and begin to envisage and plan for alternative futures with some choices.

Developing boundaries between illness and the rest of people's lives

It is important to develop clear boundaries between the illness experience and the rest of the patient and family's lives, so that the patient can feel and be seen as more than the embodiment of a disease or problem, and family members can feel and be seen as more than carers. Particularly where a disease or disability is chronic and severe, or where the disease seems pervasive or hard to locate (for example, diabetes, cancer, HIV infection, panic attacks without apparent trigger), there is a risk that the patient and the problem can seem to be one and the same thing, a dehumanizing process exacerbated by a reductionist bio-medical analysis of health problems.

Example 4

Malcolm and Anna argued with increasing frequency over the management of their 5-year-old autistic daughter's behaviour, the reason for the GP referral. Both felt angry and very tired. It became apparent in the first session that the family was already receiving a range of support and advice from many different educational and social services regarding Zuleika, and they were in fact overwhelmed by conflicting advice. They were facing serious financial difficulties as their previously successful fashion business declined, since neither was bringing in new business or developing new lines. They agreed that they spent '95 per cent' of their energies on Zuleika, which 'didn't leave much for other things'. They accepted the counsellor's suggestion to divide each therapy session in two with a short break in between, discussing Zuleika in the second part if they wanted, but focusing on their business management and relationship together in the first half. They smiled when the counsellor explained 'I'm not much of a businessman, but I know it's not a good idea to spend the year's budget on just one thing with a whole family business to run.' The conduct of the sessions modelled boundary setting to prevent the daughter's disability taking over the family, recreating the space they needed to address other normal family issues such as their business, extended family contacts and their own relationship. They began to set aside specific times for particular types of conversation at home, and stopped arguing about Zuleika so much when at work.

Contextualizing and relocating the problem

Counselling may aim at developing a broader conceptualization of the problem's location (and hence also the potential solutions and resources) away from just the identified patient to include family members and others whose quality of life is significantly affected by the patient's symptoms or disabilities.

Example 5

Stella suffered from chronic lower back pain following a ruptured disc 2 years previously. She was referred for counselling by the practice nurse for depression, which Stella related to a 'distancing' from her partner Marvin. Stella felt rejected, and believed Marvin had a new lover. Marvin agreed to attend for a joint interview to discuss 'how the back pain had been affecting them *as a couple*'. (Treating a disease or symptom as an unwelcome interloper in this way is a version of narrative therapy's externalization – White and Epston, 1990 – and can also be useful in creating a boundary between the illness and the person.) Marvin was surprised and hurt at Stella's suspicions, gradually explaining over two sessions how he had become increasingly reluctant to initiate sex with Stella because he worried this hurt her. Both were relieved at the emerging explanation of tender concern leading to misunderstanding, rather than a breakdown in their relationship. Stella and Marvin decided not to discuss their plans to revise their intimate practices further with the counsellor, and commented that they felt they could come up with some new ideas 'with a bit of practice'. This brief intervention involved a relocation of focus from Stella's back and mood to the couple relationship, and externalization of the pain.

Setting goals

The primary care counsellor may be able to help patients and/or staff reach agreement on meaningful and realistic goals (Example 6) and help provide feedback about progress towards these (Example 7 below).

Example 6

Michael was a 46-year-old man with a long history of chronic, heavy drinking. He was a frequent visitor to the practice with a variety of alcohol-related health problems. The GP referred Michael to counselling for 'depression' but at the initial meeting it became apparent that Michael was attending reluctantly. He explained that he thought counselling was a waste of time and had not found AA programmes or similar support helpful in the past, and hinted that he was only attending because his GP had expressed unwillingness to sign a sicknote unless he did so. The counsellor referred him back to the GP, but was taken aback the next day by the GP's heavy sarcasm and apparent anger at the counsellor's 'failure' to offer a counselling contract. After some tense discussion, the counsellor discovered that the GP and receptionist had been experiencing increasing difficulty managing Michael as he was turning up for surgeries more inebriated and becoming increasingly verbally abusive and threatening. The counsellor's input in a case discussion at a practice meeting played a part in developing agreement amongst practice staff on a common set of 'rules' for handling Michael's attendance. Containing Michael safely seemed a more helpful and realistic short-term aim for the team than 'curing' him. This also led to a wider discussion of staff safety issues at the practice.

Identifying what works

Counselling may help identify what is helpful so that this can be maintained and if possible amplified. This is vital to help foster a sense of control in the midst of the illness experience, and avoid undue dependence on others (for example, either by patients on their partners, by the partner on the practice receptionist, or by the GP on the counsellor) (Example 7).

Identifying what is unhelpful

It is also useful to try to identify what is unhelpful so that this can be reduced or, if possible, eliminated.

Example 7

Arthur (aged 68) had a slow-growing cancer of the prostate, and suffered considerable problems with pain in his abdomen and perineal area. He and his wife, Molly (aged 70), were referred by the practice nurse who saw the wife periodically to bandage leg ulcers. The nurse commented that Molly seemed very tired and run-down, and felt she had nothing to live for. Arthur and Molly explained that their lives seemed to have become taken over by repeated visits to the hospital for 'tests, bloody tests all the time' with several different consultants, with Molly commenting 'I dread the sound of the letter-box going each morning, all those brown appointment letters'. Arthur complained that he was 'too tired to do the crossword most days or even have a shower'. Liaison between the counsellor and the GP led to an agreement to refocus care on fatigue and managing pain within levels acceptable to Arthur, rather than eliminating pain altogether. The GP asked the practice physiotherapist to provide advice on conserving energy and related home appliances, prescribed slow-release morphine and involved the community Macmillan nurse service in place of the hospital's pain clinic. Counselling work continued, focusing on the resumption of aspects of family life (for example, seeing a new great-grandchild) which had tailed off in the face of illness, and the counsellor was able to provide feedback to the GP about the couple's appreciation of the family doctor's role as 'a reliable safety net' and information source. This helped the GP feel comfortable that he was 'doing enough' without making further referrals to the hospital.

Guidelines for developing collaborative practice

A biopsychosocial approach to health care requires counsellors to work collaboratively with other health care disciplines and family members, so that care is holistic and interdisciplinary rather than fragmented and multidisciplinary. Of course, this is easier said than done, and collaborative practice is not an all or nothing process. Varying degrees of collaboration will be appropriate and possible at different times, depending on the nature of the presenting problem, the counsellor's relationships with other practice members and the skills of those involved.

The counsellor's place in a biopsychosocial health care team

Although the development of counselling in primary care can be seen as a positive move towards more holistic practice, it can also be viewed

as an implicit criticism of the prevalent biomedical training and socialization of many medical professionals. Within any given GP practice,
there will probably be a range of different views amongst existing practice members about the purpose, value and desirability of working with
a counsellor. Other team members may see the counsellor as:

- a source of advice and consultation on emotional and psychological
  aspects of patient care, and an expert on mental health problems in
  the practice more accessible than hospital based services;
- a kind person to offer 'TLC' (tender loving care) to the 'worried well',
  freeing up doctors' time to work with patients 'who really need it';
- someone to persuade non-compliant patients to accept medical
  advice and treatments;
- the person who deals with relationship problems or family disputes;
- a fashionable accessory for a GP practice as a sop to current fads and
  trends;
- an information resource about services offered by outside agencies;
- an administrator or filter for onward referrals;
- someone to comfort practice staff who are feeling overstressed or
  burnt-out;
- a dumping ground for troublesome or 'heartsink' patients to
  provide respite for other practice members;
- a usurper of therapeutic roles that other practice members used to
  hold;
- no view, counsellor's role not understood or thought of much.

Such perceptions constrain the collaborative possibilities at any given
time. Conversely, effective collaboration can positively reshape these
perceptions. Counsellors in primary care need to consider carefully
how their work in the practice affects other members of the health care
team, and what hopes and fears colleagues might have about this. This
requires reflection on the previous history of counselling work within
the practice, changes in practice staffing and/or in local support services, funding arrangements, and so on.

Working in a small but potentially intense system like a GP practice
has some similarities to membership of a family. Counsellors who are
familiar with using genograms (McGoldrick and Gerson, 1985) to map
relationship patterns in families may find it useful to prepare a genogram
of the practice team 'family', including the counsellor, reviewing this
periodically in supervision. This can help identify opportunities for
change, or at least allow the counsellor to feel more able to anticipate
difficulties and prepare responses.

Different levels of collaborative practice would include the following.

- *Providing information* from counselling interviews to other members
  of the health care team to help them plan their interventions and
  guide their subsequent interviews.

- *Coaching patients* in the course of counselling interviews to provide relevant information, or to ask relevant questions, when they are talking with other health care team members.
- *Involving other members of the family* or significant system besides the identified patient, for example by inviting a partner or sibling to the counselling interview. A biopsychosocial approach to illness recognizes that there may be several simultaneously overlapping roles for the family when one member is unwell (e.g., Steinglass and Horan, 1988). The family can be seen as (a) a resource, (b) a cause of illness or additional stress, (c) a system affected by illness which may itself be in need of support, (d) a systemic context affecting the course, meaning and manifestation of illness.
- *Conducting joint interviews with another member of the health care team* and the patient and/or family. This could mean either the counsellor interviewing a patient in the presence of the other professional, or the counsellor 'sitting in' on another professional's consultation with a patient with an agreement about the way in which the counsellor may contribute during or after the session. It is usually advisable for one professional to take lead responsibility for conducting the interview, to avoid confusing the patient and allow the other professional space in the session to look, listen and think.
- *Modelling or teaching interviewing skills* to other health care team members, either explicitly in 'education' sessions or implicitly through demonstration in joint interviews or discussion of the counselling process.
- *Consulting* to another member of the health care team, through 'live' consultation during an interview with a patient, or through consultation with the professional on their own (see Bor and Miller, 1991 for a detailed exploration of this area).

Increasing collaboration

Counsellors will maximize their chances of developing collaborative practice (Josse, 1997) in a health care team if they:

- *learn about the system and their place in it.* As well as getting to know the practice team and local resources, a primary care counsellor should try to learn about medical culture, illnesses and treatments. Patients will benefit when counsellors and other staff speak a common language, and the counsellor has a good understanding of the psychosocial typology of particular illnesses and treatments.
- *do not oversell counselling or their own theoretical approach.* Counsellors

are not highly placed in the medical hierarchy, and so need to work by gradual persuasion and example rather than pressure-selling.

• *support the competence of others in the system.* This encourages others to give support in return, while providing them with positive feedback about what they are doing that works.

• *demonstrate their own skills and expertise.* Although it is advisable to adopt a modest approach, it is also important to demonstrate competency to others in the system. This generates confidence and helps the team understand how counselling can be used.

• *limit their role.* It is better to be seen to work effectively in some areas than work poorly in many. Further, some roles may exclude others – providing counselling to a fellow team member will make it difficult to return to a level collegial relationship for subsequent work.

• *understand and make use of other resources* (such as voluntary organizations, secondary mental health or rehabilitation services, local council advice services).

By contrast, collaboration is likely to decrease or be counterproductive when the counsellor:

• *fails to meet core demands of the job as seen by key figures in the hierarchy.* Collaboration may sometimes open up potentially fruitful avenues which need to be deferred until there is scope to renegotiate time and priorities with senior figures in the hierarchy.

• *overstretches their competencies.* Different types of collaborative practice require different skills, and no counsellor will be equally skilled in all areas. Successful collaboration in one area may lead to invitations for further work which are beyond the counsellor's current competencies to the extent that their credibility might suffer.

• *trespasses on the territory of others.* Some members of the health care team may feel threatened by overly insistent attempts to develop collaborative practice if this is seen as (a) implicit criticism of their current skills, (b) a block to the development of their own interests, or (c) an attempt by the counsellor to gain position at their expense in the practice.

• *fails to recognize others' competencies, or undermines independent working.* Collaborative practice is not a single method, such as joint interviewing, nor an end in itself. Effective collaboration requires consideration of what is necessary and economical to achieve appropriate clinical goals.

• *forms coalitions rather than alliances.* There will be variations in the degree to which collaborative practice is possible or acceptable with different practice members. Counsellors need to be wary of developing extensive collaborative practice with one member of the team where this might be perceived as a coalition against another member of the practice, particularly if the coalition is against a more senior figure in the practice hierarchy.

Conclusion

A biopsychosocial approach promotes the combination of psychological and therapeutic expertise about family life cycles, development issues and belief systems with medical expertise about diseases and disability. This allows the professional team to offer patients and families a two-dimensional map to navigate a way through illness. This stands in marked contrast to biomedical and multidisciplinary frameworks, which offer patients one-dimensional medical and psychological views which parallel one another but never meet. Combining biological and psychosocial perspectives into a truly biopsychosocial approach requires collaborative and interdisciplinary team work. This can be both challenging and rewarding for counsellors. This chapter has identified some guidelines for counsellors who wish to develop collaboration in primary care to support their clients.

Key points

- Biomedicine tends to treat patients as collections of organs and systems which can be treated in isolation. This paradigm has proved valuable against many infectious and acute diseases, but less so with chronic and complex conditions.
- Multidisciplinary approaches which assign particular aspects of care to different specialists risk a continued fragmentation of patient care.
- A biopsychosocial approach recognizes that there are complex interactions between biological, psychological and social factors, requiring interdisciplinary collaboration between health care professionals and the family.
- The experience of illness is related to the intersection between disease processes and developmental/life cycle themes, within a sociocultural context.
- Combining a range of professional and family perspectives helps create multidimensional maps of the illness experience and treatment options.
- The type and level of collaborative practice that is possible will vary, depending on factors such as the particular condition, and the current skills and attitudes of those involved.
- Counsellors need to learn about the medical system and work within this rather than against or outside it.

References

Bor, R. and Miller, R. (1991) *Internal Consultation in Health Care Settings*. London: Karnac.

Carter, B. and McGoldrick, M. (1989) *The Changing Family Life Cycle: a Framework for Family Therapy*, 2nd edn. London: Allyn and Bacon.

East, P. (1995) *Counselling in Medical Settings*. Buckingham: Open University Press.

Families, Systems and Health, 14(4), pp. 409–50. Special section on and by George Engel and the development of the biopsychosocial model.

Kleinman, A.M. (1988) *The Illness Narratives: Suffering, Healing and the Human Condition*. New York: Basic Books.

Josse, J. (1997) Personal communication.

McDaniel, S.H., Hepworth, J. and Doherty, W.J. (1992) *Medical Family Therapy: a Biopsychosocial Approach to Families with Health Problems*. New York: Basic Books.

McGoldrick, M. and Gerson, R. (1985) *Genograms and Family Assessment*. New York: Norton.

Rolland, J.S. (1994) *Families, Illness and Disability*. New York: Basic Books.

Steinglass, P. and Horan, M.E. (1988) 'Families and chronic medical illness', in F. Walsh and C. Anderson (eds), *Chronic Disorders and the Family*. New York: Haworth.

White, M. and Epston, D. (1990) *Narrative Means to Therapeutic Ends*. New York: Norton.

Wright, L.M., Watson, W.L. and Bell, J.M. (1996) *Beliefs: the Heart of Healing in Families and Illness*. New York: Basic Books.

CHAPTER 3

DOCTORS, COUNSELLORS AND THEIR PATIENTS: INTRAPSYCHIC AND INTERPERSONAL ISSUES

Susan Hopkins and Mary O'Callaghan

Counselling is essentially a relational activity. In the primary care setting counsellors are involved in a complex network of relationships, involving members of the primary health care team, and often a variety of outside agencies. Because the doctor has clinical responsibility for the health care provision for the patient, and is the most usual referrer, it is especially important that efforts are made by both doctors and coun-sellors to develop a collaborative relationship in order to ensure the most effective patient care. There is a growing literature, of which this book is part, which attempts to form guidelines for the negotiation of these relationships, and evidence-based criteria for inter-professional referral and communication.

However, because this clinical setting is so complex, many of the potential pitfalls and complications are inevitably unseen; powerful irrational processes can operate below the surface. This chapter examines some of the intrapersonal and interpersonal processes associated with the doctor/patient/counsellor relationship and its interconnections within the primary health care team. This relation-ship could be conceptualized as a 'triangle' within a complex 'system'. Further configurations and issues arise from this conceptualization. The list cannot be exhaustive, but this can be a starting point, and an aid to reflection. It should generate as many questions as it answers.

Areas of general concern to counsellors include:

- Variations in the doctor/patient relationship.
- Pros and cons of teamworking.
- Influence of internal consultation.
- Conflicts between delegation and omnipotence.

- Power and hierarchical issues.
- Conscious and unconscious assumptions about roles.
- Legal issues and accountability.
- Political and socioeconomic pressures.
- Differing models of health care.
- Differing methods of problem resolution.
- Problems of professional stress management.
- Use of supervision.
- Unexamined prejudices about gender, race and culture.
- Mind/body splits.
- Neglect of reflective practice leading to unconscious acting-out.

All or any of these factors will have an effect on the triangle of the doctor/patient/counsellor relationship. Not all members of the health care team may appreciate that these influences exist, and that their degree of awareness will, in itself, have its own effect. Just as the understanding of physics has moved through Newtonian theory to chaos theory, it emerges that everything in health care practice affects everything else. It could also be argued that a practice is like a complex biological organism, seeking homeostasis, in a state of continual change, and prone to chain and cascade reactions.

Tales of the unexpected

Any day in a health care practice can bring surprises:

Lucia arrived for her second counselling session. She was a 40-year-old housewife of Mediterranean origin, separated from her English husband, and living with her two primary school age children. She suffered from a serious physical disease which took some time to diagnose correctly, involving many visits to the hospital. She looked unhealthy and harassed. The counsellor had been told by the doctor that this patient was an 'urgent referral', but fixing appointments had been difficult because of her many outpatient attendances. The first session had seemed full of overwhelming distress to which the counsellor felt she could only listen, while wondering how she could possibly offer anything helpful ... But as Lucia sat down, she said, 'I feel so much better already – I am no longer angry with the doctors!'

It took some time to work out what might have happened here. There is a question about which problem, or indeed *whose* problem was being addressed.

At a counsellor supervision group meeting, one member, Margaret, was upset and puzzled by the behaviour of the doctors at her group practice. Their reaction to her plan to find another job (linked with changes in her personal life) seemed out of all proportion. They were full of grief and anger, and she felt 'emotionally blackmailed'. Discussion seemed to indicate that they had been using her as a confidante, even phoning her at home with their own problems. She seemed to have 'become' someone special in their minds, more than the practice counsellor.

This scenario suggests that the presence of a counsellor in a general practice has an impact at different levels, beyond the direct work with patients.

Delegation and omnipotence

Some doctors recognize that they have mixed feelings about delegation. They may hold the view that the doctor/patient relationship is central to their work, but the context of that work is changing so fast that a gap is opening between the traditional ideals of medicine and the current realities of the doctor's experience. Boundaries and roles are changing, and there are losses as well as gains. The doctor's role has always had these 'fuzzy boundaries' and the position is not becoming any clearer. Arguably there are circumstances when doctors have been seduced into taking omnipotent responsibility, and this pressure can come from several different directions. No doubt, if doctors do feel that they are responsible for patients' total well-being, they may feel this burden *will* need to be shared, although they sometimes feel vaguely guilty about it. Popular publications, both medical and non-medical, frequently run features with headlines such as 'GPs should look after [cause of the month] says X [insert pressure group, Minister, academic committee etc.]'. It is genuinely bewildering for doctors to decide realistically how much they can accomplish.

Questions have been raised as to whether patients wish to have the doctor's work delegated. There has been some evidence to suggest that patients may prefer smaller practices, non-training practices and practices with personal list systems. There have been suggestions that practice organization should be reviewed in order to ensure that the trend towards larger practices, providing a wider range of services, does not lead to a decline in patient satisfaction (Baker and Streatfield, 1995). There are grumbles to be heard about too-short consultations, and difficulty in discussing personal issues with the doctor. Patients appear to want to be truly 'heard' on several levels, and especially in a direct and personal way. Whatever arrangements the doctor makes within the practice, with or without a counsellor, patients want and need to feel that *their* benefit was intended. This has considerable bearing on the quality of the doctor/patient relationship.

Quality in relationship is linked with 'being taken seriously', and there seems also to be evidence that patients want 'listening and talking therapies'. A carefully considered referral can enhance the doctor/patient relationship, but access can be difficult. NHS waiting lists may seem long, and private help is sometimes too expensive for low-income patients. Agencies each have their own criteria for acceptance, and the patient in question may not 'fit', despite the referring doctor's request. There is some reason to conclude that lower-income group patients are less likely to be offered psychotherapy, and this has been confirmed in some simulated experimental studies (Bromley, 1995). It might therefore seem reasonable to suppose that the practice counsellor will be the person to help patients who cannot obtain therapy from other sources, for whatever reason. Awareness of this situation is also a factor which affects the counsellor's feelings, and relationships with other professionals. To feel that one is the 'first and last resort' is a powerful experience, and has many implications, both desirable and undesirable.

Evolution of the doctor/patient relationship

It is because primary health care *is* the first and last resort for many patients that the experience of working in it is so demanding and yet so fascinating. This was always an intense experience for the doctor working with minimal back-up. When Michael Balint began his action research with groups of doctors in the early 1950s, the idea of a 'practice team' was unknown. The doctor might possibly have had a receptionist, or perhaps one partner, but in essence had a one-to-one relationship with the patient. Balint saw the doctor's participation in this relationship as one of listening, understanding and using the understanding so that it should have a therapeutic effect. This contribution was likened to a dose of a drug, the drug being the doctor's use of himself or herself (Balint, 1964). In psychodynamic terms, the doctor was 'created' as the patient's 'object' during the patient's interactions with the doctor. This relationship and its use could be examined by means of discussion of the doctor's countertransference in the training-and-research group.

At that time, the doctor/patient relationship was undiluted by other health care workers unless the patient was referred to hospital or other agency. The question of *responsiveness* in the relationship was very much at issue. The most important effects of the 'drug' called 'doctor' were mediated through the doctor's response to what the patient 'brought'. It was recognized that if a referral took place, this was a new, additional factor in the relationship. This might mean more than the single issue of additional technical expertise. Either the doctor might *feel* lacking in the expertise to help this patient, or the patient might *have doubts* of a similar kind about the doctor (Balint, 1964). The salient point here is that a referral is often occasioned as much by the *feelings* of the protagonists as by the more 'scientific' criteria in the textbook. Exploration of these feelings illuminates much in the way of half-conscious or unconscious processes between doctor and patient. Exploration can uncover factors which might lead to misunderstandings, and derail the purpose and value of the referral. A common problem arises when the patient believes that the referral is made in order to 'get rid of a nuisance'. It is then understandably difficult to approach new treatments in a positive spirit and gain benefit from them.

Doctors and patients are human and fallible, and there are sometimes negative feelings around. The phenomenon of 'serial referrals' may reflect discomfort in the doctor/patient relationship, and this can lead to what Balint called a 'collusion of anonymity' with no one left feeling truly responsible. This collusion can be a defensive reaction, more easily evoked in some individuals than in others. Some patients are especially likely to elicit this reaction, and sadly, sometimes they are the most deeply troubled ones. Alternatively, the patient may be a willing participant in this tacit collusion. In any case, the one-to-one therapeutic relationship can sometimes feel intense in a negative way; as many counsellors and therapists already know. As an analyst, Balint understood this, and recognized the implications. He felt that the 'collusion of anonymity' could also be described as a 'process of dilution of responsibility'. This was a harsh but probably important insight. He also noted that 'problem patients' evoked aberrant reponses from the doctor and could 'play one doctor off against the other'. In this respect, very little has changed since the early days of the NHS, but now, in the 1990s, dysfunctional 'games' can be played with the whole practice team in a similar way. This is especially likely to become an issue between doctor, patient and psychological-health workers. In the interests of fairness and accuracy, it should be added that it is not only patients who play dysfunctional games!

Pros and cons of teamworking

It can be useful to think of the doctor, patients and counsellor, and the wider group of the practice team, as being part of a system which exhibits feedback phenomena and circularity, and makes up a complex whole which is more than an aggregate. We may need also to examine the idea of the 'team', an appealing concept, which may occasionally prove to be an oversimplification. It has been said that systems exist in the eye of the beholder. Multidisciplinary groups may not always operate like a team. The members may have different goals, trainings, affiliations and beliefs. Perhaps it is a miracle that they can work together at all (Hopkins, 1974). Nevertheless, there they are, colleagues with the best of conscious intentions (McCaughan and Palmer, 1994). When team relationships go well, the members have mutual support, and pleasure and intellectual stimulation from working with other people from different disciplines.

However, systemic theory is extremely useful in understanding and facilitating team collaboration and the relationships involved. The health care team can seem like a living system, with potential for growth, stimulated by internal activity, external influences and feedback from various sources. This system can contain sub-systems, and it may itself form a sub-system of a supra-system (for example, the NHS). Combination of systems theory with psychodynamic theories offers the possibility of applying what has been learned about the individual human system to other interpersonal systems (Hornby, 1995). The doctor/patient/counsellor relationship could be regarded as a sub-system within the practice. The practice team could also be likened to a 'family', and observation of its behaviour might give rise to an 'interactional diagnosis'. Using this idea, one might gain some insight into the situation described in the vignette about Margaret, earlier in this chapter. It may be that the practice team in question felt they were being abandoned by someone they unconsciously 'saw' as their caring mother-figure, and the counsellor then became the focus of desperate regressive wishes and child-like rage.

Practice team members need to keep in mind that every member inevitably affects every other member. Lines of communication need careful maintenance, and work needs to be done on conscious separation between professional relationships and personal needs. It may well be that different members of the team have differing personal models of the human psyche. However, we can all be surprised by something outside our own terms of reference. Interpersonal or intrapersonal phenomena can and will occur, regardless of our theoretical orientation or training syllabus!

The team itself may become the focus of care, leaving less time for patient contact. A recent report from the Royal College of General Practitioners expressed some concern on this account. This suggests that the processes that encouraged dilution of responsibility have also diminished the richness and quality of relationship, as over-efficient defences often do. Job satisfaction can be lost in this way, and the Royal College may now be modifying its previous view on the ever-expanding team (RCGP, 1996).

Expertise and internal consultation

Sometimes doctors may take the view that in employing a counsellor they have hired a psychological 'expert', and the counsellor may be called upon to act as an 'internal consultant'. Systemic theory is a useful reference point in such a task. Being invited to 'consult' indicates trust and respect from the members of the team who actually made that decision, but of course is fraught with risk. The varying beliefs and reciprocal relationships within the team need to be elicited, and note taken of the feelings that are aroused. The consultant needs to be self-reflective, since it is probable that personal bias affects the supposedly 'neutral' hypothesizing and formulating. The counsellor may have a stance that unconsciously favours the counselling service at the expense of some other facet of the practice. Never forget that you are going to be around to see, and live with the results of any 'internal consultancy'. Whatever the outcome, the other practice members will have views and feelings about that outcome, and will also remember whose consultation appeared to initiate any associated change.

Natalie was keen to extend and improve her practice-based counselling service, and successfully 'sold' this idea to the doctors. They agreed that she could use one of the better-furnished and quieter rooms, instead of the cramped one her predecessor had occupied. She would also extend her hours of work, and see patients later in the evening. Both Natalie and the doctors were delighted with this plan. But the practice storage was idiosyncratic, as it often is, having been planned in a piecemeal way. The room that the counsellor had chosen was indeed large enough for seating couples and families. It was also the room that was large enough for the extra cupboard space that the practice nurse used for some of her equipment. She often wanted access to these cupboards at times when the counsellor was working, and did not want to be interrupted. A great deal of bad feeling was generated by this apparently mundane problem. It adversely affected the nurse's view of the counsellor and the counselling service, and nobody was left in any doubt about those feelings. The nurse felt her 'territory' had been invaded. She also felt that her place in the hierarchy was threatened because she had to wait until the counsellor finished seeing patients, as if the counsellor's work was considered more important.

So it seems that a 'molehill' can easily grow into a 'mountain', and unfortunately this can be a common occurrence. Many practice problems originate in an *apparently* trivial way. It is not only the substance of the decision that matters, but what that *means* to other people. In the example above the consultation about practice services had not been sufficiently thorough, and although the counselling service might have been improved, other problems arose. It is always important to try to understand as much as possible about the effects of the consultation (Bor and Miller, 1991).

Doctors may be keen to solicit comments on the service offered to patients. This requires caution about the *style* as well as the substance. The consultant, or the new arrival, will need essential information about the not-so-obvious 'rules' existing among the group members. All interventions can have a 'ripple effect', and almost anything can influence the rest of the system. Attachments and alliances within the team may be significant, have powerful effects on role behaviour, and arouse feelings of exclusion and suspicion in others. There is always a delicate balance point between valuing one's own contribution as a counsellor and maintaining individuality while cooperating with the doctors and other team members.

Power, hierarchy and responsibility

Practices vary in their capacity to allow counsellors a real voice in the team. Having a place at the team meeting is important in order to use that voice. It is also useful to discover where power is *perceived* to be, where it actually is, and why. This is a particularly tricky issue for counsellors who may previously have worked independently, or perhaps in a specialist agency.

Counsellors may find that they are excluded from team meetings. This may be either deliberate or unintentional. Someone who only works in the practice on one day per week may be seen as peripheral and be 'forgotten'. Sometimes 'forgetting' may reflect conscious or unconscious undervaluing, or even denigration.

Patricia was trying to establish a place for herself, as counsellor, in the practice team. But both she and the Community Health Visitor had, despite several requests, been excluded from meetings. In fact, the only people who attended team meetings were the doctors, nurses and practice manager. Patricia felt that this might mean that biomedical and organizational perspectives were the only ones which were valued in that practice, and psychosocial topics were marginalized, and perhaps even considered dispensable. She felt hurt and resentful, and it added to her sense of isolation. She tried to communicate with the doctors in snatched moments in the corridor. What she did not realize, and nobody talked about, was that the doctors felt overloaded by the frequent new directives from the NHS authorities. Meetings were filled up with new plans to implement, and the doctors' minds were occupied with anxieties. There was no 'space' for the counsellor.

When doctors employ counsellors, they often imagine that this arrangement will *save time* for them. It is then difficult to accept that they may need to make time for the counsellor. Furthermore, medical culture has a strong tradition of 'busy-ness'. Crammed schedules and long working hours are considered normal. The phrase 'busy doctor' occurs so often in the media that it could perhaps be converted into a single word. There is often too much to do, and yet doctors often feel ashamed to admit that they cannot find time for further tasks; that seems to them to indicate incompetence. None of this can be easily unpacked, because they are supposed to be 'in charge'. Their NHS contract is framed in such a way that the final responsibility rests with them, since they are 'independent contractors'. Further issues arise from this, especially with regard to professional stress and its management.

The counsellor may wish to know what the practice pressures are, in order to feel genuinely useful. Or the counsellor may already know, and have ideas they want to discuss with the doctors. But it always needs to be remembered that the counsellor is also an employee of the practice and some issues are risky. Inter-doctor differences of opinion constitute one of these. Agreement about assessment and referral criteria is vital, but not always easy to arrive at. If one doctor is selective about referral, and another can fill up the waiting list in no time at all, there is potential for resentment between the partners, and difficulties for the counsellor. On the other hand, the counsellor may feel glad to be 'needed'. There may have been controversy in the practice about the cost of employing a counsellor.

Re-referral of patients to other agencies is a topic that requires careful policy discussion. To the doctors this may feel like a double delegation, and may arouse anxiety if they feel they do not really know the practitioners at the 'XY Centre for Psychotherapy'. They will remember that their contract holds them responsible for the actions of all their employees, and they already worry about what the counsellor is doing behind her closed door. They may even fear being involved in a False Memory scandal, especially if all the other members of the patient's family are on the practice list. The doctors do indeed have power, but they also have responsibility, and may feel more burdened by it than they care to admit.

Some team members may feel that the doctor has power and does not use it appropriately. But it may not feel like that for the doctor. Doctors often feel persecuted by health service authorities, and equally persecuted by patients. People who are suffering, and convey it vividly, are sometimes experienced as insatiable and attacking. The NHS complaints system is often more responsive than some people realize, and the Patient's Charter has had the effect of escalating demand without significantly increasing resources. Bureaucracy can interfere unhelpfully.

Patient/doctor relationships seem to have become more oppositional in the years following the 1990 NHS 'Reforms'. All NHS practices are contractually obliged to operate complaints procedures, and information from in-house complaints procedures will be admissible in court actions. So there are more than the obvious usual psychological issues, and not all fears are irrational. The doctor may say 'No' to an idea for a variety of reasons, and one of them may be to avoid losing control.

The counsellor might also feel that she does not want to be drawn into all these anxieties, and retreat into a narrow role where she feels safe. The counsellor may rationalize this by saying that she 'wants to concentrate on patients' or 'wants to preserve confidentiality'. Being thus cocooned may feel good for the counsellor, but can arouse envy in the more exposed members of the team. This can also conjure up the demon of gender stereotyping: 'That part-time woman . . . hardly ever see her . . . don't really know what she does . . .'

However, if the doctor/counsellor relationship is functioning well, there will probably be an improvement in the doctor/patient relationship. Patients may like to have an in-house service, and feel more at ease with it, and if the lines of communication are good, the doctors can feel reassured about what is being offered to their patients, and less anxious than they feel about outside referrals (Jewell, 1992).

The counsellor will need to address the question of what 'size' her role is. This includes what size she feels comfortable with, and which size the practice wants.

Various factors may influence the 'role size'.

- Which other psychologically orientated professions are represented in the practice team?
- Who feels competent to take on the task of psychological assessment?
- Who makes the decisions on referral policy?
- Is there any plan for psychological education of other staff members?
- Is there a place for the counsellor in health promotion activities?
- Does the practice want to provide opportunities for group-work? This requires extra organizational input.
- Is the counsellor going to take on trainees for supervision?

These are examples of areas of expansion for the counsellor's role, all of which have multiple implications for other team members, and their beliefs and feelings about their own roles.

Role size is a very significant power issue in a practice. It is arguable that the role-defining power of professionals has sometimes been used to service their own narcissistic needs. Role maintenance should not be debased into status maintenance, nor role promotion be inflated into oversell and empire-building. All these get in the way of an authentic working alliance. Any of us can be led astray by false pride in our job titles. It is probably salutary to remember our real purpose, and have in mind a 'user-centred' model of care, placing the patient at the centre, surrounded by collaborating 'face-workers' who are the relevant health professionals (Hornby, 1995).

Triangles: conscious and unconscious

Whatever psychological theory we espouse, there is a common view that relationships of three people are highly charged in emotional terms. The doctor/patient/counsellor triad may, for instance, provide an oedipal experience for the patient, who perhaps feeling needy and regressed, is passed from the doctor who performs the 'phallic' or 'scientific' functions of medicine, to the counsellor for nurturing 'maternal' containment of emotions. This may feel good or bad, according to the contents of the patient's psyche, but it is hardly ever a neutral matter.

An intra-practice referral can be conceptualized as a triangle. Referral by the doctor to any psychological service instigates a three-cornered emotional relationship, and may 'hold' the idea of referral suitability through the initial stages. As with any new arrangement, each participant has to decide whether, and how, to become involved with the others (Clulow, 1985). In the in-house setting of counselling in the practice, the question of mutual involvement of the doctor and the counsellor is at least partially pre-decided. It may be their relationship which facilitates (or not!) the patient's entry into the counselling process. It can happen that patients who were at first uncertain about using the counselling service were 'held' by the relationship of the doctor and counsellor while 'tasting' it. This may permit a kind of decision period for tentative or volatile patients, a period which may have not been 'there' for the patient in an external referral. The patient's awareness of the doctor/counsellor relationship may therefore assist the process and reduce fearful fantasies, enabling at the start. One could say that in the patient's unconscious mind the doctor and counsellor are already 'related' as a care-taking 'couple' and part of the 'practice family'. It should not be forgotten that the same kind of unconscious factors might sometimes cause an apparently appropriate referral to fail.

For the patient, acceptance of the process of referral is already a force for change. It may be experienced as a move from a 'world of two' (one-to-one with the doctor in the patient's mind) to a 'world of three', and the ability to accept this triangular relationship could be an important step in the patient's psychological development (Jones et al., 1994).

Sometimes the patient's relationship with the counsellor is very much like that with the other team professionals and/or inextricably bound up with them. It has been suggested that in the work in primary care practices there is frequently a dual transference – to the doctor, and to the counsellor – and that this is another way of looking at the 'referral triangle'. Initially a patient of the practice may be considered to be in a transference relationship to the doctor (Balint, 1964). When the patient is referred to the counsellor, there can appear to be *two* layers of transference. In psychoanalytic terms the practice could be said to be acting as the 'overall container' for the patient's anxieties; this includes the oedipal triangle and quasi-parental couple previously mentioned. Understanding of this relationship can be used, both in thinking about the patient's internal world and observing the actual relationship between them and the staff 'couple'. It is likely that these unconscious dynamics will affect the doctor/counsellor/patient relationship, and the work, *and more so if they are not addressed.* Working with awareness of the dynamics should improve care. If the double transference can be thought about it can enrich the work, but in order to do so the doctor and the counsellor must be able to cooperate. This is very much about sharing knowledge and feelings in a mature way.

Unconscious messages

It has been suggested that primary care practices have a 'special psychological atmosphere', providing a continuous relationship or 'home' where the patients could enter and re-enter over a period of time, without there being a feeling of a formal break in the helping relationship (Balint, 1964). It may be that counselling in this setting can allow for kinds of closeness, distance and variation not usually risked in standard counselling practice. This special atmosphere is a shared one; it may be broken up if team relationships deteriorate. The counsellor may need to adapt to this atmosphere, as contrasted with other counselling settings. Boundaries may be different and more 'fuzzy'. The needs and expectations of the patient may now be projected on the *group* of health care professionals rather than *one*. In the patient's mind the 'group' may be the object of transference of many complex emotions.

Richard had been registered with the practice for many years. He had been abandoned by his mother at an early age, and when his marriage broke up in his middle years the repetition of emotional loss precipitated a severe depression. He received many hours of help from the counsellor, but seemed passive, stuck and dependent. He continued to attend, and the counsellor began to feel that he had developed an adhesive kind of attachment, and could not use the help in moving on. One day, she unexpectedly had the opportunity to observe his behaviour with the reception staff, when she went into reception to look for the next patient, who was late. Richard seemed animated and chatty, almost as if he were enjoying himself! She felt that he may have 'replaced' his estranged wife and children with the practice staff, and this caused him to feel welcome and cosy, and even more likely to attend.

Sometimes we wonder why patients fail to 'get better'. The wish to be looked after is very seductive. This can apply to non-patients as well. The counsellor may be felt to be the one who 'looks after feelings', as if she were personifying some maternal archetype.

One day when the counsellor arrived for work, the harassed receptionist said glumly (and perhaps enviously?), 'What about counselling for the *staff*?' The counsellor smiled sympathetically, but resisted the temptation to go any further into what she sensed would be a minefield.

How do the staff 'see' the patients who are referred for counselling? Maybe there is a 'problem child'. One may need to ask in whose interests is the referral in question. And suppose that the chemistry between the patient and the counsellor does not seem all right. Is it appropriate to persuade those who are doubtful? At the rational level perhaps it may seem so, but these are uncomfortable questions, and the referrer may not want the patient 'back' yet. It is hard for the doctor to sit and listen to anxiety-generating material without taking some action. The doctor may find the patient's distress unbearable, for various reasons, not least his or her own. Some doctors make more bereavement referrals than one might expect, but then it may help to bear in mind that for the doctor, the death of a patient's relative, who may also have been a patient of the practice, may feel like a painful therapeutic failure, no matter how unavoidable it actually was. The doctors may not be fully conscious of their own distress. They may feel haunted by past mistakes of various kinds.

Sarah needed and requested a lot of help from her counselling supervision group. The doctor in her practice had recently referred several children with obvious psychiatric problems. She had no special training or expertise in this area, and had made this clear to the doctor. Now she felt angry and 'dumped on'. But she was new to the job and uncertain how to handle the problem of inappropriate referrals. She tried to discuss the matter with the doctor at the practice meeting, but he became very agitated, not so much about reviewing referral procedure, as by her reluctance to see children in the future. The doctor said huffily that *he* did not have the luxury to pick and choose whom *he* saw. (This comment seemed to contain a number of issues, including that of envy.) The counsellor felt it was inappropriate to isolate one of the children, an 11-year-old girl, as the 'problem', because the issues were family ones. The child already felt very alone, over-responsible and depressed. She had had to find her own way to the surgery, got lost and was half an hour late for her counselling appointment. She did not want to come to counselling, but was complying with her parents' wishes, in particular those of her father. He turned up to collect the child, and the counsellor took the opportunity to discuss the possibility of family therapy. Father was not in favour, and became angry.

The counsellor felt that some of the dynamics were mirrored in the way the team responded to the referral. The doctor made an inappropriate referral to a counsellor who felt insufficiently trained. The counsellor then felt 'dumped on', in a way identifying with the child. She then tried to hand the case back to the doctor, incurring his anger, mirroring the anger of the father who was hoping to be 'rescued' by a compliant daughter. Eventually the counsellor managed, with her supervision group, to formulate a way to communicate all this back to the doctor. This analysis offered a kind of interactional diagnosis which was freeing for both the doctor and the counsellor. Referral procedures were reviewed. Then the doctor revealed that a few years earlier he had experienced similar difficulties when the patient's elder sister had been the 'problem'. He had 'overlooked' this significant fact in his unease and urgency.

Alternatively, the doctor may be reluctant to relinquish an intriguing exploration of a patient's problems.

Valerie was asked to 'take over' and 'tidy up' a situation where a patient had been in twice-weekly 'therapy' with an over-enthusiastic locum doctor, who had no actual training in counselling. The patient had developed expectations which could not be fulfilled in the practice setting. She felt abandoned when the locum moved on, and was extremely angry, *probably with good reason*. A difficult situation had to be acknowledged, and a more appropriate referral for 'real' long-term therapy was arranged with an outside agency.

Any dysfunction in the relationships in the group may contribute to unhelpful 'splits' in the patient's psyche. Equally, the split may originate in the patient and be acted out in the group. The more team members there are, the more complex are the possibilities. Conceptualization of the team as a feedback system may seem too simple; the idea of a neural net may feel more apposite.

Goodwill can be transferable, and can aid counselling where the relationship between doctor and patient is one of 'mutual investment' (Balint, 1964). Doctors and nurses can themselves take a counselling role, and often do so, as seen in the above vignette. There is considerable scope for overlap. But there may be feelings of envy and competition within the practice team on this account. However, a sense of failure or frustration on the part of the referrer may sometimes motivate referral and the preparation for it. There may be some unconscious hope that the 'expert' will also fail. This can make the referrer feel better about their own unsuccessful struggle.

That kind of unconscious, or half-conscious communication may have a far-reaching effect. It can confirm for patients that what they find unmanageable within themselves is also unmanageable to others; a very frightening message, and one which may be echoed by the patient's family (Clulow, 1985). There may be a group countertransference if members of the professional team are unconsciously cast in 'family' roles and may 'act out' in relevant ways. Careful attention needs to be paid to the feelings and interactions in the doctor/counsellor relationship, and any other team members involved. The unconscious factors at work are not only those of the patient.

Perhaps all referrals contain an unconscious message. They may be expressions of love, hate or ambivalence. They may be manifestations of rivalry and competition, or defensive. Inevitably they reveal something about the psychodynamics of the referrer and his/her transference to the person receiving the referral, and to the patient. We all need to own up to what Jung called 'the shadow', and our less admirable motives. However, mutual respect can facilitate the use of the insights gained in counselling by *all* the parties concerned. Sometimes the doctor will find that the counsellor's report enables them to see the patient in a new light, to the benefit of all the relationships.

Thinking together and coping

Joint group work helps practice teams and/or staff groups to learn more about interpersonal and unconscious processes. Groups of this sort are now widely used in vocational training schemes for training doctors in primary care, and have contributed greatly to doctors' understanding of psychological issues and interest in counselling and therapy (Dammers and Wiener, 1995). For counsellors, it is useful to select supervisors who are acquainted with primary care issues, to help the counsellor avoid being overwhelmed and shipwrecked in this vast and stormy sea of half-understood needs and emotions.

If the professionals concerned can reflect together on their feelings about patients, considered action can be taken. Professional defences deny us important understandings (Dammers and Wiener, 1995; Jung, 1966). Study of our own professional patterns and consulting styles can be useful, as can observation of the idiosyncrasies of other team members and events in the life of the practice. Background knowledge can be very illuminating. There is no substitute for a genuine relationship with colleagues, and a true understanding of their perspectives and circumstances. There needs to be a 'meeting of minds'.

Counsellors may suffer frustration and stress connected with 'working briefly' and sometimes being expected to provide symptom relief, according to a medical model which is foreign to them. Waiting lists may be experienced as a psychological pressure, raising anxiety levels. Suicidal patients can stir fears of medico-legal problems, and echoes of 'emotional blackmail' which feel threatening to the whole team. Conversely, over-compliant patients who come to the counsellor because they are 'sent' will also trigger off uncomfortable feelings which will affect not only the counsellor, but also the counsellor/doctor relationship. They will not be usefully engaged in the counselling process. Good supervision can help to defuse difficult experiences, as it did for Sarah, and thereby contribute to better interprofessional relationships. But counsellors need to remember that this is a source of support that most doctors lack, and may also envy. If there are times when pressures in the team feel too great, one member may become 'scapegoated' as a container for all the unbearable feelings about the impossible aspects of health care. There is even a potential pitfall in believing that we counsellors are the ones who are more psychologically aware; we may still have blind spots.

Assumptions about patients may lurk in blind spots. If a patient has experienced a doctor as unempathic, there may be idealization of the counsellor, distorting the work. Other 'split' conceptualizations may be those of 'nice doctor' and 'useless counsellor'. Professionals are also sometimes guilty of contributing to this in their own way. Uncensored 'off the record' comments at conference lunch-breaks sometimes reveal surprisingly primitive feelings!

Ideally, a referral should be experienced by *all* parties as the doctor's contribution to problem-solving, and then that in turn will facilitate a good therapeutic alliance between patient and counsellor. Counsellors may find it useful to remember a subtle point: their primary care referrals have been 'assessed' under conditions affected by the patient's beliefs about *doctors,* and what patients think doctors want to know. Patients may give doctors faulty cues about their true concerns. Fear, misconceptions, deference, or different 'languages' may interfere. Experiences with *previous* doctors may also be relevant. Some patients may be inclined to tell the counsellor their problem quickly and then wait for a solution to be offered. This is the 'medical model' from the *patient's* point of view.

Every model is connected with assumptions. The counsellor receives referrals from the doctor, and is to some extent dependent on what the doctor defines as valid work for counselling. Different professions have different assumptions about their work, and such assumptions cluster into what Durkheim called 'moral rules'. These 'rules' tend to tap into deeply held and emotive beliefs; here is the potential for culture clash and negative feeling. For example, problems could arise between the reductionist and positivist approach in medicine, and the more relational and constructivist approaches in counselling.

Politics, economics and practicalities

Public and government pressures can place conflicting demands on public service organizations, thereby generating stress in staff, distorting relationships between them and with their patients. The operation of the 'internal market' and fundholding in the NHS generated a great deal of extra work and stress, and a great deal of emotion of all kinds. The introduction of management innovations such as Primary Care Groups is currently generating further anxiety and there may be some professional casualties in the course of the changes. There have, for instance, been fierce ideological arguments tearing professional groups apart and setting health care units against one another. Counsellors cannot escape these effects (Halton, 1995). Pressures may be passed on inappropriately, and the counsellor blamed for the length of the waiting list or lack of vacancies, and then designated as the one who is 'depriving' the patients. Cost-cutting 'quick-fix' solutions are advocated, avoiding the painful reality that some patients have needs that cannot be met in this way. When demand exceeds resources, it is easy to become angry with the wrong person. There is a risk that this might happen with a 'difficult' patient. Feelings of being overwhelmed by excessive work can bring about emotional withdrawal which is inimical to counselling.

It is curious that health care workers *have* accepted some of the hardships of the NHS. But perhaps it is sometimes an effective 'social defence' against the emotional pressures in primary health care work. Doctors and counsellors can both be caught up in a collusive attitude where they can feel that *they* are caring, and it is the Family Health Service Authority (FHSA) or Department of Health (DoH) that is uncaring and forces a 'bad' system on us. We ought to admit that short-term contract interventions can sometimes protect the professionals and deny the gravity of the tasks we face. Guilt and shame at our own inadequacy are particularly unwelcome feelings. Most of us would prefer to pass them around the team like a booby-trapped parcel, and conceal them in a dark corner, or hurl them at a convenient outside target.

However, it is not only the big ethical questions that cause trouble. Attention to practical matters such as pay and conditions of work is absolutely essential to the doctor/counsellor relationship in order to avoid feelings of grievance, and promote the experience of feeling appropriately valued. There needs to be sufficient space and privacy, and paid time for administrative tasks. This all sounds very mundane, but certainly affects relationships, and the quality of work done.

After discussing the trainee counsellor's work at a placement, the doctor said, almost as an after-thought, 'Do you feel that the patients take you less seriously because you are working in the Portacabin?' The doctor didn't know that some of the more extravert patients had actually made jokes about it . . . and the trainee had not felt able to say anything about that.

There is so much that is unsaid between people.

Mind/body splits

Although unspoken thoughts often appear as bodily symptoms, ideas and beliefs associated with somatization may have a perceptible effect on the doctor/counsellor relationship, as well as the doctor/patient relationship. Sometimes medical literature contains comments that subtly denigrate 'somatisers' as 'heartsinks', and it may be suggested that 'reassurance' is an adequate response. Counsellors and patients feel unhappy if referrals are made in this spirit. It seems to imply that the effect of the mind on the body is seen as a low-risk phenomenon. This is neither true nor helpful for the quality of relationship between the doctor and the provider of psychological services. Some of this half-conscious denigration may be transmitted to the patient, increasing their unhappiness. Thoughts and feelings can potentiate and even cause illness (Taylor, 1997). We need to be alert to the unity of the psyche–soma, and the scientific evidence of the neurohormonal axes which influence our general health (Dantzer and Mormede, 1995). Physical symptoms can be more than 'symbolic', and we have to be aware of the possibility of adverse metabolic change, and irreversible disease processes triggered by stress. None of that stress should be iatrogenic. Good and *safe* patient care requires mutually respectful professional relationships and discussion; and of course, compassion.

Conclusion

This chapter can only partially address the vast field of relationship factors. It is probably not possible or desirable to try to construct algorithms, since that might inhibit enquiry. This account contains a plea for the recognition of complexity. Service providers need to keep on questioning received truths, and engaging in active listening to one another, as well as to the patients. This is a different kind of learning from the conventional intellectual variety, and needs constant renewal (Balint et al., 1993). No matter how extensive our professional experience, nor how evidence-based and informed our practice may be, we cannot escape from being human, and having our various feelings and personal biases, both conscious and unconscious. There is always something new to be learned about ourselves and how we relate to others.

Key points

- There may be little correlation between professional guidelines and personal feelings.
- The counsellor may be 'seen' by the team in unexpected ways.
- Medical settings have their own particular culture, anxieties and responsibilities.
- Assumptions are unwise; check out individual beliefs and feelings of team members, including your own!
- Primary health care work is the focus of exceptionally high expectations, both emotional and political.
- Being the 'psychological expert' in the team may have complex implications.
- Be prepared for, and respect, differing value systems.
- Triangular relationships are often highly charged.
- Awareness of both conscious and unconscious dynamics improves work and team relationships.
- Even if something is not on your flow-chart or in your theoretical model, it can still happen!
- Significant problems can arise from apparently trivial factors; be vigilant.

References

Baker, R. and Streatfield, J. (1995) 'What type of general practice do patients prefer? Exploration of practice characteristics influencing patient satisfaction'. *British Journal of General Practice*, 45, 654–9.

Balint, M. (1964) *The Doctor, his Patient and the Illness.* London: Pitman.

Balint, E., Courtenay, M., Elder, A., Hull, S. and Julian, P. (1993) *The Doctor, the Patient and the Group: Balint Revisited.* London: Routledge.

Bor, R. and Miller, R. (1991) *Internal Consultation in Health Care Settings.* London: Karnac Books.

Bromley, E. (1995) 'Social class and psychotherapy revisited', *BPS Psychotherapy Section Newsletter,* 18: 35–47.

Clulow, C. (1985) *Marital Therapy: an Inside View.* Aberdeen: Aberdeen University Press/Pergamon Group.

Dammers, J. and Wiener, J. (1995) 'The theory and practice of counselling in the primary health care team', in J. Keithley and G. Marsh (eds), *Counselling in Primary Health Care. Oxford General Practice Series,* No. 30. Oxford: Oxford University Press.

Dantzer, R. and Mormede, P. (1995) 'Psychoneuroimmunology of stress', in B. Leonard and K. Miller (eds), *Stress, the Immune System and Psychiatry.* Chichester: John Wiley.

Halton, W. (1995) 'Institutional stress on providers in health and education', *Psychodynamic Counselling,* 1(2): 187–98.

Hopkins, P. (1974) 'The cons of health centre practice', *Update*, February, pp. 348–9.

Hornby, S. (1995) 'The contribution of analytic psychotherapeutic understanding to the development of collaboration in the helping services', *Journal of the British Association of Psychotherapists,* 28: 45–64.

Jewell, J.A. (1992) 'Report of an evaluative study of counselling in general practice. Cambridgeshire FHSA', quoted in Correspondence, *British Medical Journal*, 306: 390.

Jones, H., Murphy, A., Neaman, G., Tollemache, R. and Vasserman, D. (1994) 'Psychotherapy and counselling in a GP practice: making use of the setting', *British Journal of Psychotherapy*, 10(4): 543–51.

Jung, C.G. (1966) *Collected Works,* Vol. 16. *The Practice of Psychotherapy.* London: Routledge & Kegan Paul, para. 364–5.

McCaughan, N. and Palmer, B. (1994) *Systems Thinking for Harassed Managers.* London: Karnac Books.

RCGP (1996) *The Nature of General Medical Practice. Report of a Working Party. Report from General Practice,* No. 27. London: Royal College of General Practitioners.

Taylor, M.B. (1997) 'Compassion: its neglect and importance', *British Journal of General Practice*, 47: 521–3.

CHAPTER 4

DEEPER ISSUES IN COLLABORATION: AVOIDING PITFALLS AND MANAGING INTERNAL BOUNDARIES

Gilly Pembroke

The previous chapter dealt with some of the interpersonal issues that are raised in the course of collaborative practice. Professional colleagues and members of the practice may themselves ask for help from a counsellor. In this event, it is important that the general practice counsellor has her own personal boundaries firmly in place so that her seemingly good nature does not inadvertently jeopardize any professional relationship. It is suggested that a good professional working relationship cannot be the same as a good therapeutic relationship, and if the two should become confused, both may be lost. To clarify this further, we must first consider more closely the issues around how we communicate within the practice. It is important to distinguish between personal and professional communication, and this is explored below.

Personal communication

The previous chapter described how the hierarchy of a practice can be upset by the arrival of a counsellor. It is therefore important that the counsellor remain sensitive to the hierarchy which exists and to the way she may be perceived by the others. This will vary from surgery to surgery, as can be seen from the following example.

A group of primary care students were each asked to draw the professional hierarchy of their own surgery on a flipchart and to show where they thought the practice counsellor fitted into this. It was surprising how many versions were proffered. How interesting it would have been to have asked the same question of doctors and other practice members.

With this in mind, the counsellor must proceed to develop her relationships in the practice with caution. She must somehow 'belong', yet remain 'separate'; she must be able to communicate and liaise freely in any direction, yet continue to observe the agreed confidentiality of her patients; she must be flexible and adaptable to tradition, yet able to stand her ground when necessary. She must empathize with the conflicts of surgery politics, but remain essentially neutral. She must continually use all her counselling skills when communicating with other practice members, but must nevertheless refrain from counselling them. The words of Rudyard Kipling (1910) are especially apt:

> If you can keep your head when all about you are losing theirs,
> And blaming it on you . . .
> If you can trust yourself when all men doubt you,
> But make allowance for their doubting too . . .
> If you can talk with crowds and keep your virtue,
> Or walk with Kings – nor lose the common touch . . .

The practice counsellor occupies a lonely position. In order to gain acceptance from other members of the team, she will need to work hard at learning about the others around her – and they are going to have to learn about her. Working in a new environment may give rise to anxiety and/or feelings of intimidation, resulting in withdrawal or shyness, or overcompensation in the form of assertiveness to the point of being inflexible. The counsellor may feel she has inadequate knowledge of the system, or fear the discussion of issues about which she has little knowledge. It is all too easy to disappear behind a closed door, see one's patients and go home again. But every effort must be made to overcome such inhibitions and to take every opportunity to communicate with all colleagues. This may mean coming out of your room between patients, making more visits than necessary to the kitchen to mingle with the others over a coffee and taking time to find out exactly how the practice works.

Earning trust also comes in other ways. Social gatherings, such as the Christmas party, for instance, should be attended where possible. This will give further opportunity for you to get to know other members of the team in a different context and for them to learn more about you. But beware! Letting your hair down completely, or drinking too much, may mean it is difficult for you to remain discreet and confidentiality may slip. You will soon be remembered for your 'gossip', but not for your reliability. Many counsellors will have experienced the comment at parties: 'I bet you've got some good stories – tell us some of the sexy ones!' In a party atmosphere it may be hard to resist such temptation, especially when popularity can stem from entertaining those around you – but the ability to deflect such invitations must be retained.

One person who can make a huge difference to your day is the practice manager. They may also occupy a lonely role and may feel threatened by the easy relationship that the counsellor may appear to be developing with those around her, especially if there has not previously been a counsellor post in this surgery before. If you can get along with the practice manager, you could find an ally who will help to smooth your way – but if you do not make the effort to enlist the approval of such a person, you may well find you have a visiting chiropodist or dietician using your room, whilst your patients accumulate in the waiting room!

Professional communication

Educating other members about counselling

Many counsellors work behind closed doors without ever considering collaboration. Yet the benefits are potentially enormous – demystifying the counselling process, reducing stress and providing the opportunity to get more heads around a problem. This may, however, also bring with it certain pitfalls, such as someone else trying to take charge of the session or not clearly understanding what happens in counselling. It is very important to try to convey to doctors and to other members of the team how counselling works, and what actually happens in sessions. It is only too easy for that 'closed door' to stimulate the imagination of other practice members and fantasies may then need to be dispelled.

Consider the following example:

A counsellor had just brought to a close what had been a very difficult session with a particular patient. This individual had become extremely distressed during the session and was reluctant to leave but the counsellor had a busy schedule ahead of her with another patient already waiting. She therefore suggested to the patient that she sit for a while in the corridor, away from the waiting room, giving her time to gradually regain her composure. The patient accepted the offer and the counsellor continued with her next appointment. However, as this tearful patient sat and reflected her session, her sobbing only increased. She was simply allowing herself the relief of expressing grief, but passing staff were puzzled and unsure if they should intervene. One of them was heard to say 'Oh, don't worry about her – she's just been to the counsellor!' And another, rather impatiently, 'Why isn't the counsellor dealing with this?'

What do others think the counsellor is 'doing' to her patients? It would, of course, have been more acceptable if the counsellor had spoken to one of the reception staff or nurses to explain this patient's distress and her own dilemma, and to ask if one of them could perhaps have made the patient a cup of tea while she waited. The practice staff need to understand how the counselling process works, in order for them to appreciate the distress some patients may have when they leave the sessions. They also need to feel reassured that the counsellor is in command of the situation, and that she is confident that such distress is acceptable and containable, despite the unsettling effect it may have on others. Surgery staff need to be reassured in the same way as patients.

Individual counselling and the GP

In addition to regular feedback to GPs about referred patients and your attendance at practice meetings, consider inviting a doctor to sit in one of your sessions. It would of course be necessary to seek advance permission from the patient. One could perhaps say:

> Dr Smith and myself are very keen to give you the best possible help that we can and this is often better achieved if we work as a team. In order to help Dr Smith understand the issues you have raised, perhaps it might be useful to invite him to attend the session with us. The contents of the session could be kept confidential to the three of us. How would you feel about this?

In my experience, a patient will have no problem in accepting this. Not only is it useful for the doctor to learn more about their patient, but they will also learn a great deal about how the counselling process works, and will also be able to share their own perception about what is taking place between the patient and the counsellor. This is all very well in theory, but of course a doctor's time is already stretched, so perhaps a compromise would be to invite the doctor to attend the first or last 10 minutes of a session – perhaps to hear a summary of what has happened and for important issues to be clarified .

Patients who suffer panic attacks, for instance, frequently fear that they are suffering some organic disease such as heart problems or the onset of a stroke. Such anxiety will further fuel their symptoms, and the counsellor may have also learned some family history that is exacerbating their fear. Ten minutes with doctor and counsellor together can be very valuable in the doctor gaining further understanding about the patient and being able to be more specific in reassuring that patient (Bor et al., 1998). The doctor may also be able to give more precise medical information which hitherto had been misunderstood.

Other forms of collaboration might include the following example.

Roy had been suffering from depression for several months and had been attending counselling once a week for six weeks. The counsellor had been concerned at the depth of his depression and Roy wept a great deal in every session. However, Roy had managed to hide this side of himself whenever he saw the doctor in an attempt not to be seen as 'weak'. One day, he felt so depressed in the counselling session that the counsellor felt he needed to be assessed by a doctor. She called the GP and asked if he could attend the session. The counsellor and GP were able to assess the patient together and the counsellor was able to help the patient to reveal to the doctor how desperate and suicidal he felt. The doctor had a much clearer idea of the patient's problem and arranged a referral to a psychiatrist. The counsellor appreciated the GP's support, and the GP felt reassured by the counsellor's ability to recognize the limits of her professional competence.

Couple counselling and the GP

Dr Hall was becoming increasingly confused by Marion and Bob, who made endless individual appointments to see him to complain about their respective ailments and general unhappiness with each other. Both complained that the other was 'ill'. Dr Hall was convinced that both of them had emotional problems and would benefit from counselling, but was unsure which one to refer! The doctor consulted with Helen, the counsellor, and she suggested that a one-off joint assessment session could be set up for this couple to include both the GP and herself and that this might then enable all of them to work out the best way forward. The patients agreed and the resulting session confirmed the counsellor's suspicions that marital, rather than individual counselling was indicated. Not only did the session clarify a great deal of confusion around the presentation of their symptoms, but also gave the GP some insight into the interaction and projection that goes on between couples and how a counsellor might handle this.

Family Therapy and the GP

It often happens that a doctor sees different members of a family at individual sessions. A mother may bring her daughter with an eating disorder to see the GP. The father may consult because of chronic back pain. The mother may be suffering from irritable bowel syndrome. The son may be depressed. The doctor may find themselves treating each problem in isolation, but it is possible that sitting in on a family counselling session will enable them to understand that not only might there be marital problems, but there might also be intense jealousy between the siblings. The daughter might be carrying an unconscious fear that if she were to reach adult maturity and leave home, her parents might separate without her distracting presence – hence her anorexia nervosa – which served to bind the family together in dealing with her complex problems.

Two practice counsellors, both attached to a surgery in the north of England, were able to offer family therapy sessions within the surgery. Taking the collaborative idea a stage further, they invited the referring doctor to attend a family session with them. Since the GP knew each individual member of the family reasonably well, he was able to observe how they interacted together as a family. He could see how the teenage daughter needed to look after her mother, and how her father always failed to support his son for fear of confrontation with his wife. He was also able to understand the sources of family stress that lead to psychological disturbance, manifested in mother's propensity towards somatization.

It would be fair to say, that whenever doctors have had the experience of sitting in on a counselling session, most have found it enlightening, and it usually dispels some of the fantasies about what happens in counselling sessions. It is important, however, to clarify who will interview the patient or family, and the role of the other team member(s). Good intentions can be thwarted by poorly managed sessions where so-called teams try to work collaboratively.

It may be hard for a practice counsellor to imagine a scenario where family sessions are offered to patients, let alone the practice of including a GP in sessions. This is one advantage of having at least two counsellors working in the same surgery. They may be able to attend a family therapy course together, and be able to practise together with families. GPs will become familiar with a systems approach and can gradually be introduced to the idea of attending sessions from time to time.

Some GPs in the USA have taken collaboration a stage further. They invite their practice counsellor in with them during consultations (Stulp, 1991). Whenever psychological problems are thought to be contributory, the counsellor is left with the patient while the doctor continues with their next patient. Taking collaboration to such lengths is still rare in the UK, and yet the advantages are obvious: the doctor can remain focused on physical illness but attentive to psychological and behavioural issues, leaving the counsellor the more lengthy task of helping the patient cope with and adjust to issues raised. Mental illness can be treated more quickly and earlier intervention may have a better prognosis and reduce medical costs. In addition, by attending the patient together, a very important message is conveyed to the patient –

that mental health care is just as important as physical health care, making it more acceptable and easier to treat.

Setting up a collaborative session

Allowing 10 minutes before a session to brief a doctor or co-counsellor is necessary. It is helpful to clarify to the doctor their role as one of participant/observer. The counsellor conducts the interview and the doctor directs comments or questions to the counsellor, who may then respond to them. When the patient arrives, the counsellor explains the seating arrangements and restates the confidentiality that exists within the room. The counsellor proceeds with the session while the doctor observes. If the doctor does not raise any issues during the session, the counsellor may turn and invite the doctor for any feedback: 'I am wondering if anything particularly strikes you about what we have been discussing – or whether you have any questions you would like to ask at this stage?' In a similar way the patient can be given the opportunity to ask the doctor about any medical worries which may be relevant. When the patient leaves, it is helpful to have a few moments discussion and debrief of the session.

Sometimes, a doctor's attendance gives the opportunity for both counsellor and patient to learn more about some medical aspect of a disease from which either the patient or a member of his family may be suffering. It is also important to remember that practice nurses, health visitors and midwives may detect psychological distress in patients before the GP, so they also need to know how to refer to you, and may equally value the occasional invitation to attend a session.

A trainee GP requested if he may sit in on a session with a patient whom he had originally referred. The patient was more than willing and a session was set up. This was the patient's third session and because he had just started a course of anti-depressants he felt more tired compared to earlier sessions. This session seemed to the counsellor to be particularly bland and uneventful, and she doubted that it had been of much help to the GP. She was therefore surprised and delighted when the GP reported a few days later that he had been particularly impressed by her methods of reflection, paraphrasing and questioning in the session. He had been experimenting with these skills in his own consultations and was delighted with the glut of relevant information that was invariably produced each time his patient really felt *heard!*

Practice meetings

Regular attendance at practice meetings should be incorporated into the counsellor's initial contract. If this is not possible, then occasionally a whole meeting should be allocated to the counsellor when she is able to attend, so that general issues can be discussed and concerns can be aired. It also gives the individual doctors a chance to recognize how they each use the counsellor differently, whether they are referring similar kinds of patients and whether their problems vary significantly in severity.

Practice meetings may also give the counsellor opportunity to create discussion and debate about more general issues in counselling and to draw to the attention of the doctors any particular ideas for concern or improvement.

A counsellor was becoming aware that suddenly there was a huge increase in the prescribing of SSRI'S within the practice. Although these new drugs are generally safer and more effective than other antidepressants, patients still report side effects. The counsellor found it increasingly confusing to know whether a patient was experiencing side effects or increased anxiety as a result of painful conflicts addressed during the counselling sessions. This in turn made it difficult for her to monitor how fast or deep she should work with a patient in any one session. Explaining these concerns to the doctors at a practice meeting resulted in a lively debate, resulting in clearer understanding of the counselling process and closer attention to the selection of antidepressant when a patient was also receiving counselling.

Accessibility

Take the trouble to explain to others how you can be contacted and when you are free to discuss difficult cases. Be approachable; allowing 5 to 10 minutes between counselling sessions and leaving the door wide open during these spaces creates a sense of accessibility. Perhaps it is more convenient to build a 'drop-in' slot into the timetable, to allow space for general discussion with colleagues. Some thought will need to be given as to whether this is going to be paid or unpaid time, and needs to be addressed when negotiating an original contract. Staff and patients alike need to know whether they are permitted to contact you at home and at what time you are available.

Collaboration with the GP over a difficult patient

From time to time one of the doctors may ask for the opportunity to discuss a patient with whom he is having difficulty. The first consideration for the counsellor is 'How long can I give to this?' There may be a patient waiting outside when the request is made. If these requests are made regularly, and no provision has been made for consultation within the counsellor's original contract, she may find that she is giving a great deal of unpaid time to such discussions. It is important that doctors feel free to consult with you, and you with them. The counsellor must try to ascertain how long the GP would like to spend on this – will it be a quick 5 minutes, or would it perhaps be more appropriate to make time at the end of the day. How then is the counsellor going to be best able to help the doctor? It is suggested that the task of the consultant is, through a conversation, to help the consultee to define and clarify problems, and find his or her own solutions by increasing the competence of the consultee and the options or choices available to them, without blaming anyone or invalidating a particular view (Bor and Miller, 1990). Therefore, having first listened to an overview of the problem which the doctor is presenting, the counsellor then needs to address the following with him:

- What sort of help is he looking for?
- Does he simply to need to offload or does he need more intensive help?
- What would he like to feel he had achieved by the end of this discussion?
- How might the personality of the patient affect the doctor's decisions?
- How does this patient make the doctor feel?
- How might the patient feel in the doctor's presence?
- What does the doctor wish he could do for his patient?
- And is this realistic? What are his choices?
- Are there other resources which would be useful to him?
- Whom else might he consult?

The unwary and perhaps over-caring doctor can easily find himself the dumping ground for his patients' painful emotions. People are quick to find ways of shifting responsibility for their uncomfortable feelings, and the doctor may well become a target for blame, displacement, projection and transference, as is also suggested by Holland (1995) in his excellent book *A Doctor's Dilemma*. The counsellor may be able to help the doctor to disentangle his own strong emotions from those of his distressed patients, which in turn may help to diminish his sense of frustration and helplessness when a patient appears non-compliant and reluctant to accept his advice.

Dilemmas and pitfalls of working with unclear boundaries

Any counsellor who has begun to achieve even half of the above will by now have developed a flourishing working relationship with the practice members. In practice, this level of collaboration takes years to achieve. It is likely that through communication and collaboration practice members will have grown to trust their counsellor and to have confidence in the way she works. In addition to the maintenance of existing relationships, the counsellor must also put effort into developing new ones with recently appointed members of staff. Unless care is taken, she may face new demands on her as a result of the quality of her relationships with colleagues. The counsellor may find that not only do other members of the team ask for help for their patients, but they may also seek help for themselves. It is precisely at this point that the counsellor's own boundaries should be firmly in place, otherwise confusion may develop between a working relationship and a therapeutic relationship.

In order to understand how this problem may occur, the counsellor has to return to her own beliefs about the boundaries around her relationship with patients. It is generally accepted that counsellors should only work with people with whom they have no existing relationship since it is only in this context that a counsellor can remain sufficiently objective. If she were to attempt to counsel a friend or family member, she may have a vested interest in the problem (or at least some unconscious bias), and will find it hard to remain neutral. In turn, it may not be safe for the patient to go sufficiently deep into his conflict for fear of what his counsellor friend may think of him, for fear of being rejected or causing hurt. This is a scenario that does not give the counselling the best chance of success, and therefore it is inappropriate to offer counselling, though some form of collaboration may be appropriate.

Consider the following example:

A counsellor accepted what seemed to be a perfectly appropriate referral. Anthony was a married man who wanted to talk about his failing career and subsequent feelings of depression. After several sessions, it became apparent that the children of both counsellor and patient had recently struck up a friendship through some (then unknown) mutual friends. The counsellor became uneasy that if counselling continued, Anthony was likely to reveal a great deal more about his marital issues about which she now preferred not to know. Worried that boundaries could become confused through their children, she decided to refer the patient on to a different counsellor. Despite her efforts to explain, the patient found it hard to appreciate the problem, and sensed it as a rejection, though reluctantly accepted an onward referral. Some weeks later, however, Anthony found himself sitting next to his first counsellor at a dinner party. The counsellor's original concerns were justified – she was acutely uncomfortable, since the other guests were not aware that Anthony had ever consulted a counsellor, and persisted in making inappropriate jokes about her work. In addition, Anthony's wife sat opposite to her, unaware that this 'stranger' already knew intimate details about her and their family!

Consider how much worse this situation would have become if the counselling had continued. It is hard for some doctors to appreciate a counsellor's dilemma about seeing patients socially, since doctors sometimes have social relationships with their patients. But GPs may need to be reminded that there is less taboo associated with needing to see a doctor. Patients pass each other freely in the waiting room with only a fleeting thought as to why the other may be attending – it may simply be for a flu jab.

Although it may be very flattering that a staff member or a close relative be referred to the counsellor, the pitfalls associated with accepting such referrals may not be immediately evident.

Mary, the wife of one of the doctors, consulted another GP in her husband's practice. It became clear that Mary was suffering from depression. Her doctor decided to refer her to the practice counsellor. The counsellor tried to explain that she felt it would be inappropriate for her to see Mary, since her husband was one of their colleagues and she did not want to find that she was holding secrets. Nor, she suspected, would Mary's husband be comfortable working with his practice counsellor, not knowing what his wife had said about him; moreover, of even greater concern was that joint counselling might be indicated.

But the referring GP was insistent; he would not take 'No' for an answer. He only wanted the very best for his colleague and his distressed wife, and this meant the counsellor must be someone he knew and trusted. He felt he could rely totally on the discretion of their practice counsellor. The counsellor was sinking deeper! She was rapidly finding herself in a no-win situation. It seemed likely that she would upset one GP or the other. A compromise was reached. She agreed to have a consultation session with the wife so that the best options for psychological support could be explored without any expectation that the counsellor would be directly involved in ongoing care. All was resolved – but it had been very important for the counsellor to stand her ground.

Similar problems may arise when a counsellor is looking for a placement or regular work. She may find that the local surgery where she is a patient has a vacancy for a counsellor. This seems convenient – short journey to work, no travelling expenses, and since she knows some of the staff she will quickly fit in. But this can also lead to problems in the future. Consider the following experience:

A counsellor began working in the surgery where she was also a patient. For a time there seemed to be no difficulty until she gradually became aware that in comparison to the other GPs, her own doctor was only referring very 'straightforward' cases. When she confronted him about this, she realized that he could not see her as a colleague, or as a professional, but only as his patient. He was therefore protective and parental. It became more difficult still when the counsellor herself experienced a spell of anxiety. Because she did not want to be seen by her colleagues as 'not coping' she was slow to seek the help she needed. She also frequently found that when she consulted her doctor as a patient, he would then take the opportunity to liaise and consult with her about patients whom he had referred to her. This was, of course, a source of great irritation to her when she was feeling unwell and wanted time for herself. The situation finally resolved itself when one day she marched into the consulting room and said, 'You can either have me as your patient or your practice counsellor, but not both!' She remained a patient, but now works 15 miles from her home.

It can be seen from these examples how easy it is to fall outside the limits of a comfortable boundary. In order to protect herself from compromising and inappropriate professional situations, the counsellor must constantly look ahead and try to predict the outcome of her actions before they become irreversible. If a counsellor has had a good training in self-awareness, ongoing supervision and common sense she can usually identify that small chill of unease which needs addressing at the outset.

Colleagues in distress

So far, the counsellor's discussions with the doctor have been within the context of a 'working relationship' – both of them working towards the good of their patient. But supposing the counsellor begins to pick up that this doctor is himself stressed or depressed, and that his decisions are being affected by this. How can she best help her colleague to gain insight into his dilemma without it becoming a 'therapeutic relationship' and why is it so important that this does not happen? We must at this stage remind ourselves that when a counsellor is helping a patient, she may be perceived as more 'in control of her life' and therefore more 'powerful' in some way. The consultee who is struggling to cope with life may feel 'out of control' and inadequate compared to the perception he has of the counsellor at that particular time. In 'normal' counselling, the counsellor will be seeking to empower her patient and when he is recovered, he will move on, and is likely to be anxious to forget this painful episode.

If such a situation should arise between colleagues, however, they must continue to work together thereafter, and although theoretically we are all accepting of each other's shortcomings, the consultee could feel embarrassed or humiliated by the earlier exposure of his own vulnerability of which he is constantly reminded by the counsellor's presence in the surgery.

The counsellor now has to walk a precipitous boundary if she is to help her colleague without becoming his counsellor and much will depend on the depth and length of the relationship between doctor and counsellor. Perhaps one way of tackling this might be to say:

> I do not want you to answer this question to me aloud – but simply think about what's going on in your own life at the moment – and whether there could be any link there with the current difficulties you are having with this case. For instance, the patient we are discussing is 16 years of age – could the age of your own children have any bearing on how you feel about this person?

The counsellor offers insight and understanding which could even lead to self-disclosure of her own experiences, if appropriate. She should try to discourage the doctor from answering aloud. If there is an indication that she has tapped into something deeper now is the time to say:

> I can see that you may be concerned about this and it may be inappropriate for us to say more – but it might help you to discuss this with someone who is totally outside the picture. Any thoughts?

Or perhaps she could say:

> I went through something similar a few years back. It was difficult, but a few sessions of counselling helped me to continue working effectively until the problem was resolved.

It is important to return to the reasons why it is inappropriate to counsel friends and family. When patients have completed a course of counselling, they usually do not wish to see their counsellor again (and vice versa). Seeing their counsellor may serve to remind them of 'finished business'. And more than one doctor has been known to say 'I can't understand it – I spent so much time listening and trying to counsel Mrs Jones, and I really thought I'd been of help, only to find that she has now switched to another doctor in the practice!' (Mrs Jones may have well found the help valuable, but now she is back to her old self, she may have no wish to be reminded of this painful episode in her life when she felt so depressed by consulting the same doctor.) And in the same way, if the counsellor allows staff within the practice to use her for their own personal difficulties, she may well find that these people will distance themselves from her. But each case must be taken on its own merits. It is sometimes hard to tell when a colleague is just having a general moan and when it is an underlying cry for help.

The following example shows alternative ways of handling such a situation.

The counsellor was aware that a receptionist had recently lost two close members of her family through unexpected death. One day the receptionist took advantage of the counsellor's open door and came in and sat down. She told the counsellor she thought she was going mad because she kept 'hearing' these deceased relatives in the next room and dreaming about them as though they were still alive. The counsellor was able to reassure her that such experiences were a normal part of grief, but if she felt she would like to explore her feelings further, she would be happy to give her some names of other counsellors in the area (adding that sadly it would be inappropriate for her to do it herself). The receptionist replied that she felt she could cope for the moment but was glad to know of the available resource. The counsellor also lent her a self-help book on grief, so she could read for herself what experiences she might normally expect under such strain and how best to cope with them. Some time later, the receptionist called in to return the book, saying how useful it had been and how reassuring it was to read that her experiences were normal.

The counsellor was able to provide support to this receptionist without getting pulled into counselling. Nevertheless, it would have been important for the counsellor to be sensitive as to whether this was a general enquiry or an urgent cry for help.

Conclusion

This chapter has endeavoured to take a closer look at issues surrounding collaboration with colleagues and to outline the type of dilemmas which may be encountered if the counsellor does not have a clear sense of her own boundaries. Exact clarity is impossible and each situation, or request for help, merits its own considerations. If the practice counsellor has already given some advance thought to how she might cope with such dilemmas should they arise, she will at least have given herself the best possible chance of remaining utterly professional in any given situation, and will therefore continue to be a valued asset to her surgery.

Key points

- A good working relationship is not the same as a therapeutic relationship. If the two should become confused, both will be damaged or lost.
- Make every effort to learn about the work of the others in your practice.
- Take every opportunity to educate other members of the practice about your work.
- Clarify your own boundaries in your mind and help others to understand them.
- Stay involved, but neutral and non-judgemental.
- Have a list of resources available and a list of alternative counsellors at the ready.

References

Bor, R. and Miller, R. (1990) *Internal Consultations in Health Care Settings*. London: Karnac.

Bor, R., Miller, R., Latz, M. and Salt, H. (1998) *Counselling in Health Care Settings*. London: Cassell.

Holland, J. (1995) *A Doctor's Dilemma*. London/New York: Free Association Books.

Kipling, R. (1910) 'If', in *Rewards and Fairies – Brother Square-Toes*. London: Macmillan.

McDaniel, S., Hepworth, J. and Doherty, W. (1992) *Medical Family Therapy*. New York: Basic Books.

Stulp, C. (1991) 'Counsellors/Psychologists and Primary Care Medicine: Challenges and Concerns of an Emerging Relationship'. Paper given at 'Who Needs Counsellors in Primary Health Care?', Derbyshire Health Authority.

CHAPTER 5

MANAGING REFERRALS

Teresa Schaefer, Jenny Chesshyre and Susan Kendal

Referral is the nodal point of primary health care counselling. As the initial focus for contact between doctor, patient and counsellor, the referral is the pivot for both professional collaboration and the counselling process itself. But, prism-like, it can also highlight those differences – the interdisciplinary rivalries and fantasies – that can so bedevil working relationships and a productive sharing of the care-giving role.

The context

In primary care, where doctors and counsellors usually work in the same setting, there is rarely a complete handover of care, but rather concurrent treatment by different professionals using different models and skills. Referral in this context is a reciprocal act – it is offered and received and informs the ongoing process – and as such is a dynamic with responsibility for its success lying with both participants. Clearly, then, effective patient care depends on the quality of the providers' cooperation. But the peculiar characteristics of the primary care context – the implications of both the physical and occupational structures, the impact of professional ideologies and health care economics – all mean that the potential for collaboration, whilst inviting and exciting, is also plagued with difficulties (Small and Conlon, 1988).

Advantages

Ostensibly, all parties stand to gain from the possibility of referral for counselling within general practice: counsellors obtain access to a wide range of clients; doctors have a ready means of passing on work they feel less able or willing to undertake; and patients gain a relatively accessible and stigma-free specialist resource in a setting that is both familiar and convenient (Small and Conlon, 1988).

From this perspective, the counsellor's location on site in the practice would appear to facilitate the referral process in a number of ways. Doctor and counsellor already know each other, and there is no substitute for knowing a referral source personally (McDaniel et al., 1990): the setting validates the large numbers of patients who present their problems in the form of physical illness and allows for a more biopsychosocial concept of illness and health; mutual accessibility on the same premises should promote the preparatory consultation and ongoing monitoring essential to a successful referral.

Disadvantages

The structural characteristics of the setting can, however, also fudge issues and confuse communication. Relieved of the automatic requirement of a letter to an outside agency, GPs may skimp on both the initial consideration and relevant information necessary to referral. The brief exchange snatched in a corridor enabled by close proximity may be an inadequate substitute for a more structured forum, leading to frustration and misunderstanding, and may even threaten confidentiality.

Moreover, the interdisciplinary dynamic that underpins the doctor/counsellor relationship has traditionally been a problematic one, beset by differences in professional paradigms and cultural hierarchies. While doctors and counsellors may share a common purpose – to comfort and rectify – they seek to do this from very different perspectives, from different assumptions about human behaviour, methods of care, the use of time and giving of advice, that stem from different ideologies and training and are expressed in different languages. GPs are trained to think quickly, to make snap decisions and to issue brief, focused communications. They have to bear enormous responsibility for the never-ending care of their – often demanding and intractable – patients. The notions of well-stated boundaries, of the '50 minute hour', of acknowledging limitations and setting limits on work undertaken, of lengthy discussions of interpersonal dynamics, may all appear alien and precious to the harassed GP to whom such luxuries are denied (Graham and Sher, 1976: 99–104). Inequities of power and status, defined both culturally and structurally, where the GP effectively employs the counsellor and determines the counselling caseload, may make it harder for the latter to find a comfortable balance between undue deference and hostile competition – to act as an independent professional with valuable skills as opposed to a resentful appendage. Having respect for the doctors' view of psychological problems, accommodating their codes of behaviour and communication and, above all, acknowledging the centrality of the GP/patient relationship in the practice system does not make the counsellor a slave to the medical model (Dimmock, 1993).

While no referral system is likely to work smoothly all the time, avoiding difficulties from such variables as patients' attitudes, work-load pressures and clashes in personality, key issues of suitability, accountability and confidentiality can be overlooked if the referral is poorly set up in the first place (Irving, 1993: 63). If the counsellor is to be an effective member of the team then rules and procedures regard-ing the referral system must be clear and agreed by all concerned. But a caveat: preparation, however thorough and tactfully conducted, is no panacea. Merely to produce a set of ground rules in a situation where the parties may already be apprehensive and easily threatened will not necessarily obviate all the pitfalls of the context outlined above.

Furthermore, practices, like families, are different (Bor and Miller, 1991), with their own cultures and styles, their own myths and *modi vivendi*. The task for the counsellor is to adapt to the group ethos and interactional process while adhering to professional standards and boundaries – to maintain good work as an integrated team member rather than a pushy or precious outsider.

In considering the various components of the primary care setting, then, it is necessary to look at those beliefs and expectations and in par-ticular the GP/counsellor relationship and GP/patient interaction that shape a referral and so influence its success.

GP perspectives and reasons for referral

Any counsellor working in general practice will notice differences in referral patterns from the various GPs. These may reflect differences in how a GP views his role in relation to the patient, what expectations he may have of counselling, and the nature of the relationship with the patient, as well as wider issues to do with ethnicity, sexual orientation and gender.

In one practice the counsellor noticed that a high proportion of those patients who failed to attend their initial appointments were referred by one particularly old-fashioned, autocratic partner and may merely have been giving lip-service to his advice, while those who had an opportunity to discuss their fears and expectations with more patient-oriented doctors were more likely to present for counselling.

Another counsellor noted how trainee GPs tended to refer more frequently than the more experienced partners. Is this a result of their comparative lack of confidence in dealing with psychological problems, or does it reflect an increasing awareness of psychosocial factors in current medical training?

Referral patterns may also reflect individual doctors' special interests or prejudices.

In another practice a particularly maternal female partner was very sensitive to issues concerning loss and attachment, while another doctor who specialized in addiction and mental health difficulties was more likely to refer problems relating to low self-esteem and isolation.

Attitudes to a counselling referral may be rooted in beliefs and perceptions relating to ethnicity or gender.

Valerie, a young Afro-Caribbean woman, went to her GP with feelings of depression and worthlessness following troubles at work. In the consultation she felt stereotyped as 'pretty but thick' and had the impression that her difficulties were dismissed as a 'chip on her shoulder'. She refused a referral to the counsellor, both because she saw it as an attempt to get rid of her, and because she feared a practice colleague would share her doctor's views. Instead she re-registered at a different practice where, once she felt heard as an individual with pressing concerns, she was willing to be referred for counselling and explore her lack of self-belief in the context of both her family and the wider society.

Tricia went to her doctor as she was worried about a loss of libido which was damaging her relationship with her boyfriend. She felt that the male doctor was taking her partner's side and that a referral to counselling was with a view to adjust her behaviour to his expectations. She was only able to engage in the process when the counsellor explored the differences between the doctor's and Tricia's views of the problem, and, by inviting her partner to join the sessions, redefined the difficulty as an interactional one.

These examples underline the importance for the counsellor of considering and checking out – of being curious about – what happened before the first session to bring the patient there, of how the referral, which includes a definition of the 'problem', was negotiated between referrer and patient, and how each party viewed the meaning and possible outcome.

Some questions the counsellor might think about asking include:

- Does the GP rely heavily on the medical model of his training? If so, will he regard emotional difficulties as outside his domain and treat them by prescribing medication, or by a blanket handover to the counsellor?
- Does the GP regard himself as psychologically minded and prefer to take on the counselling role rather than relinquish it to another professional?
- What are the GP's expectations of the counsellor? To work with patients who could benefit from more time than he can offer? To relieve him of a patient with a chronic problem? To take a quick referral of a worrying patient as an alternative to waiting for a psychiatric referral when mental health services are scarce? Or to offer a different opportunity to the patient to change and find his own solutions?

Clearly, the importance of a good working relationship between professionals is indisputable: no referral is a neutral act and a successful referral begins with a successful contact between doctor and counsellor (McDaniel et al., 1990). But it could be argued that the success of any referral also depends on the quality of the preceding doctor/patient interaction.

The GP/patient relationship: the problem of the referring person

In their seminal paper entitled 'The Problem of the Referring Person', Palazzoli and her colleagues (1980) begin by stating that 'The problem of the referring person in family therapy is one of the most insidious and potentially compromising to the success of the treatment'. They consider the question of whether the referrer has become an important member of the patient's system, and argue that how the referral is handled moulds the process and outcome of counselling. The doctor may, for example, have experienced the patient's initial gratitude then felt himself trapped in the system and finally, in exasperation, sent the patient for therapy. The patient, responding to the doctor's wishes, may accept the referral but have a vested interest in not changing in order to retain the original relationship.

Gladys, aged 63, had a history of heart trouble, for which she had been treated, but still felt unwell and worried about her health. She consulted her GP frequently but never found a cure for her ailments. After various referrals the GP sent her to the counsellor as a last resort. Gladys did not know why she was there, and did not see her problems in a way that enabled her to engage in counselling – although she did have the somewhat hollow satisfaction of proving that no one could help her.

The counsellor needs to be aware of this type of situation and may either choose to convene a joint meeting with the doctor and patient – the evidence from one family counselling project in a general practice was that this was the best way of disengaging over-involved patients from their GP, so that counselling could be effective (Dimmock, 1993) – or to ensure that the patient's relationship with the referrer is respected.

Thus a referral for counselling risks being perceived as a rejection by the doctor, with accompanying dangers of splitting and resistance. Communication between doctor and counsellor – a communication that is apparent to the patient – is vital to minimize such difficulties and keep the feelings around the issue of referral to the forefront, as a focus for the counselling work.

Lisa was referred for help in dealing with a history of childhood sexual abuse by her uncle. She had been brought up by her grandparents, and while she had felt protected by her grandfather, her grandmother had never been able to accept the allegations of abuse within the family. At her first appointment she stressed how her GP was the only person in the world that she trusted, and indicated that she felt the counsellor would never believe her story. In fact, her doctor admitted that she drained both his time and his emotional energy. By exploring her feelings about the referral and liaising closely with the doctor, the counsellor (whose hypothesis from a psychodynamic perspective was of a split transference, with the GP as good grandfather and herself the bad grandmother) was able to address those issues of trust and betrayal that underlay her experience and engage her constructively in counselling.

This example illustrates how collaboration, by explicitly focusing on the meaning and process of the referral, can enhance the working relationship and improve patient care. However, it should be emphasized that in this particular case the doctor and patient enjoyed a relationship which allowed them both to acknowledge 'unprofessional' feelings of anxiety and helplessness, and, by recognizing their relative stakes in the referral, to try to avoid the pitfalls these presented (the doctor ridding himself of a problem, the counsellor pitting her professional status in competition for the patient's confidence). In this way, as McDaniel et al. have pointed out, the investment of the referring person need not be seen as part of the problem but as an opportunity to provide alternative views and enable more effective work (McDaniel et al., 1992).

Of course, there are many ways in which the patient's relationship with the GP, and indeed, with the practice as a whole, will colour their experience of a referral for counselling. Often GPs have known their patients over a long period and been a consistent figure through key life events such as births, deaths and serious illnesses. Such a trusting relationship can withstand shortcomings of the practice such as an impatient response from a receptionist, and provides a positive framework in which a referral is seen as a resource that the GP is offering.

Margaret, aged 60, had recently lost her husband, having nursed him through a long and painful illness. During this time he had been very difficult and abusive to her and his other carers, including his GP. Margaret felt that her doctor understood the difficulties she was experiencing and supported her through it as well as providing excellent medical care. When Margaret was referred for counselling, because of her trust in her GP, she was able to take the opportunity in the sessions to resolve some of her conflicted feelings towards her husband.

But feelings brought into the counselling can also be less positive:

It emerged during counselling that Sandra, aged 40, had previously been referred to the Social Services because of concern by her GP about one of her children. She was left feeling that her GP did not believe in her capability as a mother and this lack of trust spilled over into the counselling relationship, where Sandra felt under further scrutiny.

It may be important, therefore, to explore the patient's perceptions of the GP's reasons for making the referral, for example by saying 'Your doctor has told me a little about your situation. What do you imagine he has said?' or 'What changes do you think your doctor sees happening as a result of our meetings?'

When considering any referral in general practice, the counsellor needs to ask:

- Who initiated the referral – doctor, patient, family, friend?
- What is the patient's relationship with their GP? Trustful? Deferential? Suspicious?

- What changes does the GP/patient want from counselling? Were these agreed between them?
- How does the patient experience the referral? As rejection, an obligation, an opportunity to view the problem differently?
- How does the patient see the GP/counsellor connection? As collaborative colleagues? Rival professionals? Social friends? How might this affect the counselling process, especially regarding issues of boundaries and confidentiality?
- Why was the referral made now?

It is worthwhile exploring this last question more specifically, as the timing of a referral can be of critical importance.

Timing

It is axiomatic in counselling theory that motivation for change is a requisite for successful therapy; but sometimes the GP may be more motivated than the patient. This may mean that the patient does not appear for his first appointment, or seems unable to engage in counselling. Such a patient may be seen as the bane of both the doctor's and the counsellor's caseload, as either dropout or difficult. But as has been pointed out (Miller et al., 1997), motivation should no longer be seen as some stable personality trait; rather, it can be understood as a dynamic process, 'determined as much by context as by personality'. The patient's expectations may simply not match the doctor's or counsellor's at the time of referral.

For example, a patient may not feel that they have a problem, or may not make a connection between difficulties they are experiencing and their contribution to these. Such patients may perceive themselves as under duress but explain this in terms of bad luck or circumstances beyond their control. If they do not attend for counselling, the counsellor may discuss with the doctor how he can better manage them in their consultations and slowly introduce the idea of counselling. Or, if a patient presents at the GP's behest but is not ready to think about change, the counsellor may need to recognize that, at best, they can keep the door open by creating a climate where the patient can consider change – as implied by a counselling referral – without feeling under pressure to make a commitment to the process.

There may be other important factors in the timing of a referral.

Xania, a 35-year-old woman, had been seeing her GP once a month for nearly a year after the sudden death of her husband. She had long term physical problems which required monitoring, but the GP was also concerned about how Xania was managing and wondered if she would benefit from counselling. She had apparently depended completely on her husband, who was much older than her, having given up her job when they married. Her doctor felt that she should be trying now to build an independent life, returning to work and finding new social supports.

The GP had offered a counselling referral just before the anniversary of the husband's death, which Xania was planning to mark with a special meal with friends, and she had politely declined it. Talking it over, the counsellor felt that the doctor had a good relationship with her patient; she did not feel burdened by their regular consultations, which she saw as both medically appropriate and generally positive. Rather, she had thought of referral because of her own goals for Xania's recovery from mourning. The counsellor wondered if referral at this point, coinciding with the anniversary of her husband's death, might be experienced as another loss – i.e. of a trusted support – and discussed with the GP the idea of continuing the existing arrangement for the time being while gradually exploring her thoughts about counselling, focusing also on the anniversary meal and its possible significance for her as a landmark event.

In the event, doctor and counsellor were able to work collaboratively to bring about an effective referral. But such cooperation depends on the kind of communication that is possible within the system, and this will be determined by the particular characteristics of the individual practice. Referral systems range from a brief conversation 'on the hoof' to regular practice meetings, where possible referrals can be discussed and a collaborative treatment plan agreed. The success of any referral rests on how it is made.

How the referral is made: meetings, letters and forms

Where surgeries have regular meetings, the counsellor may attend as a recognized member of the health care team. The presence of a colleague specifically trained in interpersonal relationship problems may help team members develop an increased awareness of the emotional and social dimensions of patients' problems and, as prior discussion is possible, referrals are more likely to be appropriate. The counsellor also has the opportunity to offer suggestions, such as a joint session, or to support a GP in exercising his own assessment and interviewing skills, as in the example above.

In addition to the information which has been shared at the practice meeting, or in the absence of such a forum, the counsellor may require a referral form to be completed by the referrer – and although discussion here has centred on referrals from doctors, this might also be a nurse, health visitor or the patients themselves. Forms usually include basic information – name, address, contact number – and a brief description of the problem and reason for referral, as well as the expected outcome from counselling, and sometimes psychiatric history and current medication. What can usefully be covered on a form raises the question of how much information is helpful for the counsellor to have. Diagnostic labels and strong opinions may bias the counsellor's own impressions and limit creative work. This is especially so in a team environment, where the counsellor may overhear gossip in the reception area, or be tempted to pre-judge patients by their reputation in the surgery. In this way, a form may serve to limit information as well as elicit it. An example of a referral form is given in the Appendix to this chapter.

Allocation

How counselling referrals are allocated will depend on the characteristics of the individual practice. Where the referring agents include other practice workers – nurses, health visitors, physiotherapists – this may be in practice meetings or, where all referrals go through the GPs, they may meet regularly with the counsellor(s) specifically for this purpose. At practice or allocation meetings the counsellor has an opportunity to discuss alternative resources available, as well as determining how soon the patient would be seen, particularly where a waiting list operates and appointments are not available for some weeks. If the practice offers direct self-referrals, then the counsellor may use the meeting to consult other professionals about the patient.

Where there is more than one counsellor, the allocation of referrals will depend on a number of factors – the counsellors' different areas of expertise, experience or special interest, their relationship with the referrer and availability of space for a new patient as well as issues of gender and ethnicity and the patient's perspective. Some situations may be inappropriate for a particular counsellor, for example where there is some pre-existing connection with the patient or where a pregnant counsellor would be offering therapy to an infertile couple.

John was referred for help with a fear of shaming himself in public, by wetting himself. After discussion in the practice meeting, it was decided that he should be seen by the male counsellor, who was trained in cognitive behaviour therapy, rather than by the more psychodynamically orientated female counsellor.

Soraya was a young Moroccan woman struggling with her need to commit to a long term relationship with her English lover, which she felt would automatically entail rejection by her family. The GP wondered whether she would benefit from discussing her dilemma with someone who might understand the cultural conflicts involved, and suggested a referral to the male counsellor who also came from a Middle Eastern background. When Soraya refused to see a man she was convinced would share her family's expectations of women's roles, her GP was able to offer an appointment with the other practice counsellor, a woman.

Such issues can be discussed in allocation meetings or when practice counsellors get together regularly to decide workload management. Where there is no such opportunity, counsellors need to negotiate allocation by some other means so that referrals are appropriately shared and not abandoned to the vagaries of the system. Some GPs, for example, may prefer to work with a particular counsellor (perhaps because of the opportunity for feedback), or a female counsellor may receive more referrals than her male colleague, reflecting possibly the greater number of women seen in general practice or the referrer's assumption that they would prefer a counsellor of the same sex.

Most practices operate some form of waiting list, and where this is long, patients may need to be prioritized, rather than seen on a first come first served basis. This may mean, for example, deciding between seeing someone with a work based problem where their job is at risk, a patient with long term depression presenting with suicidal feelings and someone complaining of anxiety and panic attacks.

Emergencies

Some referrals may be designated an emergency by the GP or other referring agent. Here, the counsellor needs to bear in mind those issues considered earlier and ask themselves for whom it is an emergency. As we have already seen, an emergency may reflect the anxieties of the referrer. It might be that the problem can be more effectively dealt with elsewhere, in the mental health department of the local hospital, for example, if the patient is reporting seriously suicidal thoughts.

Most counsellors offer all patients an initial appointment to make an assessment of the problem and determine what, if anything, the course of treatment will be and when it can commence. This can provide an early response to the patient, who might construe his situation as an emergency, and may be sufficient to allay fears and create confidence in the idea of treatment at a later date.

Certain situations are of necessity an emergency: the patient requesting termination counselling does not want to wait 2 months for an appointment. One or two sessions followed by a further appointment after the termination would be a more effective way of helping. Someone who has just suffered a bereavement, experienced a trauma, or been given a diagnosis of cancer may find an initial appointment helpful and be re-assured to know where to turn in the future. Blakey, Sinclair and Taylor (1994) suggest that early contact, with an interval before follow-up, may be clinically effective.

Providing the space for an initial assessment or emergency session for two or three patients a week, depending on the size of the practice, can help process referrals of this kind.

Knowing that the counsellor had a regular appointment set aside for such situations, a GP referred Chris as an emergency after he had been turned away for treatment at the mental health department of the local hospital. Having explored with the counsellor his feelings of rejection, Chris began to develop an understanding of what he could be offered within the GP system and was ready to wait for ongoing appointments.

Andrew had recently taken an overdose and was referred by his GP as an emergency. In the session, he came to trust that there was someone willing to listen to him, offer support and provide ongoing treatment at a later date.

Of course, anticipating an emergency session may raise the counsellor's anxieties before meeting the patient. It is reassuring to feel able to call on appropriate resources should the need arise, or to encourage the patient to seek medical assistance that is easily accessible. For these reasons it would be inadvisable for counsellors to schedule their emergency sessions when they might be alone in the building. Sometimes an emergency only comes to light during the session – or all too often towards the end – and this requires all the counsellor's skill to manage the situation in a short space of time. All this is demanding for the counsellor, who may in turn want to consider these issues in supervision.

Acting on the referral

Once the counsellor has accepted the referral, the patient needs to be contacted and an appointment made. This may be either by telephone or by letter from the counsellor themselves or the practice receptionist. Where the counsellor chooses to telephone patients directly, they should be aware that to do so initiates the counselling relationship and process, and some patients may want to use the opportunity to discuss their perception of the problem prior to the session – a point to note, particularly when the referral is for couple or family work. It is important for the referrer to clarify with the patient their feelings about being contacted at home or work, and whether or not they would like to be offered an appointment at short notice, in the event of a cancellation. Where there is no waiting list, the GP may ask the patient to make an appointment directly.

A referral, of course, is no guarantee that the patient will show up for their first appointment. Some counsellors require the patient to contact the receptionist after they have agreed a referral with their doctor, and specifically request their name be added to the waiting list, before they can be offered an appointment. For some patients, making the appointment itself may be part of the solution, and they may not take it up.

Feedback: reporting to the referral source

> Treatment without communication is like two blindfolded drivers on a race-track; not colliding is a matter of luck. (McDaniel et al., 1992: 57)

Effective collaboration in the practice team will benefit from regular feedback from the counsellor of summary information on referral numbers, 'problem' categories and patient satisfaction. This important issue will be dealt with more extensively in a later chapter, but in the context of individual referrals feedback both reflects and influences the working relationship between referrer and counsellor.

The nature of communication between counsellor and doctor will be patterned by their expectations and views of each other, and in turn will shape and inform both the collaborative relationship and the counselling process itself. In the medical model, a referral to a secondary or specialist provider is met by a brief letter in reply, regarding assessment, treatment plan and sometimes recommendations for the referring doctor. While counsellors may be accustomed to reflective debates about cases, or seek validation by reporting therapeutic successes, the pace of GP working requires that any communication should be brief, timely and to the point (Dimmock, 1993). Formal communication, then, may consist of short intake and termination letters, the first describing the treatment contract with the patient (definition of the problem, goals, number of sessions) and the second giving a summary at the end of counselling. This style of communication may be especially appropriate in the early stages of a counsellor's post or where the GP prefers not to deal with psychosocial difficulties. Where the doctor is more concerned with the patient's emotional problems, or where contact with the counsellor is mutually interested and supportive, greater communication, whether through chance meetings or more formal discussions, should enhance both patient care and the working relationship. If the doctor is very involved with the patient, communication may include convening a joint session. Thus, the frequency, form and content of reporting back reflects the context, and colours the ongoing process. In this way, for example, some counsellors include a feedback section on the referral form which the counsellor completes together with the patient.

This raises an important point and one which touches on the delicate and sometimes contentious issue of confidentiality in primary care counselling. The nature of communication derives from the GP/counsellor relationship, but it should also accommodate the doctor/patient relationship and be congruent with the counsellor/patient relationship. While all patients should be advised of the practice policy regarding confidentiality (see Chapter 7), the counsellor should be respectful of what information can be usefully shared. Joint completion of a feedback form invites input from the patient on the counselling process, demonstrates communication between counsellor and doctor, and makes the patient party to what is recorded between professionals. In this way feedback, like referral, requires assessment of all the relationships in the GP/patient/counsellor triad.

Thus, when considering a referral system the counsellor may want to ask:

- What sort of system is feasible within this particular practice ?
- How can the characteristics of the practice be employed to support and implement the system?
- How will the system encourage collaboration?
- What information is necessary? What reciprocal information can be fed back to the referrer and how?

The range of issues involved here reflects that collaboration develops not only through feedback regarding case progress, but also through the process of making changes in the referral system and convening procedures (Dimmock, 1993). The following account of the introduction of a referral form in a general practice illustrates some of these issues.

Introducing a referral system: an example

Context: the practice

This inner-urban practice functions like a big friendly family where boundaries are somewhat blurred and newcomers are expected to muck in and get on with it. The atmosphere is informal, relaxed and collegial, dress is casual, first and nicknames are used throughout and there is an active social life involving staff and their families. However, the other side of this system is an anti-bureaucracy attitude that belies administrative imperatives and organizational realities. Here the myth is that everyone shares an ideological conviction and therefore both like and agree with each other; conflict and constraint are projected outside – onto the wider, impersonal economics of health care bureaucracy. While celebrated in the form of social eccentricity, difference is denied in professional perspective, so that hierarchies and power struggles tend to operate covertly, planning and policy-making is conducted outside surgery hours among social sub-groups, and there is no formal arena for addressing conflict or managing change. Full practice meetings are held infrequently with staff appearing unfamiliar with notions of formal authority – the 'chair'- and organization – the 'agenda'- and tending to dismiss the process as ineffective.

Thus the prevailing culture at the practice posed a dilemma for the counsellor. On the one hand the service was welcomed and supported, while few demands or constraints were imposed on the way it was delivered; on the other hand, there was no on-site management and no established system for referral or consultation. The need was to introduce improvements – as a fellow professional – in a situation where attempts to define structures could be viewed as presumptuous posturing.

Reasons for changing the referral system

With this background there were a number of reasons for introducing a referral form. Most immediately, there was a need to improve efficiency by focusing attention on the referral process and standardizing– as far as possible – the various methods used, which ranged from telling the patient to give necessary information to the receptionist, through a name scribbled on a piece of paper to a brief letter. It was also hoped that addressing these issues and canvassing the doctors' views on referral and feedback would establish a more collaborative working relationship, while underlining counselling as an effective and professional component of the practice's service to patients. Moreover, and especially if completed during the clinical consultation, a written form would encourage consideration of the suitability of referral, while also providing a graphic demonstration of doctor/counsellor cooperation, thereby minimizing the dangers of splitting or of the patient viewing referral as a rejection. After all, if a referral constitutes 'a powerful primary care intervention in and of itself for a patient' (McDaniel et al., 1990: 356) then a form focuses all participants on its meaning and implications.

In this way, the introduction of a form was designed to improve efficiency, enhance collaboration, raise the profile of counselling and hence, both directly and indirectly, advance patient care.

The process of change

If, as we have seen, consultation is a helpful prelude to referral, the same is true of devising a referral system, since no one party can expect to impose a procedure or prescribe a role for the other. Thus there were two imperatives to the management of this change: to conform to the practice culture and to engage the doctors' cooperation by emphasizing the advantages to them. Accordingly, the intervention was timed to follow one of the annual parties, when 'esprit de corps' was high, and stress levels relatively low. The groundwork for change was also laid by providing each GP with a directory of local resources – designed to facilitate the direct referral of those patients who might not require assessment, and also to demonstrate the counsellor's commitment to supporting the doctors in their work. This seemed successful, since each GP made a point of thanking the counsellor.

It has been suggested that innovation in general practice (Spiegal et al., 1992) requires a team approach, fostering ownership of the proposed change by identifying all key people, and addressing the costs as well as the benefits to those concerned, both individually and in group meetings.

At this practice, such a model proved unrealistic, given the time pressures and the 'anti-meeting' culture. However, the counsellor tried to adapt the principles involved by respecting power structures, and minimizing costs and highlighting benefits to those involved.

For example, although in this practice managerial responsibilities were not always clearly delineated, the practice manager had been active in recruiting the counsellor, and was therefore approached first, and her advice sought. Similarly, since the commitment of 'low status' workers is also pertinent, reactions and suggestions were elicited from the receptionists, who have charge of the appointment book, and take messages if the counsellor is not there. In the absence of meetings, each doctor was presented with a written pack including a brief outline of the objectives of the change, and drafts of both the proposed form and a handout on counselling for patients. The latter was included to reinforce the idea of a form as *helpful* to the referring doctor, relieving them of the task of explaining counselling.

The form

On the form itself the information required was reduced to a minimum, to forestall objections that it was too time-consuming to complete. The outcome section – to be filled in by counsellor together with client – was given equal space to the referral, lending graphic representation to the notion of the process as mutually beneficial. Theoretically the doctor gains feedback in an accessible and standardized form while the patient is party to what information is recorded between the professionals. Thus the form was intended to embody and respect the principles of collaboration and confidentiality.

Outcome

In the event, the doctors accepted the change with little difficulty. There has been an increase in initial consultation before making a referral and efficiency has improved to the extent that there are significantly fewer administrative errors and referrals that go astray. But, while conforming to a prevailing culture that abhorred conformity, each doctor adapted the change to their own individual style – one resolutely refuses to complete the form and still refers by letter, another regularly omits the section on expected outcome, and yet another dislikes completing the form in the presence of the patient. This example illustrates both the centrality of referral in the wider system of the practice and ways in which the characteristics of that context will determine the nature of the referral process.

Referring on

In their study of counselling in an inner city group practice, Webber et al. (1994) suggest that a single counsellor in an average-sized practice would be unlikely to have the time or expertise to respond to the full range of patients' counselling needs. Moreover, the pressure of the waiting list means that most counsellors operate in short term contracts and are unable to offer longer term therapy. Perhaps one of the tasks in this setting, rather like GPs themselves, is to help patients identify a problem and find an appropriate specialist agency where they can work towards its resolution. Patients are entitled to the best possible service, and counsellors should be ready to acknowledge the limits of their competence. There may be various reasons for referring patients elsewhere: their difficulties may be better addressed by family or group therapy when these are not within the counsellor's experience or expertise; their problem may respond better to a different orientation – for example, a psychodynamic counsellor might refer someone with an obsessive compulsive disorder to a colleague skilled in cognitive behaviour therapy; or the patient may want and be likely to benefit from a longer term therapeutic relationship.

Referring on, then, means being familiar with local resources, those agencies offering specialized services, and the work of other therapists working privately in the area. Many patients find it helpful to be given a name rather than being referred to an organization, or sent to the local library. Where counsellors are working in short term contracts, it may emerge during counselling that the patient is suitable for long term therapy. Knowing that referral on is an option will, of course, colour the nature of the work undertaken in the short term. This may focus on preparation – giving the patient an experience of the process and exploring their expectations and concerns about entering a more open-ended arrangement. As in receiving a referral, consideration must be given to timing, to the nature of the counselling relationship, to the patient's perceptions of a referral elsewhere and, where possible, prior consultation with the new therapist, to ease the transition.

Angela, a young Afro-Caribbean woman, was suffering from depression and difficulties in her family relationships. The counsellor felt that she needed the security of a long term relationship to resolve her deep-seated problems but Angela could not afford private therapy. However, she did fit the criteria of a local voluntary agency that offered free long term counselling to ethnic minorities, so the counsellor suggested a referral. Initially Angela seemed suspicious of the idea and, in further discussion, it became apparent that she associated a black counsellor with her own experience of authoritarian parents, and a family where she felt she did not fit in. It was only after careful exploration of her fears and communication with the proposed counsellor that Angela was able to embrace the referral and engage in a new therapeutic relationship.

This example shows the difficulties of referring on when the individual has few financial resources and public sector services are scarce and over-stretched. With waiting lists of several months for secondary NHS treatment, this may mean 'holding' the patient by, for example, monthly appointments. Here is one of the imperatives for primary care counsellors – the need to use their skills flexibly.

Conclusion

Referral is the nexus of the complex interactions that characterize the primary care setting. Finding common ground and mutual trust among the professional rivalries and power differentials in general practice requires persistence, imagination, respect and not a little humility. Negotiating roles, liasing with busy GPs, prioritizing and processing work, dealing with emergencies are all tasks inherent to primary care counselling, required and defined by the referral system. Working in an environment where stress levels among staff are often high and having to adapt to the stark realities of, for example, shortfalls in communication and lack of room space, can create a fine line between maintaining professional boundaries and alienating harassed staff by insisting on rigid structures. This can feel like constant pressure and, given the not uncommon isolation of the counsellor in the primary care setting, contact with colleagues in other practices as well as regular supervision can provide invaluable support. But it is the referral process, which both furnishes and is fashioned by the working relationship between GP and counsellor, that forms the foundation for creative counselling and effective patient care.

Key points

- Think about *context.*
- Who initiated the referral?
- What are the implications of the relationships involved – GP/patient, GP/counsellor, patient/counsellor?
- Do the parties concerned agree on problem definition and aims?
- Why was the referral made *now?*
- What is the best way of taking up the referral?
- How can feedback enhance the working relationship and patient care?
- Could the patient be better served by referral elsewhere?

References

Blakey, R., Sinclair, J. and Taylor, R. (1994) 'Patient satisfaction with short clinical psychology contact', *Clinical Forum*, July: 13–15.

Bor, R. and Miller, R. (1991) *Internal Consultation in Health Care Settings*. London: Karnac Books.

Dimmock, B. (1993) 'Developing family counselling in general practice', in John Carpenter and Andy Treacher (eds), *Using Family Therapy in the Nineties*. Oxford: Blackwell.

Graham, H. and Sher, M. (1976) 'Social work and general practice', *Journal of the Royal College of General Practitioners*, 26: 99–104.

Irving, J. (1993) 'Practical and training issues', in R. Corney and R. Jenkins (eds), *Counselling in General Practice*. London: Routledge.

McDaniel, S., Campbell, T. and Seaburn, D. (1990) *Family Oriented Primary Care: a Manual for Medical Providers*. New York: Springer-Verlag.

McDaniel, S.H., Hepworth, J. and Doherty, W.J. (1992) *Medical Family Therapy: a Biopsychosocial Approach to Families with Health Problems*. New York: Basic Books.

Miller, S.D., Duncan, B.L. and Hubble, M.A. (1997) *Escape from Babel: Toward a Unifying Language for Psychotherapy Practice*. New York: Norton.

Palazzoli, M., Boscolo, L., Cecchin, G. and Prata, G. (1980) 'The problem of the referring person', *Journal of Marital and Family Therapy*, 6: 3–9.

Small, N. and Conlon, I. (1988) 'The creation of an inter-occupational relationship: the introduction of a counsellor in an NHS general practice', *British Journal of Social Work*, 18: 171–87.

Spiegal, N., Murphy, E., Kinmouth, A., Ross, F., Bain, J. and Coates, R. (1992) 'Managing change in general practice: a step by step guide', *British Medical Journal*, 304: 231–5.

Webber, V., Davis, P. and Pietroni, P. (1994) 'Counselling in an inner city group practice: analysis of its use and uptake', *British Journal of General Practice*, 44 (April): 178.

Appendix

Counselling Referral Form

Patient's name: ....

Reason for referral: ....

....

....

....

....

Patient's previous experience of counselling: ....

....

Is this a crisis? ....

....

Do I need to be aware of any other issues? ....

....

What are your expectations? ....

....

Date of referral .... GP ....

FOR GP'S INFORMATION

Patient's name: ....

Number of sessions offered: ....

....

....

Work done/completed with patient: ....

....

....

....

....

....

Reasons for ending: ....

....

....

....

Date: .... Counsellor ....

CHAPTER 6

MANAGING PATIENT FLOW: WAITING AND ABSENCES

Carole Waskett

As practice counsellors, our work is challenged and shaped by the regular ebb and flow of patients entering and leaving the counselling room. Ideally, each patient or family would get an appointment quickly after referral, would arrive promptly and would leave comfortably before the next person predictably arrived. The assumption here is that, in an ideal world, there would be no

- long wait between patients making their appointment and coming to it;
- cancellations;
- patients who do not arrive (and do not tell us why) – (DNAs in the jargon).

For the purpose of clarity, DNAs and cancellations will be referred to as absences. The difference is that some of our patients tell us they will not be coming, while others do not.

As practice counsellors we are absurdly and perhaps unnecessarily vulnerable to our absentees and to our waiting list. If we admit that a fair proportion of patients who book to see us simply do not come, what does that say about us?

One interpretation could be that we are bad, inefficient or unhelpful counsellors. At the other end of the scale, if it becomes clear that there is a very long wait before we have a space to see someone, we may be seen as ineffectual, 'going on for ever', unable to let our patients go, and not able to help enough people over time to make our work viable.

In practical terms, it can be a worry that we might be held responsible for the 'waste' of booked contact hours unused, or for the huge tailback of waiting patients. Of course, these problems dovetail; people who are waiting to see us could be seen much sooner in the spaces left by the cancellations and DNAs, if only we could arrange it.

This chapter presents a view of these difficult challenges which leads us away from blaming ourselves, or worse, our patients, and towards acceptance and understanding. Absences may not in fact be 'faulty' at all. They are, of course, an inescapable part of the fabric of primary care counselling, part of the texture of the interface between our own professional lives and the rich and varied personal and working lives of our patients. Even if not interpreted as unconscious messages (as counsellors using a psychodynamic/analytic model of therapy may do), we may still be able to understand some absences as important communications or 'teaching aids' used by our patients to help us to help them. We can do a great deal to make ourselves more available for more patients – thus shortening the time they have to wait to see us – while maintaining our self-esteem and the enjoyment of our work.

Links between absences and waiting time

Our own availability and our patients' absences are two quite separate areas, both involving somebody waiting for someone else, which overlap and interlink at a few points.

If the patient has to wait a long time for an appointment, they may

- find help elsewhere
- recover spontaneously
- find that their problem deteriorates.

Any of these factors may account for the person not arriving when their appointment finally comes.

Absence slots could be filled by someone else waiting, with some simple administrative sleight of hand. This is not only a bureaucratic issue. Because counsellors and therapists so often invest so much of their self-worth in their work, a long list of patients waiting to see us can make us feel important and needed. Counselling and therapy, like other helping professions, have their dark side. We can easily be seduced by the idea of being sorcerers, uniquely possessing magical powers. A long waiting list can give rise to a secret pride (Guggenbuhl-Craig, 1971).

On the other hand, a high rate of unattended appointments can deflate our ego and produce a sense of inadequacy or shame. Perhaps each balances the other out. One practice counsellor said:

> My absence rate is about 1:7, pretty consistently. To stop myself getting tense or upset about it, I book a couple of extra patients into my administration time, so that I feel I've seen as many in the week as I'm supposed to.

TOURO COLLEGE LIBRARY

This counsellor highlights the typical effects of absences upon the practitioner. She admits candidly to the possibility of getting 'tense or upset', and is taking the burden of responsibility upon her own shoulders for making up to the practice for the unfilled sessions by cutting into her administration time to see 'extras'.

It is worth noting the possibility that simply *making an appointment* may have such an effect on the patient that they may not need to come at all, rather like the apocryphal story of the toothache vanishing on the very day of the dentist's appointment. Psychological pain may be even more susceptible to psychological 'shadow' moves, so that simply by being there to be made an appointment with, we may be serving a function, even if that appointment is not kept. Counselling is not confined to the counselling room.

After 7 years together, Angela and Diana, a lesbian couple, find their relationship is in trouble. It has taken weeks of courageous, honest talking to admit their unhappiness to each other and agree to make an appointment. During the 4 weeks they have to wait, their talking continues, and they are able to make a few important changes which begin to nurture the relationship again.

The week before their appointment, their cat is run over and killed, and the way they are able to comfort each other over this small tragedy makes them realize they no longer need to draw in an outsider, at least for the time being. Diana rings to cancel their appointment.

Recording absences

Even if absence rates in UK primary care were readily available in the literature, there are so many possible ways of measuring them that we cannot be sure we are comparing like with like. 'Dropout rates', for example, have been investigated. A figure of 17 per cent has been found for treatment delivered in centres of excellence, and between 30 and 60 per cent for psychotherapy offered at mental health centres (Hunt and Andrews, 1992). American studies suggest a 'dropout' rate of about 25 per cent, increasing to 60 per cent or more (quoted in Miller et al., 1996).

The problem is that 'dropout' does not have the same meaning as 'a patient not attending a session' and indeed has a rather more pejorative tone. Some people simply do not come for a session, and if they have more sessions booked ahead – which they attend – they cannot be said to have 'dropped out'.

Others do not arrive for a session, and have no more booked. Because we never see them again, we may label them 'dropouts'. Yet they may have found the counselling invaluable, feel better and take a healthy personal decision not to re-book. Dropping out may have many meanings; as counsellors we may be pleased with several of them.

The following are just a few examples:

- The patient found the counselling useful and made enough changes to continue without counselling help.
- The patient found after a taste of it that counselling was not, after all, what they needed; that discovery was enough to motivate them to find what they *did* need elsewhere.
- The *fact* that the patient was attending counselling (not the content or process of it) made such an impact on people close to them that things changed rapidly for the better; the counselling did not need to continue.
- As a result of a small amount of counselling, the patient's life improved and became busier. Consciously or unconsciously, they became 'too busy' to fit in a visit to the surgery.
- This was not the right time in the patient's life to use counselling, and they were aware enough of this to stop coming.

In recording rates of absences, it is important to separate those of

- unseen patients (that is, those who are referred and book to see the counsellor but then never actually arrive), and
- patients already seen at least once by the counsellor.

This is because there are very different influences upon each group and therefore the interventions and arrangements we may make to influence each group are likely to be very different.

Group 1: patients who book but never arrive

A proportion of patients are referred and go as far as to book an appointment with the counsellor, but never arrive in the counselling room. There are many possible causes for this.

1 The referrer, the relationship between referrer and patient and the way the referral was made. Was the patient trying to please the referrer by agreeing to see the counsellor, while not actually wanting to? Did the patient feel rejected by the referrer? Did the referrer know enough about the counselling on offer to make an effective referral?

2   In the intervening period between making the appointment and the time of the appointment, did the patient solve their problems themselves? Or did they find alternative help?
3   Did the patient decide that the times when the counsellor was available were too inconvenient? Some working people do not get paid if they take time off; others face criticism or even disciplinary action if they do so, and others again – many care workers, for instance – are all too aware of the extra burden they place on already hard-pressed colleagues if they are away from work even for a short time. Parents often have to look after their children and have no one to step in.
4   Did the patient receive prior information about the counselling which either put them off or made them decide that counselling would not be helpful for them at this time? Did they talk to someone who dissuaded them from coming, or did they simply get 'cold feet' or lose interest?

People who make an appointment but never arrive can only be influenced indirectly. A patient the counsellor has never seen is not yet a counselling client. These non-attendance rates can only be influenced by relationships within the team, by the way we manage our appointments system and by the preliminary information we may give to patients intending to come for counselling. A telephone reminder system may be a possibility, but weighs heavily upon whoever is charged with undertaking it. And one might argue that, if a first counselling appointment is important to the patient, they will make sure they come.

Until research *tells* us why these patients did not come, although we can speculate, we shall never know. It seems that the length of time they may have to wait, plus the way the counselling is initially presented, are probably the strongest predictors of whether someone will arrive. There are a few small ways in which we can influence non-attendance rates in this group, but we cannot influence them anywhere near as much as in the second group.

Group 2: patients seen at least once

This group of patients have become counselling 'clients'; they have already seen the counsellor at least once, but subsequently do not arrive for another booked session.

In this case the possible influences are quite different, and may include:

1   The way we as professionals behave and work.
2   Our competence and ability.

3 Our appointments system and our arrangements regarding the timing of sessions.
4 The chemistry between us and the patient.

We are always inclined to take responsibility, but this can sometimes arise from an inflated idea of our own importance. There are many other influences, such as patients' work and domestic arrangements.

Using this split categorization, the author has found over the past 10 years in four different practices (some running concurrently) that the *total* rate of absences is 24 per cent, or just under one in four. But only about half of these – about 12 per cent – are sessions of people who have actually been seen at least once. This division brings into focus the fact that the patient's arrival or non-arrival in the counselling room is something to do with all *three* parties in the arrangement: referrer, patient and counsellor. In a general practice setting, for the group of patients who never arrive the referral procedure should be the first step to be investigated.

Making appointments

Systems of making appointments vary, and obviously affect both absences and waiting times. The very first contact the patient has with the counselling service is bound to affect whether they come to an appointment or not. It is advisable for the referrer to ask patients to make appointments for themselves, that is, come to the desk, or telephone whoever is responsible for making the appointments. This is both simpler and more respectful of the patient's time than sending an appointment by post which may or may not be convenient. It also establishes that the patient really does want to see the counsellor, rather than the referrer or the counsellor deciding what *they* think is best.

Some counsellors have their cohort of continuing, perhaps fairly long term patients, and then hold a waiting list which is accumulated by the reception staff. As the counsellor becomes ready to take on a new patient they contact the next one on the list and arrange things accordingly. Others book new people ahead as there are spaces, and the current patients simply fit round them.

The latter method can be very effective. Patients choose the time of their next appointment and a slot is negotiated for them as close as possible to their chosen time. It is the patient who chooses the interval between one appointment and the next. Those intervals are often quite long, and people may be booked in two or three months ahead, but there are plenty of spaces in between for new patients. There is no

underlying meaning or interpretation given to their choice or the counsellor's offering of any particular slot. Waiting time tends to decrease
overall if it is possible to use this method.

Many counsellors reserve the right to arrange appointments themselves, giving no role to others in the practice. But particularly for first
appointments, receptionists or other allocated staff can be very helpful
in managing the appointments book or computer screens. Counsellors
are fortunate if they can have a pair of staff members dedicated to this
work (two so as to cover for each other). In general, it seems beneficial
for administrative staff to be encouraged and trusted to help manage
the appointments list. There are several reasons for this:

1   The counsellor, usually a part-time worker, should not be making
    calls in her own time, especially from home. This may lead to the
    undesirable practice of doing ad hoc counselling over the phone. In
    addition, some of the many practical problems might be: reim-
    bursement of the phone bill and payment for the counsellor's time;
    the maintainance of confidentiality; and the business of answering
    machines, relatives and patients calling back. Obviously, if the prac-
    tice computer is used for appointments, as more and more are, then
    making appointments from the counsellor's home is impossible. If
    the counsellor is given time to make appointments on site at the
    practice, it is still difficult for patients to contact the counsellor,
    because of necessity, most of her time will be spent in counselling,
    which of course should not be interrupted.
2   Clerical staff, on the other hand, are paid to be available during
    working hours at the practice for just this purpose. They are bound
    by the practice rules of confidentiality.
3   Within the team, it is probably beneficial to team working to demon-
    strate trust and a reasonable amount of openness regarding the
    practice's patients. There is no particular reason why the counsellor
    should be any more strict about confidentiality rules than the doctor
    or the health visitor, provided the patient's privacy is properly
    respected (but see Chapter 7 on confidentiality).

The following is an example of administrative good practice.

Caryl, an assistant practice manager, sees most of the referrals, who are
funnelled through from the main desk or put through to her telephone
extension. She is careful to protect the patient's privacy, taking them dis-
creetly away from the reception area to make the appointment. Caryl
explains where the counselling will take place, that it is confidential, and
that the patient will be seen alone. The patient is given an information sheet
and a note of the appointment time, and often takes the opportunity to tell

Caryl a little of what is bothering them. Caryl says the sense of relief is often great and the tissues are sometimes in evidence; counselling is already beginning! It is starting to be noticeable that patients who see Caryl at first are more likely to arrive for a first session.

Absences of patients seen at least once

These are absences of people who have already met the counsellor at least once, and have booked another session in consultation with the counsellor, but then do not arrive for it. The cost of these unfilled sessions is the price the practice pays for offering a counselling service.

We can take comfort from the fact that all counsellors have unattended appointments. Our patients are human beings who have babysitting problems, lose bits of paper, have illnesses – or their children do – and live lives which take up time, energy and nifty footwork. They get tired, they take their responsibilities seriously, their transport arrangements break down, they work hard, unexpected things happen, life gets to be just too much to pile on one more thing.

Sometimes they are rightfully wary of professionals, and sometimes they feel uncomfortable with us, or do not feel we are being helpful. Conversely, perhaps we *are* being helpful – so much so that we are becoming redundant. Patients, like the rest of us, make their own decisions, and we cannot always expect to understand those decisions. They may not always feel the need to terminate sessions formally and tidily in the way mental health professionals would like. If these patients have had enough counselling, for whatever reason, they may simply vote with their feet. The counsellor is very seldom the most important person in the patient's life, in spite of our fantasies of sorcery or rescue.

This counsellor's story is illustrative:

Some time ago, I made an appointment to see a therapist I know and trust, to work on a specific treatment goal for myself. This entailed my travelling to London, three hours' journey each way, so I had to cancel my work for that day. When I added up lost earnings (I'm a self-employed practice counsellor), travel costs, and therapy fees, the total sum for an hour of therapy turned out to be astronomical.

Over several weeks I did manage to go twice, and got considerable benefit from it. But the last straw came when my dog became ill. I was worried about leaving him alone for too long, and there were vets appointments – and bills. I cancelled further sessions. Therapy was valuable, but not that valuable. The therapist assured me that if and when I wanted to return, he would be glad to see me, and that helped too.

One possible meaning for the absences of patients who have already attended is that we have simply set up too many sessions, or that the interval between them was too short. Setting up sessions to suit our administrative purposes may not suit the patient. Arranging, say, six sessions, one every week, a common package, may be unhelpful to this particular person. There is no particular therapeutic magic in the interval of seven days. By simply not arriving or by cancelling one or more of those sessions the patient may be tactfully telling us something about what *they* need, rather than obligingly fitting in with what *we* need, or the surgery expects.

Our purpose should be to try to offer each session at exactly the right point for this particular patient, and to expect change at any time. Working in this way, as the GPs already do to some extent, requires us to become more flexible, and leave rather more control to the patient than we may be accustomed to. The simplest way to arrange appointments is to ask the person what they need each time. This also recognizes that if patients are working on changing something about their life or feelings or behaviour, they need time to assimilate the changes or their beginnings into their real life, and this may take different periods of time depending on the person, their relationships and their life. If we get it right, we facilitate their progress outside sessions too.

Mary was very tired of having panic attacks, which had been going on for 2 years, since her brother Terry killed himself in prison. She had a good clerical job in a bank and therefore appreciated a 5 o'clock appointment with the counsellor. Sometimes this meant she had to wait longer, because there were only a limited number of appointments available at this time of day. Mary was very creative and positive about her psychological work, writing letters to her dead brother, recording on a 1–10 scale her improvements and what she did to care for herself on 'good days', and talking to a loved and loving aunt, and later to her mother, about how they all felt about Terry.

Given the choice of the timing of her appointments, Mary attended a total of five times. The second session was 3 weeks after the initial one, then she left it for a month. There was another meeting after six weeks, and a last, follow-up, session 3 months afterwards – a total of around 6 months' treatment.

Mary visited the GP twice in this time, saying she felt he was very sympathetic and she would not hesitate to go if she needed to, but she believed this was a matter of time and 'coming to terms with things'.

By the end of therapy she and her family were beginning to get on to a reasonably even keel once more and her panic attacks had diminished in frequency and intensity, until in the final 6 weeks of treatment she had not suffered any more. At this point she said she was ready to finish counselling, but would appreciate an 'open door', which the counsellor was more than happy to offer.

Using this way of working, sessions are aimed at dovetailing into the patient's work outside the counselling room, coming at just the right moments to support and further it, rather as fenceposts support a long fence at just the right spaces. Too many fenceposts, too close together, and the beginning of the fence is rigid while the rest is floppy and unsupported.

Alex had a frightening accident at work, dealing with storage tanks containing various toxic substances. He was a strong and independent man, and physically he had recovered. He had found it helpful to talk to the counsellor, Peter, about his accident and recovery. He was now back doing shift work and coping quite well.

Alex really appreciated the fact that Peter had said Alex could come to see him whenever he wanted, provided there was an appointment free. Alex chose to book an appointment 3 months ahead. He said he found it reassuring to have a 'safety net' appointment, though he might not need it and could cancel if he wanted to. But a couple of weeks later, Peter saw that Alex had made an earlier appointment. Peter was happy to see Alex and his wife, Susan, to talk about their relationship, which was going through a rocky patch. Later, in a feedback exercise, Peter noticed that Alex particularly liked the way Peter was 'there for him' whenever he needed it. Peter had not heard from Alex now for some months, although one day he happened to hear from the GP that Susan was expecting another baby.

If we respect the patient's time quite carefully and specifically, by not being late for them, by being sensitive about when they want their sessions and how often, and so on, then it is more likely that they will respect our time too. The more we can cooperate with our patients, the less compliance will be a problem. In fact, we are not really interested in patients complying with what we want; it is more important that *we* comply with what *they* want. So the question 'What would be helpful for you?' in terms of timing as in other issues, is probably one of the most helpful questions we can ask. This question can be asked towards the end of sessions, so that we do not slip into a rut of 'once a fortnight' (or whatever) if this is not what is really helpful. This also keeps on the agenda the joint monitoring of how helpful the counselling is being.

The question of how the competence of the counsellor affects the rates of absences and the length of the waiting list is an interesting one. Assertive patients may vote with their feet if they realize that the counsellor is not helpful. On the other hand, many patients may continue to attend sessions even though they are unhelpful, perhaps in the belief that 'it has to get worse before it gets better' or some similar myth about therapy. Worse, they may blame themselves for being 'bad patients' if they do not progress. Thus, particularly inexperienced or poor counsellors may see patients for very long periods. This leads to the frustration of referrers who find that there are no spaces for new patients, to damaged patients and to overwhelmed, ineffectual counsellors.

The only real remedy for this state of affairs is training, experience and good regular supervision. Ideally, employers will encourage counsellors to partake of these, rather than conclude that practice counsellors *per se* are a waste of resources.

'The mountain teaches the climber how to climb'

So, our patients usually have very good reasons for what they do, and our job is to make it as easy as possible for them to cooperate, by being sensitive to their wishes and as transparent as possible in our own work of helping. The most important part of our job is to invite and facilitate an atmosphere of mutual collaboration on the task of helping the patient to progress in the direction he or she wishes to go. In this context the patient is our teacher, teaching us how to help them.

As therapists, we can choose the position from which we view patients. We may see them as basically incompetent and full of pathology, or we can take the stance that they are competent and make decisions which are the best they can do in the circumstances (Durrant and Kowalski, quoted in Miller et al., 1996). The patient's absence can be framed and attributed to pathological factors, such as a neurotic transference reaction, or a repressed dislike of authority leading to passive–aggressive moves. Or, if we choose to take a stance of believing in the patient's competence, we may let ourselves see adult decisions, such as needing to take care of a sick child, to avoid upsetting an irritable works manager, or to get the faulty car to the garage. In making our choice of how we see people, we may ask ourselves which view of the patient is most helpful for them, for this is one of the cornerstones of doing therapy.

It is certainly possible that not coming to sessions is the patient's way of showing us what they need. De Shazer and his team in Milwaukee declared that there was no such thing as resistance (de Shazer, 1984). An unexpected absence may be a nudge from the patient to remind the counsellor of their needs. When patients apologize and say that they 'just forgot to come', one can pathologize this 'forgetting', relabel it 'resistance', and suggest some underlying and unspoken factor which may or may not be the cause. Or one can sometimes say, well, maybe that's a sign you're getting better, or yes, I would have made that decision in the circumstances too. The patient may be surprised by this, but often they are heartened by being encouraged rather than having devious or fearful motives attributed to them.

So we have to read the meanings of the absences, reframing them and using them somehow for the successful progression of therapy. In these absences patients are teaching us something, and it is our job both to cooperate with them and to learn the lesson they are trying to teach us about how to help them.

Absences of unknown patients (first session absences)

Lisa was sent by her GP to a psychiatrist because she had an eating disorder. The psychiatrist rather scared her, and recommended that she was seen by the counsellor at her own general practice. Several weeks later she received a letter from the practice, signed illegibly, giving her an appointment at 3.00 pm on a Thursday in about 6 weeks' time.

Lisa's bulimia was getting worse. She did not know who had sent the letter, or what to expect when she went for her appointment. Would she sit opposite a dour middle-aged man across a desk, who would tell her, as the psychiatrist did, that she was 'being silly'? Would there be other people there? Would she have to bare her soul? She was frightened. Then she noticed the time of the appointment. She had to pick up her two young children from school at that time.

Lisa thought she ought to feel grateful because she was being offered some help, so she didn't like to ring and ask about changing the appointment. Maybe they would think she didn't really want to get better, or was making excuses. She didn't know what to do. There was no one who would pick up her children (one of them had behavioural difficulties). She worried. She ate and vomited. The time of her appointment got closer. On the day, she collected her children from school, bundled them in front of the television and had an enormous binge. She knew that she would now find it difficult to go back to the practice for *any* kind of health care in case the counsellor or the receptionist challenged her.

At the surgery, the receptionist was indeed tetchy. 'If only these people would just *ring* if they're not going to come,' she said crossly to the waiting counsellor, who noted another DNA in her appointments book.

It is easy to see what could be put right here. It is also clear what damage can be caused by the clumsy handling of referrals and appointments.

- As previously mentioned, it is always better for the patient to make their own appointment in person, rather than being sent a letter. This would have enabled Lisa to choose a time when her children were in school.
- The patient should be told the full name and status of the person they are going to see.

- The patient should also be informed of what is likely to happen, how long it will take, and about issues like confidentiality and complaints, and what to do if they wish to cancel or change their appointment.
- As much as possible should be done to put the patient in the 'one-up' position, in which they are able to feel confident about using the counselling as they wish and for their benefit rather than feeling dis-empowered. Asking the patient when they would like to come, rather than telling them when their appointment is, is one way of doing this.

Incidentally, soothing the irritation of receptionists about absences should probably be part of the counsellor's job. Patients quickly absorb prickly feelings from staff. A calm, accepting attitude to absences can help staff to feel that they are all part of the day's work and nothing to get upset about.

People waiting

Waiting lists are almost (but not quite) inevitable in the British health service. In a recent Suffolk-wide survey (Mayes and Waskett, unpublished, 1997), it was found that most of the practice counsellors in Suffolk who gave information, had patients waiting only 1 or 2 weeks. These counsellors were using a variety of counselling approaches and appointment systems. It appears that the stories of patients having to wait for months for psychological attention are less common than we may have supposed. It may be that as counsellors become embedded into teams, they and their referrers become skilled at using other agencies, referring appropriately and offering more focused help, thus streamlining the whole system.

Most counsellors (though not all) have a list of patients hoping to access therapy and waiting for the call. This is because by far the most common way of arranging therapy is to see patients regularly until they are 'better'. Once a patient load is taken on (say 10 patients for 10 contact hours) the therapist is 'full' until a patient becomes 'better' and stops therapy, at which point the practitioner contacts the next person on the waiting list to come in.

Some counsellors are restricted by their employers to a limited number of sessions per patient, but this is rarely less than six, which means that for most patients at least an hour once a week for 6 weeks is booked. Some patients have to wait for up to 12 weeks or even more before they are seen. This first visit may be only for an assessment, after which the wait goes on.

This can be a very turgid way of working which can easily bring the whole counselling service almost to a halt, and there are several dangers inherent in it. One is the obvious one that many patients who might benefit from counselling have to wait so long that they are put off, or at the very least continue to suffer for longer than they need to. Another is that doctors and other referrers stop referring because they can see no space in the list in the foreseeable future; consequently, their overview of practice counselling may be tarnished. And a third is that the counsellor has a very difficult time, which may lead to burnout.

The disaster scenario

Here is the strained and overloaded counsellor with the burden of a heavy waiting list, in the unfortunate and uncomfortable position of carrying a full load of ongoing patients with no clear goals or review dates. Patients often expect – because this is part of our cultural inheritance – that the counsellor will see them for as long as they wish, at regular intervals, and the counsellor often hopes to be able to do that too. Patients are often seen as needing ongoing work with no end in sight. There is no indication of how patient or counsellor will know that the work the patient wants has been done. There is nothing on paper about the service offered, no evaluation of any kind is being done, and there are no slots in the week available for new patients. Gridlock.

Worse, the willing, conscientious counsellor is doing extra unpaid hours to see patients or to do paperwork, phone calls etc., either at the practice or at home. Likely results for the practitioner are:

1 a feeling of helplessness in the grip of a relentless tide of referrals;
2 the counsellor becomes steadily more incapable of establishing boundaries with either referrers or patients;
3 resentfulness;
4 passive aggression to colleagues/clients;
5 workaholism;
6 chronic anxiety;
7 possibly physical ill-health;
8 burnout.

Anyone in these circumstances has little time or inner resources to think creatively about them; they are too busy running to keep up. Supervisors may feel powerless to intervene. In the worst possible scenario, supervision or consultation is reduced or even abandoned because there is too much 'real' work to do.

Ambivalence

Before we go on to look at what contributes to this sorry situation and what might be done about it, perhaps we should recognize a sense of ambivalence for many counsellors around the issue of a large waiting list. There is of course a sense of pressure and perhaps guilt. All those distressed people having to hold on . . . you're working as hard as you can but . . . Such counsellors often lose their sense of boundaries and self-worth because they feel that somehow the endless waiting list is their fault.

On the other hand – less often admitted – there can be a sense of comfort, albeit with a high price attached. The waiting list 'proves' I'm needed. All those people are waiting for *my* skills, *my* care, *my* listening ear. Perhaps I'm important; crucially so in today's uncertain employment climate. It is also part of the British health service culture to wish to be *seen* to be 'working very hard'. Buried deep in all this is the siren call to persuade oneself that one is 'special' – perhaps more magically skilled, and harder working, than anyone else, as Guggenbuhl-Craig (1971) suggests.

There may therefore be some ambivalence about taking charge of the waiting list. Bluntly, we have to choose between the living proof of a long waiting list, which shows to whomsoever might enquire that we are needed, and the greater genuine effectiveness of organizing things so that patients get the help they need quickly. This has to go alongside the inner admission, to ourselves, that we are *not* uniquely powerful sorcerers, able, with a wave of the wand, to heal all the ills of the world.

But there is some useful analysis, and consequently some action, that may improve things. When the counsellor is working well, the flow of clients is efficiently managed; patients are seen without a long wait, briefly and effectively; and the counsellor is restored to energetic, creative, respectful, well-supervised and enjoyable counselling.

What can be done?

In this situation there are four main factors to consider:

1   Referrals.
2   The use of other services.

3   The use of brief forms of therapy.
4   The question of hours.

Influencing referrals and providing information

Referral sources range from doctors only, to doctors and other clinical staff, to anybody in the practice, to a completely open referral system including self-referrals. Obviously, the more open the gate, the more will come through. Counsellors are fortunate in being able to influence referrals, by making it clear to referrers and potential patients what they do, and who is an appropriate referral. A *succinct* (one side of A4) information sheet for the doctors and team is a good idea. This could contain details of the expected wait and perhaps of alternative helping agencies.

There are several benefits. Referrals will be more finely tuned and accurate. Patients benefit because those who *do* arrive in the counselling room know something about what to expect (through information from the referrer and/or from the counselling information leaflet) and are therefore more able to use successfully what the counsellor has to offer. Their – and the practitioner's – optimism about the work goes up immediately – and optimism is the lifeblood of success.

Aside from being better for patients, the counsellor's influence on referrals will ensure that they see appropriate patients to whom they can offer something helpful within a reasonable period of time. This will help to maintain a steady throughput, and will help the counsellor to feel they are doing an effective and worthwhile job.

Using other services

Counselling is only a segment of the pie chart of services for psychological health. It has to be admitted that some quite ferocious infighting occurs between different parts of the 'pie'. At bottom this is usually about resources, status, and/or basic beliefs about what is really helpful to patients.

Whatever we may think about what our colleagues do, we are all part of the spectrum of services offered to our patients. None of us can do magic. To assume that only 'our' sort of service is truly valuable to people is arrogant and untrue. We (not to mention our patients) need a range of services and we need to cooperate with each other.

This means having easily accessible and up-to-date information about all kinds of local services and agencies in the business of psychological care, and not being afraid or reluctant to use them. *We do not have to do it all ourselves*. Often, the local community mental health team, a self-help group, or even a national telephone helpline, for something like, for instance, pre-menstrual syndrome, can be just as much help as counselling, or can be a valuable adjunct to it. Given contact information, patients can normally be trusted to explore these things for themselves; they do not need nannying. Just because someone has been sent for counselling, it does not mean that this is necessarily the only, or even the best thing to help them.

Working briefly

'Brief therapy' is not of course simply short; it entails using specific techniques. It has not been developed specifically to save time, but to be 'smarter'. Just because it works more effectively, patients incidentally seem to require fewer sessions. Counsellors who use this method do not see it as a second-best 'short-cut' but as the best they can give their patients. They offer as many sessions as necessary, but not a single one more.

There are several different kinds of brief therapy. For instance, solution-oriented therapy is structured in such a way that patient and therapist negotiate the few sessions they have together according to the patient's sense of when meetings are needed. Because they also carefully clarify the patient's realistic goals, both patient and therapist can see when these are met and it is time to stop. Repeat sessions are often strung out at lengthening intervals and can be placed amongst the new bookings ahead (George et al., 1990).

The crux of solution-oriented therapy is to clarify the patient's goals, to help the patient work towards them, and to recognize together when they have been reached. Therapists undertake to work hard to help the patient to change in the patient's preferred direction. They are not there to provide ongoing social support, although they may very well agree on helping a patient to find social support elsewhere.

What is 'better'? When is it time to stop? The answer is, when the patient's goal or goals have been reached. One of the many joys of general practice counselling is that we see patients and their families over the years. That sense of continuity means that if a patient has achieved success in therapy once, they are often happy enough to come back again for a little more help to reach another goal. It is not the therapist's job to 'finish' a patient in the sense of turning out someone who is completely 'adjusted', balanced or trouble-free. That would certainly be an unattainable fantasy.

As an example of how brief techniques can produce more effective and elegant therapy, we might look at scaling. This can be applied not only to behavioural matters, but also to feelings, for example: 'On a scale of 1–10, where 0 is as depressed as you've ever been, and 10 is completely back to normal (completely better) where are you now?' 'How come you're not one step down from that?' 'What would you notice if you were one step up?' It is thus possible to begin to discuss and clarify, in small identifiable steps, what the patient wants, today and tomorrow. Finding out together what the patient wants in clear detail is the first (sometimes the only) step in brief therapy (Talmon, 1990). Solution-oriented therapists have come to expect to see change within, say, six sessions, and it is certainly possible to make a difference in just one (Cade and O'Hanlon, 1993; Hoyt, 1995).

Does the service have enough counselling hours?

This is a much more complex question than it seems. Clearly, if only 3 hours a week are allocated for a general practice population of 10,000, then something is probably awry, although if surgery staff make vigorous use of other services (see above), the doctors like to do much of their own counselling, and the counsellor is very specialist (say, a family therapist with specific referral parameters), then even this may be quite satisfactory.

Adjustments in other areas will alter the demand for counselling hours. But after all the adjustments are made, you do need enough time effectively to deal with all the appropriate referrals. Only the counsellor will know whether this is the case. If you really believe the service does not have enough hours, there are two approaches to take. One is persistently to present well-argued evidence to employers and paymasters/ policy-makers (not always the same). The other is to cultivate clear boundaries. Saying 'no' is vitally important in these circumstances. If counsellors take the other route and work themselves into a state of barely adequate functioning, this may well have the effect of making employers and patients feel that this is *not* a service they need more of!

Conclusion

The aspect of our work dealt with in this chapter is really about waiting. The patients wait to see us; we wait for patients who do not come. Waiting is not easy, for patients or therapists. For the therapist the unease may be compounded by anxiety about 'wasting' time, about the security of our jobs, and about our standing in the practice team. Yet it is, inescapably, part of the job, and we have to tolerate and manage it as best we can.

We do not seem to be particularly powerful regarding the absence rates of our patients, nor should we act as if we were teachers chasing truants, which would be demeaning for us and our patients. Instead, we can learn useful lessons from absences. And we can do a great deal to make ourselves more available to patients who wish to see us.

Allowing a huge waiting list to continue is not good practice, and often it can be brought under control by using some of the above strategies. However, the first and most important step, which will make all the others possible, is the recognition that the counsellor is not a magical, all-powerful sorcerer who can rescue everyone in the world. Patients will often choose not to come, put counselling in second or third – or last – place on their priority list, or, like all of us, get caught out by the exigencies of life. The best we can do is to accept our limitations, keep on respecting and learning from our patients about what is, and is not, useful to them, and work within human limits, with the skills we have learned or developed, and in the time we are paid for.

Key points

- Absences are part of the fabric of counselling in primary care. Blaming our patients, referrers or ourselves is not useful or appropriate.
- Absences can be understood as useful communications or 'teaching aids' from patients. An absence may be a good sign.
- It is helpful to record and attend separately to the absences of patients who (a) have never been seen (initial appointments) and (b) have been seen at least once by the counsellor.
- Patients are likely to feel empowered by being asked to choose and make appointments for themselves, both initially and for ongoing appointments.
- Administrative staff may be beneficially involved in making appointments; this can be helpful for patients, the counsellor and the cohesion of the primary health care team as a whole.
- Making the choice to view patients as competent rather than incompetent/pathological, may make a positive difference to the way we see absences and the waiting list.
- Useful factors in influencing the counselling waiting list are: controlling referrals; using other services; using brief therapy techniques; having enough hours.
- Counsellors/therapists are not sorcerers. We can only do so much, in collaboration with our patients and other professionals.

References

Cade, B. and O'Hanlon, W.H. (1993) *A Brief Guide to Brief Therapy*. New York: W.W. Norton.

de Shazer, S. (1984) 'The death of resistance', *Family Process*, 23(1): 11–17, 20–1.

George, E., Iveson, C. and Ratner, H. (1990) *Problem to Solution*. London: Brief Therapy Press.

Guggenbuhl-Craig, A. (1971) *Power in the Helping Professions*. USA: Spring Publications.

Hoyt, M.F. (1995) *Brief Therapy and Managed Care: Readings for Contemporary Practice*. San Francisco: Jossey-Bass.

Hunt, H.C. and Andrews, G. (1992) 'Drop-out rate as a performance indicator in psychotherapy', *Acta Psychiatrica Scandinavica* 1992, 85: 275–8.

Mayes, M. and Waskett, C. (1997) Suffolk Practice Counsellor Evaluation Project (unpublished). Suffolk Health Authority.

Miller, S.D., Hubble, M.A. and Duncan, B.L. (1996) *Handbook of Solution-Focused Brief Therapy*. San Francisco: Jossey-Bass.

Talmon, M. (1990) *Single Session Therapy; Maximizing the Effect of the First (and often only) Therapeutic Encounter*. San Francisco: Jossey-Bass.

CHAPTER 7

CONFIDENTIALITY IN A TEAM SETTING

Carole Waskett

Confidentiality in the primary health care team can be seen as a combination of sacred cow and hot potato. For the counsellor, it is probably one of the issues that on the one hand commands most respect, while on the other causes most concern. Patients and their families should certainly be assured of immaculate respect for privacy; trusting, productive work between client and therapist depends on it. But at the same time, the counsellor must be able to work collaboratively with colleagues in the team (and the counselling supervisor/consultant, who may be outside it) in order to give the best service of which they are all capable. Reconciling these two imperatives is the dilemma with which all general practice counsellors are faced.

We can think about confidentiality in this setting as a careful balancing act, in which every patient and every situation may require a different degree of security. This exposes several underlying issues for consideration:

- the nature and use of gossip and privacy;
- the implications of working in a team, with colleagues from different disciplines and professional cultures;
- the position of the counsellor as a lone worker versus as a team-worker;
- the counsellor's (and team's) stance of collaborative transparency with patients and families, combined with respect for confidentiality *between* family members;
- the tension between offering therapeutic, private conversations, and the external ethical requirements on the counsellor to report on such issues as child protection, or suicidal ideation;
- the question of just how much personal, painful material needs to be revealed in therapy in order to be helpful.

Part of this chapter has already appeared in *CMS News*, February 1997, pp. 8–11, and is reproduced here with permission.

Presenting ideas about confidentiality to the patient may be done in different ways. For example, this is the statement used in the leaflet given to patients in one group of practices before their first counselling session:

> We understand that confidentiality may be very important to you. If you would like more information about the level of confidentiality we offer, please ask the counsellor about it when you meet her. Questions or comments are most welcome.

In these practices, the counsellor reports that it is not often that anyone queries it. In any case, when patient and counsellor do meet, the counsellor adds:

> We do like to work as a team here, so if I need to speak to Dr X [or the health visitor/the district nurse etc.] about you, will that be OK? I might also need to speak to my consultant about you. And was there anything else you would like to know about how we handle your privacy? Do ask at any time if you think of anything.

Sometimes things need to be clarified a little more, but it is rare for anyone, in these practices at least, to demur. The vast majority of patients trust that the clinical workers in the practice will, individually and as a professional team, do their best for the patient and the family. Indeed, they usually seem to expect that staff will communicate between themselves on their behalf.

The way counsellors ought to ensure confidentiality is clearly and comprehensively dealt with in the various counselling and therapy Codes of Ethics. Yet the primary care setting makes demands and calls for decisions that cannot be covered completely by any Code, and throws up dilemmas and challenges with which most practice counsellors struggle. This chapter examines some of these interesting and important issues.

Degrees of confidentiality

The boundaries of confidentiality should be well understood by all primary health care team members, and properly negotiated and agreed with the patient and, if need be, family or concerned friends. The counsellor, like other citizens, is subject to the law of the land. Notes and even the counsellor's spoken evidence can be subpoenaed. There are other times when the counsellor is properly required to be pro-active; for example, in reporting child abuse or terrorist activities. But aside from these reservations to do with legal issues, the professional's paramount protection of and consideration for the patient/family's privacy should never be in question.

Even so, in a team setting, an insistence on strict, one-to-one confidentiality may actually debase the service, depriving both patient and counsellor of the knowledge, support and helpful perspective available from other professionals in the team. It is more helpful to look at this matter as one of degrees of confidentiality, dictated by the unique needs and best interests of each patient, and also guided by the requirement on the counsellor to give the best and most ethical service possible. The very idea of confidentiality can be transformed by the attitudes of the team (including the counsellor) to such issues as blame, fault and the arbitrariness of luck.

Ideas from the literature

In the literature a continuum seems to be laid out. At one end is what, if we were generalizing or even stereotyping, we might call the 'British' perspective. This tends to draw from the analytic/psychodynamic tradition, and, exemplified by Bond (1995), assumes that total *confidentiality* between patient and counsellor is best, but that in certain circumstances it can or even should be 'broken', preferably after negotiation with the patient. That word 'broken' is telling, indicating an innate dissatisfaction with broaching the ring of privacy between the two (and usually only two) protagonists.

At the other end of the continuum is what, again generalizing, we could call the 'American collaborative' view. This comes mainly from a family systems perspective and its later developments. We might call McDaniel, Hepworth and Doherty (1992) this school's spokespeople, although the literature is growing rapidly in this area. These people take the stance that *collaboration* is the ideal, providing the most effective care, but that this should, of course, be negotiated with the patient/family – a rather different emphasis.

We could lay this out in the following fashion, aligning a few representative workers and writers with different parts of the continuum:

- **Confidentiality**: Hoag (1992); Human Fertilization and Embryology Act, 1992.
- **Discretion**: British Association for Counselling Code of Ethics and Practice for Counsellors, 1992; Bond (1995); Hudson-Allez (1995).
- **Collaboration**: Doherty and Baird (1983); Jones et al. (1994); Marsh (1991); Mayer et al. (1996); McDaniel et al. (1990); Rolland (1994).

Professionals under the 'Confidentiality' heading would put a very high priority on keeping the patient/counsellor dialogue completely confidential, almost sacred, although naturally they advocate being flexible enough to 'break' this trust if it becomes necessary for the welfare of the patient.

Under 'Discretion' the professional values collaboration to some extent, and in some circumstances would wish to take this path. And under 'Collaboration', writers would say that teamwork between the helping professionals caring for the patient is crucial to offering the best possible care, and that this not only expands and strengthens the quality of care the patient receives, but is intrinsic to the way the successful team works together. These are very different viewpoints.

Three useful ideas

In what can be an extremely confusing picture, three ideas from very different backgrounds may give us some helpful leads.

First, recent postmodernist models of therapy (for example narrative therapy, neuro-linguistic programming, solution-oriented therapy), question the more linear, problem-centred explanations of psychological distress. Ways of working have developed which, instead of facilitating the expression of painful experiences and feelings as a means of healing, focus on the creative use of language in therapy, and attend to the way the patient wants the future to be.

Solution-oriented therapists, for example, while being willing to hear and understand 'problem stories' if they are freely expressed, would refrain from probing for these difficult or embarrassing experiences, and respect the patient's restraint (sometimes called 'resistance'). These therapists believe it is more useful to move instead to enlisting cooperation for solution-building. Thus, even within the therapy room, the patient's privacy is respected, and less painful or humiliating material is exposed. This stance of respecting what the patient chooses to tell, and not professing to know any of the answers (but working with the patient to help discover them) seems to be empowering. In terms of confidentiality, working in this way means that very often material that might embarrass or worry the patient is never even expressed, and is certainly not seen as the key to the therapy (DeJong and Berg, 1998). This is one way of doing therapy which is highly respectful of the patient's confidentiality, even within the privacy of the session.

A different, but perhaps equally considerate and helpful approach, is taken by Susan McDaniel, an American medical family therapist who has talked and written extensively about a systemic perspective on biopsychosocial health in the medical setting. Her view – and many others' in the same school – can best be described as inclusive, rather than exclusive. These writers advocate a generous and cooperative way of team working, within a clear boundary of confidentiality accepted by all concerned (McDaniel et al., 1990).

Thirdly, Pritchard and Pritchard (1992), who focused on the British primary health care team, did some comprehensive and practical (though sadly under-utilized) work on team functioning. In the present context, it would be useful to pick out their idea of the 'intrinsic team' – a selection of specified helping professionals around the patient and/or family.

Pritchard and Pritchard suggested that there are three different types of team within the general practice. The one of most interest to us in considering confidentiality issues is the 'intrinsic team'. This is the group of people clustered around a patient or family, comprising those who have contact with or regularly see the patient(s) in question. This is a dynamic team, with people joining or leaving as and when necessary. If, for example, you are working with a young mother with post-natal depression, the intrinsic team may consist of

• the GP (and in a practice without personal lists, our patient may see several GPs, all of whom may be included in the intrinsic team);
• the health visitor;
• the husband/partner;
• and the counsellor.

There is also the possibility of others outside the practice being part of the intrinsic team, for example a psychiatrist at the local hospital, or a social worker or occupational therapist.

To illustrate the practical use of these three ideas, we might look at the case of Alan and Marilyn:

Alan and Marilyn's marriage was coming apart at the seams. He had had two affairs. She had recently taken an overdose. Recent events had destabilized Alan's diabetes. Alan's mother, recently widowed, was frail and Alan was terrified that she would find out 'what was going on'. Their daughter Laura was about to take A-levels, and both parents agreed that this was not the time to worry her. This was a small town and confidentiality was very important to both of these clients.

The therapist quickly established a collaborative atmosphere in which several members of the primary health care team were identified by Alan and Marilyn as part of the team working to help the couple; the practice nurse (who knew Alan well and was knowledgeable about his illness); Marilyn's and Alan's doctors; a worker at the diabetes clinic at the hospital; a community psychiatric nurse who had first seen Marilyn after her overdose. Each of these knew how important it was to preserve confidentiality for the couple.

Working in a solution-oriented way, the therapist asked 'What would be helpful?' 'What will you both be doing differently when things are better [on a previously established scale of 0–10]?' 'What's the first small step for each of you towards making that happen?' and so on. When Alan had an unexpected hypoglycaemic attack, the practice nurse, who was very knowledgeable about diabetes and knew Alan well, was asked to come and join part of a session to explain things. The therapist also spoke to Alan's doctor about how anxiety might be affecting the illness, and fed back to the couple. Marilyn regained some confidence as her strength and creativity were recognized and complimented, and decided she wanted the marriage to continue. Alan found himself wanting to stay with her. He got a new and more interesting job. Slowly, things settled down, and the pair expressed their appreciation of how everyone at the practice was 'rooting for them all the way'.

Combining a solution-oriented model of therapy with a more collaborative, team perspective, as well as using this precise idea of the intrinsic team-within-a-team, here made an effective package. Being carefully respectful of confidentiality, it also used all the professional skills and resources available to help this couple, who were struggling to get back on track in their lives and to protect other members of their family from the worst effects of distressing events.

These ideas may help us to make sense of some of the complexities of confidentiality. However, before we continue on this logical trajectory, perhaps we should look at some very basic psychosocial drives which can make this issue difficult for us and the teams in which we work.

The nature of gossip, and why we like to blame

Human stories are what bind us together. Gossip is the telling of somebody else's story, and the sharing of speculation about it. Advanced gossips might make up the bits we don't actually know, or change things a little to make the story more interesting. Gossip serves several distinct and valuable functions in society:

- It refines and maintains the group's *norms*.
- It binds the gossiping group together by saying in effect '*We* would never do anything like that, so all of *us* are OK and mutually approve of each other,' – a nice safe feeling of *group cohesion*.
- The one who carries the secret and tells the original nugget of gossip wins *special status* in the group.
- Gossip enables 'us' to blame the one gossiped about. This has a primitive magical function. It says: 'Oh, she got run over. Well, it

serves her right for not using the crossing'. *Blaming the victim* is enormously reassuring to 'us' because, of course, 'we' would never dream of crossing the road away from the crossing. And if we had been secretly thinking of it, we've learnt by her behaviour – and by the censure of our fellow gossips – and we will certainly always use the crossing now!

- This 'blame the victim' function has two further advantages. We don't have to feel sorry for the victim (because it was her fault) so it *reduces the anxiety* aroused by hearing emotionally painful stories. In addition, most importantly and most magically, we can delude ourselves that as long as we do the right things (or avoid the wrong ones) *we will stay safely in control* of our lives, and nothing bad will ever happen to us.
- Finally, while we are part of the gossiping group we are *safe from censure* from them – for now, at least.

So gossip is imbued with the comforting magical notion that if bad things happen to people it is likely to be their fault. But the reality is that troubles come because of a million different reasons, hardly any of which we can discern or understand. Mostly, trouble falls arbitrarily, without 'fairness', on the heads of the wise and the stupid, the good and the not-so-good. This idea is basic to an understanding of confidentiality.

If we work in an organizational culture which can accept this idea, then two things are likely to happen. One is that the level of gossip will fall (although staff may well continue to talk about each other and their clients, this talk will not contain that nugget of blame); and secondly, the idea of confidentiality will change its shape. If people are not seen as blameworthy, but as ordinary people doing their best in a difficult and arbitrary world, then plain consideration and understanding will take the place of the protection of humiliating secrets.

Here are two scenarios:

Story 1: Setting – a quiet evening behind the reception desk

Receptionist: You know that young chap Danny Brown? He's just been sent to prison – look, it says here – 2 years for drug dealing.
District nurse: I'm not surprised. That whole family are crazy. Do you remember – oh, years ago – his mother had two men living with her in the house at once? And one of them was a transvestite! Weird! She was claiming benefits as well. If my son tried drug-dealing – well, I just wouldn't have it, would you?
Health visitor: All those children ran wild, right from the early days. I mean, wouldn't you think she'd protect them a bit? But no. Chips with everything

and no proper bedtimes ... [to the counsellor] haven't you just seen her this afternoon?

Counsellor: Yes I have as a matter of fact. And you won't believe who's living with her now ...

This snippet of conversation reveals a good gossip, with many of the psychosocial functions of gossip being well served. But, in the next scenario, as interested faces turn towards the counsellor, a firm authorial hand covers her mouth, for here she has a more honourable role.

Story 2: Setting – the same quiet evening

Receptionist: You know that young chap Danny Brown? He's just been sent to prison – look, it says here – 2 years for drug dealing.

District nurse: Oh dear, poor Bella, his poor mum. I bet she's beside herself. She had a really difficult life, never any money, but she did her damnedest to bring those kids up as well as she could. She's still got two still at school, hasn't she? I wonder if I can manage to pop in some time today. Or perhaps I shouldn't; I wonder. She's beginning to get arthritis too.

Health visitor: Yes, they had chips with everything, but she was a pretty good mum; plenty of cuddles. And I bet all the family will rally round. They really look after each other in a crisis. I'll show this to Dr Clarke; she'll want to know in case Bella comes in. [*To counsellor*] Oh – haven't you just seen her?

Counsellor: Yes [*no point in denying it; the appointment is on the front desk computer*]. I should think they might all be glad of our support if anyone else comes in, although I think they'll look after each other pretty well. Let's just keep an eye out for them.

These are very different ways of looking at exactly the same set of facts. In the first scenario, the participants are using the story to blame, feel better about themselves and improve group cohesion. For the moment, they have forgotten about being professionals. In the second scene, they are still chatting, but they know life gets tough sometimes for us all, express faith in the unfortunate family and think about how they, as a practice team, can help.

Keeping our counsel

As practice counsellors, we hear 'secrets' all day long. Specially trusted, not because of our personal qualities but because of our job title and role, people tell us about what they see as their failures, their shames, their temptations, their unhappiness and their struggles. Unlike schoolchildren, or neighbours enjoying a good gossip, we have to think carefully about our trustworthiness and our consideration of the patient as a general policy, and about what confidentiality means. We have to forgo the pleasures of communally picking extraordinary stories to pieces, feeling the comfort of being at one with others who agree with us in our judgements, and blaming the person gossiped about. We learn not to rush off in search of a repository for any delicious secret we have learned: 'You'll never guess what I just heard!'

Time and experience help. Sadly, after quite a short time in this work we find that sexual and violent abuse of children and adults, bullying, marital disharmony, eating disorders, suicidal desperation, obsessions, neglect, depression and a hundred other miseries become the unremarkable stuff of our working lives. We become stronger and more flexible, more able to hear and hold the distress. The urge to unload what we hear onto somebody else diminishes.

At the same time, if we choose to, we can marvel at the ways people survive desperate lives and terrible events, and create stability, love and warmth from almost nothing. A notable and very common example is the way that parents, abused or neglected themselves as children, bring up their own children with great tenderness and care.

It is still true though, that, like everyone else, health professionals are human and weak. Our egos often need boosting, and so the temptation can be strong to use the stories we hear to enhance our own standing and image: 'I'm seeing the wife of one of the consultants at the moment; talk about passive–aggressive!' Being a counsellor is a lonely job, for unusually, we cannot use any of the stuff of our work to join us together with others.

The high-profile aspect of the confidentiality issue conjures up an image of the heroic counsellor in the witness box, refusing against the majesty of the law to inform on her patient. But there are other times when something *should* be done, and perhaps the counsellor is the only one who is able to do it. And there are very many other times when the confidentiality issue is nowhere near so clear-cut, and where it may be right to talk about the patient to someone who is not the patient. For instance:

Bob is awaiting trial for the sexual abuse of his son, and is temporarily living in a local hostel. He tells you that his family has disowned him. He is under great stress. Later he says that in the evenings he often goes out and walks the streets. He likes the look of a young boy who lives near the hostel, and has started to chat with him and his mother.

Most counsellors would certainly want to discuss this case with their supervisor, and probably with the GP involved. The counsellor may even feel that they would not want to talk to the patient before discussing him with these other professionals. Further action may need to be taken, not only for the patient's sake (a further incident may clinch his miserable imprisonment, whereas the first may have only earned him probation), but also for the sake of local children. Clearly there are several different and conflicting pressures which the counsellor, GP and supervisor will have to weigh up before taking further action.

It is generally mandatory to report any suspected danger of abuse to children to the local Social Services child protection team. And unfortunately, one of the pressures to be coped with will be the one known as 'covering our backs', familiar to everyone working in today's NHS. It can be tempting to resist seeking advice (from supervisor, GP or child protection professional) when alarm bells are ringing about a patient. It may be clear to us that if we break confidentiality we will lose the patient and any possible progress. Yet if we continue to work with the person without advice, we risk harm to others, the patient and ourselves. These are very difficult decisions which can, ultimately, only be made by the counsellor.

Two issues arise which have been well documented in specific detail by Bond (1995). Broadly, these are:

- respecting the patient's privacy, even in the face of the authorities; and
- knowing when it *is* important to discuss the patient's issues with appropriate others.

There is another important aspect of this issue, though, which hinges on the emphasis we give on the one hand to confidentiality, and on the other to collaboration within the primary health care team. It is this perspective which we now address.

The influence of teamwork on confidentiality

Primary care counselling is a comparatively new field in Britain. The primary care team is a specialist environment, different even from other medical settings such as hospitals. Most importantly, it is a team in which every member contributes their part to the well-being of the practice population. The meaning of this word 'teamwork' in primary care is complex: much vaunted, but not so easy to put into practice (Waskett, 1996). The fact that a counsellor works within the primary health care team and is part of it has a profound influence on the issue of confidentiality.

If the counsellor is to be seen as *part* of the practice team, rather than just a luxury bolt-on module, then there must be more to good practice counselling than just doing the counselling, one-to-one, with a single patient behind a closed door, and then going home. The counsellor must consider herself a team member, helping, with the rest of the team, to give a service to the families and individuals that comprise the practice population. Obviously this viewpoint has implications for the many dilemmas of confidentiality.

It would be wonderfully reassuring to have an all-embracing, universally agreed confidentiality policy which told us exactly what to do in any given situation. Many policies have been formulated, but nothing has really been agreed across the board, with all the professionals who might be involved. One of the reasons for this is that we work in multidisciplinary teams, where one person's professional culture is often completely different from another's.

On most training courses, for example, trainee counsellors are still taught that patient confidentiality is virtually sacred, while doctors and others in medical professions are socialized into the understanding that health care teams *share* information, so that they can stand in for each other as need be and give the patient a good experience of integrated care. Nevertheless, counsellors, nurses, doctors and the rest of the treatment team need to find ways to collaborate with each other, and with the patient and family, in order to give an excellent service (McDaniel et al., 1992).

Example: What would you do?

You have seen Susan three times and she has told you about her terrifying marriage. Last time you saw her, she reported that during a row, she had told her husband she was going to leave him (the first time she has ever said this to him out loud). He got the carving knife and threatened to kill her and then himself if she ever tried it. You saw the small cut on her neck. Where '10' meant feeling completely safe from violence, she rated her level of safety at about '2'.

Today, she has not arrived for her appointment. Looking at the computer, you see that she has never been late or unreliable before for any appointment. You are worried. Telephoning or visiting may endanger Susan further. Doing nothing may leave her at risk or actually being harmed. Should you do anything? If so, what?

The British Association for Counselling's general guidance is as follows: 'In the event of a possible break of confidentiality, the client should be involved in any discussion, if possible, and preferably before the counsellor consults the counselling supervisor, or other experienced counsellor/s if the supervisor is unavailable, and a fast decision needs to be made' (*Counselling*, August 1997, p. 71). This sounds very sensible, but because it has been written as universal guidance, here is a case in which such advice is useless.

You need to be able to talk this dilemma over with someone before your next client arrives in half an hour (you've spent 20 minutes waiting with increasing concern for Susan to turn up). The rest of the day is full of clients and a meeting, and you are then away from the practice until the following week.

Obviously, Susan is not here to be asked. Your supervisor is away on holiday for a week. You are the sole counsellor in the practice so there is no counselling colleague to turn to. You keep asking yourself, am I over-reacting? Perhaps she just forgot? But the concern keeps pushing you; you must at least talk to someone, even if you end up doing nothing. You decide to speak to Susan's GP, who knows her well. But you are told he is on a course elsewhere. The senior partner is also absent. The two remaining GPs are wading through heavy surgeries as a result of their colleagues' absence.

In the end you decide to loiter outside one of the doctor's rooms and catch them between patients. It is helpful just to describe your dilemma. The GP remembers the patient vaguely and once visited Susan at home; she thinks you are right to be worried. Together, you try to work out what to do . . .

Should you also be worrying about 'breaking' confidentiality?

Together you conclude that a telephone call is a possibility. If Susan answers, you can merely remind her of her appointment. If it is someone else, you can follow the usual practice policy of asking for Susan. If she is not available, you do not leave a message unless pressed, in which case you ask if she can ring the surgery at some point, but stress that there is nothing to worry about. This strategy may at least get you a little further, and is unlikely to provoke trouble.

In fact, Susan answers. She has been delayed by problems with the domestic plumbing, and is happy to make another appointment.

Keeping strict confidentiality

There are several arguments in favour of adhering to strict patient confidentiality. Some of these are:

- It promotes psychological safety for the individual patient. Some therapists working at the psychodynamic or analytical end of the scale might argue that this discretion and safety magnifies the concentration and the transference issues in the work, rather like a broad, slow river, channelled between the unforgiving walls of a canyon, becomes an energetic torrent. Not everyone, of course, works with the transference.
- The patient stays in complete control of their own information. 'What is heard in this room, stays in this room', other than in exceptional circumstances which would be negotiated, piece by piece, with the counsellor. There is no worry about the receptionists, the secretary, or the doctor finding out anything about the patient's business. Nor can it leak out to other family members or neighbours.
- The counsellor does not have to be concerned about what is, and what is not, disclosed. Nothing is disclosed, apart from to the supervisor. The counsellor does not have to take any decisions or live with any tension about what is the right thing to do. It makes life easier for the counsellor.
- Because the counsellor is *known* not to discuss patients, other workers do not need to put aside time to do so. Some doctors and nurses, trained to take individual, autonomous responsibility, may be quite glad of this. The counsellor comes, does her self-sufficient and somewhat mysterious work, and goes. She does not request any time to consult or jointly consider patients, nor does she hope or expect to be involved in any joint thinking about patients. She certainly does not expect to share any responsibility with the doctor or other members of the team for the patient's welfare. That most precious of commodities in the health service, worker time, is saved.

The movement from 'strict confidentiality' to . . .

There is nothing like this issue for triggering discomfort and guilt in the counsellor. Most of us long to have some inviolate, monolithic code of practice on which to depend. But in general practice, it is probably more realistic and helpful for counsellors and other professionals to view confidentiality as an open, live issue, one in which our baseline is *respect and consideration* for the patient, the family and the community. This is a much more flexible attitude, which demands constant attention to keeping carefully alert and maintaining cooperation with both the patient/family, and with the other professionals in the team. Often we can watch and learn from our colleagues the GPs, many of whom deal calmly, respectfully and effectively with confidentiality issues.

Codes of Ethics are carefully thought out, and in many ways excellent, but in some ways such Codes (for example, that of the British Association for Counselling) are rather like the traffic lights on pedestrian crossings. If we ignore the evidence of our own eyes and ears and simply obey the lights, they certainly keep us more or less safe, but there are many occasions when we could stand like idiots facing an empty road, watching for the green man to tell us to cross, when in fact we might have been over and on our way minutes before. At other times the green man will light up just as a lawless motorcyclist screeches around the corner, and we need to take back responsibility for our own safety once more.

In the general practice team, we have only to look at our own experience to tell us that if we attempt to maintain complete and sacred silence about every one of our patients, this will not be beneficial to the patients and families of the practice population. Often, we have to make up our own minds on the spot about 'whether to cross the road'. Many counsellors would feel uncomfortable about abdicating this responsibility just because they have traffic lights – a Code of Ethics – in front of their eyes.

So there are also several strong, practical arguments *against* maintaining strict confidentiality.

- The counsellor is unable to benefit from other professionals' often more extensive knowledge of the patient and family, more general clinical wisdom, or encouragement. Equally, other staff cannot benefit from interacting with the counsellor.
- The counsellor may unwittingly be working against other professionals. You cannot offer coordinated care if none of you talks to each other. This can become even more complicated if you are working with a couple or a family, and if the family members visit different GPs, nurses or other staff in the practice. Patients often assume that the relevant members of staff do in fact communicate with each other, and find it difficult to understand why this is *not* happening (Marsh, 1991).
- The separation of GP and counsellor (to put the most simple case) can promote unhealthy collusion, secrecy or splitting between the patient and counsellor and patient and doctor pairs. Most practice counsellors have had the experience of finding that, somehow, they have been seduced into becoming the 'good counsellor' as opposed to the 'bad doctor'.
- An important part of the practice counsellor's job is to foster and nourish the patient/doctor relationship in whatever we say to the patient, as well as welcoming the doctor's input and offering clear and helpful feedback as appropriate (McDaniel, Campbell and Seaburn, 1990). It may be tempting for the practice counsellor to inhabit the 'angel's corner' at the expense of the way the doctor is

viewed by the patient, but the counsellor should not go along with this. The patient needs a good relationship above all with the GP, who is the central figure in the health care offered by the practice.

- The GP holds a central place in taking medical responsibility for the patient. It is probably unwise to cut him off from any knowledge of this sector of the patient's treatment in the surgery. Where personal lists are not used, the patient may see several doctors at different times, and this point becomes even more complex.
- The counsellor may easily gain the reputation of being aloof, secretive or pretentious. This will probably have knock-on implications for the sort of referrals they get and the conditions they are afforded (which in themselves have a knock-on effect on the patients).
- Working under strict confidentiality makes a distinction between the biochemical and the psychosocial areas and encourages the Cartesian split in the patient and family – not to mention the rest of the team. In fact, mind and body are, of course, inextricably intertwined and need to be attended to together – one of the more powerful arguments for having counsellors in the practice at all.

Why not be inclusive rather than exclusive?

In the Western world we have a cultural history of being treated as individuals rather than as groups or systems. Many of us are not used to thinking in collaborative ways. Psychological health care in particular is dominated by the towering figure of Freud, and individual attention on a single couch. So the collaborative, systems-oriented instinct to enlarge the group – either in reality or just in consideration – may be very disconcerting for patients. Most health care professionals are, of course, imbued with this identical cultural history. The doctor or nurse normally sees just one patient in the surgery, and family or friends alongside are sometimes seen as an irrelevance, a nuisance or even an unwanted interference.

To become more aware of the importance – and involvement – of family, friends and community in health care takes a conscious effort. Involving other health care team members, or other family members when appropriate and helpful to the patient, may at first seem alien to us all for these reasons, and may take some time to become familiar. One of the concerns always mentioned when more than two people are in the counselling room is the worry about confidentiality. But this can be securely maintained, even with a working intrinsic group of a whole family and several health workers, if every one – of the health workers, at least – has a clear and rigorous understanding of where the limits of confidentiality lie.

Confidentiality between family and friends – a very delicate balance

Maintaining confidentiality between the patient, family and friends is a much more complex and demanding task than holding the cordon firm from the professional point of view.

Linda and Evan visit you together several times to talk about their experience of Linda's benign brain tumour, surgically removed under particularly unpleasant circumstances 18 months ago. Linda was very frightened by some of the treatment. The couple are deeply devoted to one another and it is hard to say which of them was more traumatized. Each has been making light of the experience to spare the other's feelings, and they have come to a point of feeling sadly distant from one another.

Adding to their difficulties is Evan's mother, Monica, who is very fond of Linda and very much aware of how much she means to Evan. Monica has recently stopped visiting the couple after a row in which Evan accused her of making things worse by constantly and fearfully asking how Linda was? This usually drove Linda out of the room and led to much uncomfortable meaningful eye contact and nudging between the young couple. Monica's marriage seems a little rocky at present and Evan is also worried about his parents' relationship. The underlying implication (feared by all, of course, but never actually mentioned) is that Linda's tumour may return.

Although this is a close, supportive and highly competent family, anxiety levels are very high, and you are not very surprised when Evan's father makes a separate appointment to see you. He has been having severe migraine-like headaches which he has not wanted to mention to his wife for obvious reasons. They have been making him bad-tempered and inclined to drink rather too much.

This family presents a real challenge to the counsellor's delicacy of touch, requiring multiple psychological pirouettes, and with several interweaving decisions to be made at every turn. Plunging into the terrors of brain surgery and chemotherapy with Linda and Evan together may distress either of them so much that they may call a halt to therapy, yet they come knowing – and saying – that this is what they wish to discuss. Should you suggest that they come separately to ease their fear of upsetting each other, or would this simply separate them further? You have so far had two occasions when Linda on her own 'caught' you in the waiting area and began to blurt out something about her nightmares.

Evan doesn't know [she said] I get out of bed quietly and go downstairs to cry and shake; I don't want to worry him, and he needs his sleep.

You have to be careful not to reveal this in the joint sessions, but if Linda should want to talk about it there you mustn't get in the way either. This is real tightrope walking.

As a lone counsellor in a surgery to which all the family belongs, you have also to give a good service to Evan's father, Mike. You must not give away to Mike Linda and Evan's misgivings about Monica, even though Mike talks to you about the row his wife had with their son and daughter-in-law. And you must not give any of your knowledge about Mike and Monica's marriage away to Linda and Evan. Somehow, you must maintain your manoeuvrability and lightness of touch while rigorously respecting each person's, and each couple's, boundaries of confidentiality.

It is possible that the whole family may be able to get together (with or without you) and you must do nothing to impede this. If different family members manage to talk to each other outside the counselling room, this can only be good, and yet your credibility can easily be lost if you do not appear to 'know' facts that different family members tell you in sessions and of which you already have prior knowledge.

A careful explanation of the boundaries of confidentiality to each person will help, but may not make keeping your own balance very much easier. There is no avoiding the fact that you may well look slightly stupid at some point. There are no easy solutions, except developing the skills by practising them.

Confidentiality in violent partnerships

A fairly common situation in which an acute awareness of confidentiality is extremely important is that of working with a couple where there is violence. The most usual circumstance is that of a heterosexual couple where the man has been violent to the woman.

The Brief Therapy Practice in London has developed some valuable policy thinking for the counsellor approaching such a situation, and this may be useful even for those counsellors who use very different models of work from the solution-focused brief therapy used and taught in the Practice. The following discussion is based on George, Iveson and Ratner's suggestions (1996).

- Seeing such a couple together can promote danger. If a woman is asked to say what has happened to her, or why she is here in counselling, in front of her partner, this may provoke later retaliation by the man.
- If only one partner wants to come then that one is seen alone. If both partners want to be seen then they are first invited to come in

separately. Each is asked to agree to the counsellor putting the question of safety from violence at the top of the counselling agenda. Each is invited to add any other goals they wish to the agenda.

- Practice workers in the Brief Therapy Practice continue by asking the man to assure the therapist that he will not be violent during or between sessions. This would take the form of solemn promises. It is only under certain protective circumstances in which the man explicitly makes this promise, and the woman explicitly believes him, that joint therapy takes place. Otherwise, each person is seen individually.

In this situation the counsellor has to be very careful both to respect each person's privacy, and to promote the couple's welfare as a couple. One does not want each member of the couple forming, as it were, an alliance with the counsellor against the other member. Challenges abound for the counsellor:

On Tuesday, she tells you that last weekend he hit her again. She doesn't know whether to go home to her mother or 'give him one more chance'.

On Wednesday, he tells you that things are going well, he is using his strategies for avoiding hitting her, and he hasn't laid a finger on her for a couple of weeks.

Our job is not to find out 'the truth' nor sit in judgement. Neither can we leak even an inkling of either of their stories back to the other partner. It may be more important to take a macro-position and explore their views of what keeps them together. They may well say love. This should be respected and taken seriously. If we can be curious about this and explore it, we avoid confrontation, and may learn things that each will find valuable about the relationship (George et al., 1996).

Anxious relatives

Another area where care has to be taken is when relatives of the patient contact the counsellor.

You are seeing Sally, a young woman of 20, who has had to return home halfway through a university course because of her bulimia. Her very anxious and loving mother, Angela – a single parent – rings unexpectedly to ask how Sally is doing and how she, Angela, can help.

Some of the issues here are:

- Angela is also a patient of your practice and therefore part of your responsibility. She is also in distress.
- You cannot discuss Sally there and then because you do not know how Sally will feel about it. But there are several creative possibilities:
  (a) you could ask Sally if she would like her mother to come in for a session or part of one with her daughter;
  (b) you could ask Sally if she would like you to talk to her mother either in person or on the telephone, and if there is anything specific she would or would not like you to say;
  (c) you could write a letter to Angela, perhaps with Sally's help, courteously answering her questions.
- You can, of course, explain about confidentiality to Angela, talk in general about bulimia, maybe suggest some reading, and encourage her to discuss her own anxiety about Sally and how she deals with it most successfully. If Angela wants to see you for her own sake – it is never easy living with someone you love who is bulimic – you can offer a session or more.
- Finally, you can be humane, empathetic and do everything you can to offer psychological help to Angela without broaching Sally's privacy.

Another area to consider is how counsellors should conduct themselves *outside* the surgery, especially if they live within the catchment area of the practice they work in. When we meet a patient in the supermarket, at a party, or on the bus, we have to find ways of remaining friendly but professional (first intuiting whether the patient wants to be recognized at all!). Sometimes, too, it is necessary to sidestep any direct questions by people accompanying the patient, for example, 'So where did you two meet?' However honest and transparent we may wish to be, acting skills are sometimes necessary.

Final thoughts

The few examples above may begin to indicate the many and various dilemmas around confidentiality which present themselves in everyday practice counselling work. Ideas about the more recently developed brief therapies, the inclusive and collaborative ideas of McDaniel and her colleagues (McDaniel et al., 1990, 1992) and other family therapists, combined with the notion of Pritchard et al.'s intrinsic team (Pritchard and Pritchard, 1992), help us to conceive of a different idea of confidentiality which enables us to use and value the input of whoever might be helpful to the counselling task.

The most useful understanding of the difficult concept of confidentiality in health care seems to arise out of a culture which has a systemic perspective, and holds transparency, respect and collaboration as its key characteristics. Perhaps it is easier to describe this by contrasting two fictional practices.

In Practice A:

- Patients are seen very much as individuals. Others in the patient's system are barely recognized, let alone welcomed. Amongst the staff also, little is shared, and people are left to get on with their jobs and shoulder responsibility alone.
- Professional gossip about patients (and between staff) is rife. These are often speculative 'sightseeing' conversations which are judgemental and full of blame. While couched in professional jargon, such interchanges often reinforce the gossiping group's perception of the patient's 'damaged identity': 'She's a jealous, overpossessive mother; no wonder the whole family's dysfunctional.'
- The notion of strict confidentiality in this practice is fiercely defended, because the helping professionals are quick to see people as blameworthy, and therefore of having 'secrets' to be ashamed of.

Across the town in Practice B:

- Staff welcome the involvement of the patient's relatives and friends, provided the patient wants this to happen.
- When workers discuss a case, which is often, their views are full of acceptance, respect and hope. Almost any conversation here could easily be tape recorded and heard by the patient and family. Helping professionals acknowledge and respect the fact that, in a difficult world, patients and families are working towards healing and change in the best way they can manage at that time. Sometimes we have bad luck, but change is always possible and indeed likely. Staff see themselves as cooperating with their patients, assisting them and cheering them on.
- Staff at all levels work well together on the whole, and there is a lot of sharing and collaborative work.
- All conversations relating to cases are kept firmly within the confines of the relative intrinsic teams, and bounded by ethical considerations. Other than this, there is an openness and respect which permeates the practice, its internal workings and all its dealings with patients.

Although there seems to be no easy, catch-all solution to the many dilemmas thrown up by this important issue, perhaps the greatest help

is in our own attitudes and styles of working. It seems that understanding and respecting the complexity and arbitrariness (and sometimes even absurdity) of human life helps us to move closer to the ideal
of transparent, collaborative work with our patients. Thus a concept of
confidentiality can grow which will seem innate and natural to us as a
practice team, and comfortable, secure and helpful for the patients and
families we see.

Key points

- In the primary care setting, patient confidentiality and team collaboration are equally important and interdependent.
- Different professional training, socialization and cultures mean different views of confidentiality within the team. But collaboration is
  essential to offering an excellent service.
- Confidentiality may be seen as a matter of degree, guided by the
  unique needs of each patient/family.
- We have a choice about how we view patients. To see them as competent and notice their strengths is empowering for patients and the
  team.
- Gossip serves important psychosocial functions in the health care
  team; but to nurture the confidentiality/collaboration principle, the
  team has to sacrifice many of these functions.
- Three useful ideas are:
  solution-focused interviewing;
  the inclusive biopsychosocial model;
  the intrinsic team.
- Confidentiality can and should be maintained rigorously within the
  working 'intrinsic group' agreed by the patient/family. This may be
  patient/counsellor/GP/supervisor (the basic group) or include other
  family/friends or professionals.
- The concept of confidentiality seems to flourish and function best in
  a non-judgemental team atmosphere, in which we collaborate
  respectfully with patient/family and team.

References

Bond, T. (1995) *Standards and Ethics for Counselling in Action*. London: Sage.
DeJong, P. and Berg, I.K. (1998) *Interviewing for Solutions*. Monterey, CA: Brooks/Cole.
Doherty, W.J. and Baird, M.A. (1983) *Family Therapy and Family Medicine*. New York: The Guilford
    Press.

George, E., Iveson, C. and Ratner, H. (1996) Unpublished handout.

Guggenbuhl-Craig, A. (1971) *Power in the Helping Professions*. USA: Spring Publications.

Hoag, L. (1992) 'Psychotherapy in the general practice surgery: considerations of the frame', *British Journal of Psychotherapy*, 8 (4).

Hudson-Allez, G. (1995) 'Issues of confidentiality for a counsellor in general practice', *CMS News*, August. pp. 8–9.

Jones, H., Murphy, A., Neaman, G., Tollemache, R. and Vassermann, D. (1994) 'Psychotherapy and counselling in a GP practice: making use of the setting', *British Journal of Psychotherapy*, 10 (4): 543–51.

Marsh, G.N. (1991) *Efficient Care in General Practice*. Oxford: Oxford University Press.

Mayer, R., Graham, H., Schuberth, C., Launer, J., Tomson, D. and Czauderna, J. (1996) 'Family systems ideas in the 10-minute consultation: using a reflecting partner or team in a surgery', *British Journal of General Practice*, 46: 229–30.

McDaniel, S., Campbell, T. and Seaburn, D. (1990) *Family-Oriented Primary Care: a Manual for Medical Providers*. New York: Springer-Verlag.

McDaniel, S., Hepworth, J. and Doherty, W.J. (1992) *Medical Family Therapy: a Biopsychosocial Approach to Families with Health Problems*. New York: Basic Books.

Pritchard, P. and Pritchard, J. (1992) *Developing Teamwork in Primary Care: a Practical Workbook*. Oxford: Oxford University Press.

Rolland, J.S. (1994) *Families, Illness and Disability*. New York: Basic Books.

Waskett, C. (1996) 'Multidisciplinary teamwork in primary care, and the role of the counsellor', *Counselling Psychology Quarterly*, 9 (3): 243–60.

CHAPTER 8

DOING THERAPY BRIEFLY IN PRIMARY CARE: THEORETICAL CONCEPTS

Christine Parrott

Traditionally, people have viewed therapy as a long process, an engagement of many sessions over a lengthy period of time. This view dates back to psychology's beginnings, when in-depth psychoanalysis was the standard of therapeutic practice. However, the First World War created the need for more immediate psychological services and, as such, the development of briefer approaches emerged. Today, the need for brief perspectives is more salient than ever. It is not only a contemporary trend but a necessary method in handling the realities of today's modern health care environment.

Primary care settings, whether private or NHS-governed, place demands upon mental health professionals which can not always be managed effectively by long term approaches. Limited resources and an increased public acceptance of counselling and therapy have contributed to the almost insatiable need for mental health services in recent years. Long term therapeutic approaches are simply ill-equiped to deal with the pressures of general practice. Brief therapeutic approaches are thus a practical and ethical necessity. As such, like all effective therapies, brief therapy should be approached thoughtfully and competently. The following two chapters aim to encourage this perspective. This chapter explores the theoretical underpinnings of brief therapy while the following chapter will cover some of the key elements required in practising effective, proficient and professional brief therapy.

The primary care setting

One fundamental element to effective practice, of all kinds, is an appropriate context. For brief therapy this can be found in the primary care setting. It is a fertile environment for successful brief interventions. First, the current medical establishment practises from a time-aware perspective: promoting effective and lasting change as rapidly as possible. It is also an arena where attention is increasingly being paid to preventative, rather than reactive, assistance. Brief therapy mimics this approach. The methods are concerned with quick yet effective intervention, while the foundational beliefs emphasize the prevention of entrenched emotional difficulties. Second, primary care settings are often the first point of contact for the patient: it is here that the patient is introduced to the world of medicine while more in-depth specialized procedures are carried out elsewhere. Brief therapies foster the same pattern of care: focused, effective and necessary intervention at the level of primary care with more specialized, in-depth and long term approaches located elsewhere. Furthermore, as brief therapy may seem less overwhelming to a patient than years of treatment, it may also help to reduce some of the present reservations about therapy, ultimately reinforcing therapy as a 'primary' health concern.

Viewed in this way, the practice of brief therapy is not a compromise. It is a powerful and comprehensive therapeutic approach. In fact, studies comparing the effectiveness of time-limited and open-ended therapies document little difference in outcome (Koss and Butcher, 1986). Research has also suggested that brief therapy is the most prevalent mode of treatment in practice today (Hoyt, 1995), with many clients terminating treatment without notice. These findings indicate that therapy is often made brief by the client. Counsellors need to respond to this reality and brief therapy is one method of doing so. It enables the counsellor to practise effective therapy within the parameters dictated by client and setting.

Defining brief therapy

Brief therapy, as described in this chapter and the next, is a method of applying various treatments rather than a distinct branch of therapy (as has been described by de Shazer, 1985). It is a philosophy of change that is congruent with many, if not all, theoretical orientations. Although in the past cognitive and behavioural treatments have been viewed as most compatible with brief therapy approaches, psychodynamic, systemic, humanistic and existential orientations have all begun to explore this approach to treatment.

Brief therapy refers to any method of treatment which specifically aims to effect change within as short a time period as possible. It is an approach to therapy that embraces the effective use of time and utilizes time as a therapeutic tool. Although no strict time definition has been set, the general consensus is that brief counselling refers to treatment plans up to 20 sessions in length, although usually between six and ten. The aim is always to address change and patient growth within a restricted time frame. Technically, 'time-limited therapy' specifically establishes an end date whereas in brief therapy no such specific deadline is made despite the aim of brevity (Dryden and Feltham, 1992). For the purpose of ease, the two will be used interchangeably in these chapters to denote any short term therapy.

The philosophy of 'doing therapy briefly'

Doing therapy briefly, and effectively, involves embracing a particular philosophy. Included in this philosophy is the conviction that *change is possible at any moment*. This stems from the belief that change is a fundamental, essential and non-negotiable aspect of life. It is the aim of brief therapy to help direct this change in a more positive direction for the patient. As change is constantly occurring, therapy does not need to be lengthy in order to facilitate this directional shift. Change has occurred before the patient has entered the office and will continue to occur after therapy has been terminated. Hence, effective counselling can be accomplished in a condensed period of time.

This 'change' can be defined in a variety of ways according to various theoretical orientations. It can be behavioural, cognitive or emotional. It may even simply be a matter of enabling the patient to engage in a reflection process with which he was not previously involved. However defined, the underlying philosophy of brief therapy maintains that this change does and can happen in a brief time period. Moreover, that change may be permanent. A well-timed and focused intervention can be the catalyst for multiple improvements in a patient's life. Problems are often inter-related, so that improvement in one area will facilitate change in another (Strasser and Strasser, 1997). Good therapy does not solve every problem for the patient. Instead, it gives the patient the tools and skills to effect change by himself. Brief therapy maximizes this therapeutic technique.

Brief therapy also embraces the idea that *the process of therapy belongs to the patient*. The power is more with the patient than the counsellor. The counsellor is merely a catalyst for transformation as the ability to change ultimately resides within the patient. Moreover, therapeutic shifts can and often do occur outside the counselling room. This ability is increased when the independence of the patient is heightened. As with almost all theoretical orientations, the goal of brief therapy is to make the individual a free agent, someone who can reflect upon the process of life and effect change through his increased knowledge or awareness. What distinguishes brief therapy from more open-ended approaches is the primary importance it places on the ability for each person to create change for himself. The power of the patient becomes a central and defining factor in brief therapy. It underscores every intervention and moment in the approach.

Brief therapy requires a shift in the counsellor's basic assumptions about change and pathology. It recognizes that the patient has the power to change and that some change has already occurred before the patient arrives for a session. Change will also continue to occur outside each session and after counselling has ended. Because of this philosophy, more than any other theoretical stance, brief therapy is a non-pathology based model. It is a way of approaching every therapeutic moment with the belief that the patient is capable of change and that the patient does not usually require extensive treatment, though the course of counselling may be intensive. In this way, brief therapy is an ethical and humane method of practice. A brief therapeutic approach recognizes that more treatment is not necessarily better treatment (Hoyt, 1995). Some changes are best made with focused short interventions. In certain circumstances, only time will strengthen a patient's conviction, transformation, or newly acquired skill. More therapy will not necessarily increase such ability.

Language

Because brief therapy derives from a philosophy of problem maintenance and resolution, it pervades every aspect of the therapeutic encounter, including the language. Language is among the most powerful tools available to counsellors. Changing a single word in a sentence can affect the entire meaning of that sentence. For example, notice the difference between saying, 'He's a short man' versus 'He's a small man' or 'She's a great woman' versus 'She's a large woman' or 'You are so far from me' versus 'You are so distant from me'. In each of these sentences, a word has been replaced with another word almost identical in meaning; however, this small modification is able to alter the entire flavour of the sentence. Similarly, small modifications in the language of therapy can also create an entirely different atmosphere. Language can cultivate a ripe environment for therapeutic change. Suggestions that change is already happening or that the patient has initiated change himself, are characteristic of the brief therapeutic approach. They reflect the overall philosophy of change, as illustrated below.

Consider the language involved in a first encounter with a patient. Traditional approaches may prompt the patient's story with a statement such as:

> I have heard from your doctor that you have been experiencing some prob-
> lems. Why don't you tell me what has been happening in your life?

Although nothing is essentially wrong with this statement, a brief
therapeutic approach would advocate some small but, none the less
meaningful, changes. For instance, a brief therapeutic statement of
similar purpose might be:

> The referral from your doctor said that you wanted to make some changes in
> your life. Why don't you tell me what you would like to accomplish through
> our meeting here today and perhaps in the future?

The first statement of this brief therapeutic approach emphasizes
'change' rather than 'problems'. This helps to convey the non-pathology orientation of brief therapy while it also creates a more positive
focus. The second statement highlights the power of the patient. It
marks the patient as the agent of change: 'What would *you* like to
accomplish'. By contrast, in the first example the counsellor's words
'What has been happening' suggest that the patient is a passive agent
to life's events. The brief therapy approach also states that accomplish-
ments will be made *today*. The focus is on the present, conveying the
belief that change can happen within the moment. 'Perhaps in the
future' adds the possibility of future meetings but does not take such
meetings for granted: it stresses the here-and-now ability to change.

Time

In brief therapy every session is approached with the aim of making
that session meaningful on its own. This does not mean that connections cannot be made between sessions and that recurrent issues cannot
be highlighted. However, it does mean that the issues addressed in any
one session are contained in such a manner that the session will be
useful without further meetings. In this way, if the patient were suddenly to terminate counselling, the ideas of the last session would be
complete and would not need further elaboration. Re-emphasis of ideas
is often ideal but it is not always possible. As such, the brief therapy
approach uses only the time that is guaranteed: the time of the present
session.

Time is constantly an issue in brief therapy, and its efficient use is
always a priority. This affects everything from the length of each
session, the use of time between sessions, and even the timing of events
within a session. For instance, each session is punctuated by a beginning, middle and end phase. Such structure provides emphasis and
meaning to events which can be useful for the therapist and client. The

topics which are addressed at the beginning and/or end of each session will tend to be heightened (Hoyt, 1995). As such, these will be the issues that the patient may focus on between sessions.

Brief therapy recognizes that this time between sessions is often the most therapeutic, as it is the playing field for all that has been discussed in session. The value of the events in the session can only be tested during the course of the patient's 'real' life. Counselling is not the true playing field for patient issues and dilemmas, only life outside sessions is. Although brief therapy aims to make each session whole, it is whole as a catalyst for patient growth and change. The intrinsic worth of each session will ultimately be tested outside the therapy room. Thus, in brief therapy, time between sessions becomes a therapeutic tool and it is managed with as much care as the time within the session.

Benefits and limits of brief therapy

The efficient use of time is one of the many benefits of brief therapy. Its management as a tool allows many theoretical orientations to work within the parameters dictated by today's health care environment. With brief therapy, many patients receive care who would not previously have been helped by traditional long term therapies. The more focused and patient-driven approach of brief therapy is also more 'user-friendly' both for the counsellor and patient. It allows the counsellor to manage a greater patient load within the limited time and resources available while it also enables the patient to approach counselling with less trepidation. The prospect of help contained within a few meetings as opposed to treatment over many months, or years, may make counselling more appealing to many individuals. In addition, counselling that maintains a focus on the present may seem less overwhelming than counselling that delves into the unconscious or deeper meanings of events. With these benefits, brief therapy becomes an effective and suitable treatment approach regardless of limited resources and economic pressures. Therefore, the decision to practise brief therapy can be a positive option. It is a choice made because of a belief in the ethos of brief therapy: that more treatment is not necessarily better, that quick treatment is often the most ethically sound, that brief therapy maximizes the potential of the patient, and that time is a valuable resource which needs to be utilized optimally.

These beliefs are not exclusive to brief therapy: long term approaches are based on many of the same convictions. However, the degree to which these beliefs are embraced differs between long and short term approaches. Long term approaches simply do not place the same priority on time. The benefits reaped from extended exploration and patient–counsellor contact are seen to outweigh the benefits of time efficiency. For example, with some counsellors, the value placed on in-depth analysis will constitute more of a priority than focused interventions. Yet, for most practitioners, the values and goals of counselling are essentially the same: optimizing patient potential, creating growth, or facilitating change. It is the preferred means of reaching those ends which will influence the choice to practise through a long or short term perspective. In the end, each counsellor must determine for herself which type of approach is most compatible with her personal philosophy. This is an issue which must be as carefully explored as the particular theoretical orientation with which a counsellor chooses to practise.

Brief therapy is not a suitable mode of treatment for all patients. Some patients will have entrenched personality characteristics or complex presenting problems which may need the expertise of more long term care. Patients who do not have the capacity to act independently or reflect upon their own actions will not be appropriate for brief therapy approaches. Moreover, some patients may be seeking a long term approach. They may be looking to explore their lives, values and personality by engaging in discussions over the course of several months or years. These patients will not be satisfied by the brief therapeutic approach and as such may need to be referred elsewhere.

Summary

The practice of brief therapy provides unique opportunities to the counsellor. It not only enables a counsellor to foster change and growth more quickly, but it provides the counsellor with a viable means of working within the parameters dictated by today's primary health care settings. Primary care is a ripe environment for the advantages of brief therapy. Not only can practice within primary care help to promote psychology as a integral part of modern health care, but it also supplies an opportunity for counsellor and patient to work collaboratively, efficiently and preventatively. The combined dynamics of primary care and brief therapy also afford a suitable and unequalled context for research. The benefits of brief therapy in primary care, both to patients and to the psychological field, could be enormous. From this perspective, the need for more in-depth training in brief approaches is urgent. The relationship of training to practice is almost reversed: the briefer the approach taken, the more intensive the training needed. Put another way, a brief approach requires a long time in training.

The following chapter aims to address some of the practical issues that will need to be addressed in any brief therapy training programme.

The philosophical shift of brief therapy requires certain changes in counsellor perspective and approach which invite more rapid change. Language and time need to be managed effectively while the potential of each patient needs to be maximized. Focused interventions aimed at creating this experience are the cornerstone of brief therapy in practice.

Key points

- The primary care setting is a fertile environment for successful brief interventions.
- Brief therapy reflects the underlying ethos of primary care: quick, effective interventions aimed at the prevention of long term difficulties.
- Brief therapy can be defined as any method of treatment which specifically aims to effect change within as short a time period as possible.
- Brief therapy is a philosophy that affects the entire approach to therapy and yet is compatible with various orientations.
- Language and time are valuable tools within the brief therapeutic approach and need to be considered accordingly.
- Brief therapy is not an appropriate method of treatment for all patients. Patients must be selected according to need and suitability.

References

DeShazer, S. (1985) *Keys to Solutions in Brief Therapy*. New York: W.W. Norton.

Dryden, W. and Feltham, C. (1992) *Brief Counselling: a Practical Guide for Beginning Practitioners*. Buckingham: Open University Press.

Hoyt, M. (1995) *Brief Therapy and Managed Care*. San Francisco: Jossey–Bass.

Koss, M.P. and Butcher, J.N. (1986) 'Research on brief psychotherapy', in S.L Garfield and A.E. Bergin (eds), *Handbook of Psychotherapy and Behavior Change: an Empirical Analysis*, 3rd edn. New York: Wiley, 1986.

Strasser, F. and Strasser, A. (1997) *Existential Time-Limited Therapy: the Wheel of Existence*. Chichester: John Wiley.

CHAPTER 9

DOING THERAPY BRIEFLY IN PRIMARY CARE: APPLICATIONS

Christine Parrott

The previous chapter addressed the theoretical basis of a brief thera-peutic approach. This basis has important implications for the practical application of counselling. Each moment and phase of brief counselling will be affected by this shift in focus. The emphasis and value placed on time and patient potential in brief therapy demands certain changes in the counsellor's approach from assessment to termination. New and revised techniques must be implemented to achieve effective coun-selling within this more limited time frame. These practical changes and techniques are the focus of this chapter.

Issues prior to assessment

As time is limited in brief therapy, it should be treated as a precious resource. This does not mean rushing through each phase of treatment but rather using time wisely. This practice begins well before the first meeting. The foundation for sound and productive counselling is laid by the position and respect that a counsellor creates for herself within the primary care setting. Every counsellor should know about the setting in which she is working and should take the time to get to know the people working within that setting. The connections made with col-leagues will ultimately help to make a counsellor's job more effective and efficient. As people become familiar with counsellors, both on a practical and personal level, the more likely those individuals will be to make referrals, enquire about appropriate actions, encourage patients to attend and help link services within the practice. A sound reputation will facilitate setting the right atmosphere within the clinic and, most importantly, within the therapeutic context. A patient who has heard genuine positive remarks from not only his GP but from nurses and receptionists will be much more at ease and ready to engage in a relationship with the counsellor. This may reduce the time needed to build a working relationship. Counselling, therefore, has begun before the patient ever reaches the counselling room.

The referral process

The referral process can also facilitate brief therapy. The art of eliciting appropriate referrals has been discussed previously in this book (see Chapter 5) and the reader is advised to refer to that chapter for a more in-depth discussion. However, a few points need to be highlighted in relation to brief therapy. Good referrals are established *by the counsellor*. Time taken to discuss appropriate referrals with all referring agents is well spent. Referrers should be well aware of the strengths and limitations of the counsellor with whom they work. They should know how and when to contact the counsellor with any questions regarding a referral. In this way, inappropriate referrals are kept to a minimum and patients' needs are handled efficiently. The referral process should be made explicit to all concerned agents. They should understand how to approach patients about counselling, how to prepare patients for their first meeting and what to include in the referring letter to the counsellor. All of these issues help to make the referral process as efficient as possible.

Information included in the referring letter will help to prepare the counsellor for the first meeting with the patient. A good counsellor will also make additional preparations for the first session, as she would for any session in brief therapy. For instance, if the referred patient has a medical condition with which the counsellor is unfamiliar, then the counsellor should take the time to read or ask the GP about that condition. If the referring letter alludes to an extensive medical history, the counsellor might take a few moments to familiarize herself with the patient's medical notes. If the client will be bringing her child to the session due to lack of child care, the counsellor may want to have a few toys at hand in order to help the child feel at ease and remain occupied. This will not only help the counsellor to gain a better understanding of the presenting problem but may help to establish a good working relationship with the client.

Initial contact

A good relationship in brief therapy will also be forged by the initial contact. Whether this be by phone or letter, the contact needs to be professional. The counsellor should be able to talk openly and freely about her practice and to answer any questions the patient may have about counselling. Lengthy descriptions of the client's problem(s) at this point should be avoided. This is why contact by letter is often preferable. It allows the counsellor to control the first impression which may impact the client's decision to continue with the counselling referral.

The initial contact should be made with care and within the ethos of brief counselling. This means considering simple things such as the proper spelling of the client's name and more complex issues such as whether or not to include preparation suggestions for the initial meeting. Such suggestions will help the patient to use the time of the first session more efficiently and to set the stage for future out-of-session work. The letter may also include assessment measurements which can either be returned to the counsellor before or at the initial contact. If used, however, such measurements need to be chosen with care as too lengthy or technical measures may seem overwhelming or too clinical, and thus may deter some patients from attending the session.

The wording of the initial letter should also be considered carefully. It will help to set the atmosphere for the counselling services on offer. Consider the difference between receiving the following statements as part of an initial contact letter:

Dear Mr Blue,
As requested by your GP, we have arranged an appointment for you with the counselling services on ____ at ____. If you cannot make this time and date, please notify the surgery. Enclosed please find several forms to be completed and brought to your first session . . .

---

versus

Dear Mr Blue,
Thank you for your interest in our counselling services. We have arranged an initial consultation to meet and discuss your concerns on ____ at ____. If you are unable to make this appointment, please contact the surgery on ____ and we can reschedule another appointment if you so desire. Enclosed please find a few forms which you might like to complete and bring to your initial session. These are to help both you and your counsellor gain a better picture of your life circumstances . . .

Note that the second example not only sets a more receptive atmosphere but also introduces the ethos of brief therapy. In the first sentence, the patient is thanked for his interest in counselling, making him the agent of change rather than the GP. The initial session is referred to as a 'consultation to meet and discuss . . . concerns' rather than as an appointment. This emphasizes the collaborative aspects of counselling and sets the stage for patient participation in the process. Finally, the introduction of assessment measures is explained to the patient rather than dictatorially administered. The wording of this explanation is aimed at creating both an atmosphere of collaboration and of patient control. These may seem like small changes but brief therapy advocates a precise use of language and requires the efficient use of *all* time.

The assessment

The assessment session is probably the most important session in brief therapy. Other sessions may help to develop insight and to develop and monitor strategies for problem-solving for the patient. Like every previous action, the first session sets the stage for effective therapy and initiates the counselling process. The assessment session goes further, however. The *assessment session is therapy* and is not simply time to gather information, meet the client and formulate hypotheses. It is therapy for the patient. This is probably the most overlooked aspect of the assessment session, and yet it is the most important. When a patient steps into the counselling room, he is there to engage in the process of counselling, not to hand over bibliographic details and to recount a story.

By making the decision to attend counselling, the patient has already begun to think differently about the difficulties he faces. At the very least, the patient has recognized his problems as worthy of attention. This change in attitude and focus is something that needs to be maximized. It reflects the belief that change is initiated by the patient. The power of change lies within the patient and this is made visible when that patient steps through the counsellor's door. During the assessment, the counsellor seeks to facilitate and accelerate that transformation already in progress. To overlook this opportunity is to be remiss in addressing the needs of the patient.

Two types of patients will most likely be encountered at the assessment session: one who has nothing to say and the other who has everything to say. For some, counselling will be a strange and daunting experience. These patients may arrive apprehensive about the counselling process and will therefore be less willing to talk. Conversely, their anxiety may prompt lots of conversation! Others may be more relieved at the prospect of counselling and will come to the session ready to pour out their difficulties. Whatever the patient is like, the power of the first session lies in a positive experience for the patient. If the patient needs to talk, a good counsellor remembers to listen. If the patient is more withdrawn, a good counsellor will remember that solid relationships are gained through genuine warm encounters, not through the gathering of dry biographical details. Although a counsellor needs to gain information from the first meeting, this must be done within the parameters of a therapeutic session.

Assessment as treatment

In brief therapy, assessment and treatment are inextricably linked. One cannot treat without assessing and one cannot assess without treating. This stems from the belief that everything a counsellor does within an encounter will have an effect on the patient. The goal of brief therapy is to make this effect continually positive. A considerable percentage of patients will only be seen for one session (Hoyt, 1995) which underscores the need to consider the assessment as a therapeutic encounter. If not viewed in this way, the counsellor runs the risk of stifling the momentum set by the patient when he initiated the meeting. The assessment may be the only opportunity that a counsellor will have to act as a catalyst in the change process. As such, the assessment should be used wisely. In the words of a famous old adage, 'Never put off to tomorrow, what you can do today.'

Any energy brought to a session, whether excitement or nervousness, should be utilized by the counsellor. This may mean commenting on the process of counselling. For instance, if a patient arrives to the assessment and with a little prodding begins to pour out his story, the counsellor, after listening, might point out the client's manner of speech:

> I noticed that you have been speaking very quickly about what has been on your mind. It obviously is a very important issue for you. I was wondering, because of its importance, if we might be able to go over the issues more carefully and perhaps explore some of the areas in more detail. I was thinking that this might help to organize some of the elements for you.

In this way, the counsellor has conducted an intervention while allowing for assessment information to unfold. The counsellor continues to gather details while aiming to help the patient construct his story in a more manageable fashion. With such a statement, the counsellor may be trying to break down the problem into more manageable elements, to increase the reflection process, or even emphasize the various options available for change. Whatever the exact aim of the intervention, the approach works from a time-limited perspective as it achieves assessment and treatment objectives simultaneously.

Assessment objectives

With this philosophy in mind, the assessment consultation will have several unique objectives separating it from other treatment sessions, not least of which will be the counsellor's goal to select and prepare patients for brief therapy. As noted above, not all patients will be suitable for the brief therapy approach. The counsellor will need to assess client motivation, expectations and the complexity of the presenting problem. If a low level of motivation and commitment to change is apparent, continued counselling may not be appropriate. However, in all cases, the assessment session should still be used to the benefit of the patient. The brief therapy approach maintains that every interaction will affect the patient so that, even if termination or referral is expected, the counsellor will need to take care to remain attentive and focused on the needs of the patient.

Selecting appropriate patients for brief therapy is critical to the development of time-limited skills and, hence, ultimately to the development of effective practice. Such practice will also require that patients be prepared for the approach in which they will be participating. This will mean discussing issues of time, orientation, collaboration and commitment. The client will need to know what is expected of him from the start. The patient will need to understand that counselling is not open-ended. An immediate understanding that therapy will eventually come to an end will help the patient to focus on his goals more readily. Every person is familiar with how much more rigorously people will work when a deadline is set. Although some people may feel stressed by end dates, an experienced counsellor will be able to judge the length of counselling necessary to minimize this frustration. As the end of counselling draws near, such stress can be an indicator of underlying fears which still need to be addressed. Remember, brief therapy is about utilizing all the resources available. Sometimes stress can be a therapeutic tool.

Patient collaboration is another issue that will need to be discussed during the assessment. The nature of this collaboration will depend on the theoretical approach taken and, as such, these two issues can often be linked when addressed. For example:

> You may have noticed that I have been asking you questions during our meeting. Unlike some therapies you may have heard about where the

counsellor may say very little, I will actively participate in the session. At the same time, this means that you will need to be active in our discussions as, although I am here to help you, the benefits that you reap from our meetings will ultimately be a result of your hard work. This will often mean thinking about issues or trying new things outside of our meetings. How does this sound to you so far? . . .

Notice that the counsellor explains only as much as is necessary for the patient to understand what may be expected of him. This creates the opportunity for the patient to ask more about the approach, if he is interested, but does not burden the patient with unnecessary information. The counsellor also sets up future expectations concerning the style of interaction and patient collaboration, including out-of-session work. Such statements will help the patient to become more familiar with the therapy on offer and prepare him for the work ahead.

While helping the patient to orientate himself to counselling, the assessment allows the counsellor to orientate herself to the presenting problem. No matter how one works, all counsellors need to listen to the patient's story during the assessment. The story is ripe with information as it not only addresses the details of a situation but it also allows the patient's character, values and coping methods to be demonstrated in session. Thus, a good counsellor will pay attention to the many layers exposed by the patient's concerns. Eye contact, pace of speech, logical thoughts, emotional reasoning, self-blame, accusations and the amount of emotion displayed will all help to build a picture of the patient, the problem and the context in which the patient and problem exist.

In order to gain a more complete picture, the counsellor will often have to seek out additional information from the patient. Perhaps one of the most important questions a counsellor will ask during assessment (whether directly to the patient or to herself) is 'Why now? Why has this patient decided to seek help *now*?' With this question, a counsellor can begin to focus on what is important to a patient. For instance, if a patient has been in an abusive relationship for several years and just decided to come to counselling after her husband was arrested on a drugs charge, one might suspect that the patient was finally given the opportunity to seek counselling through the absence of her husband. However, upon the counsellor asking 'Why now?', the patient may reveal that she has been left financially stranded while her husband is awaiting trial and cannot cope with this added pressure. In this scenario, the question 'Why now' helps the counsellor to understand the priorities of the patient. It helps the counsellor to locate the level of change sought by the patient as well as the contributing factors to the patient's distress. It clarifies the triggers associated with a particular problem and the related fears that may be involved. 'Why now' also helps to assess the patient's motivational level and expectations. As such, this single question covers a broad spectrum of issues which can help to assess the situation and to direct change.

Past attempts to alleviate the problem and the patient's previous experience of counselling are also key factors for the counsellor to address during assessment. These areas allow the counsellor to determine what has and has not been helpful to the patient. If the aim of brief therapy is the efficient and successful use of time, reattempting ineffective solutions is counter-productive. This can be bypassed by discussing a patient's history. This is also an opportune time to begin redirecting the focus of the patient away from his difficulties and towards the successful aspects of his coping methods. No matter what the level of distress, the patient has coped effectively in some way: he has at the least made it to counselling! Moreover, patterns of behaviour, coping methods and personality traits develop for a reason. Although such patterns may now be ineffectual, they once served a purpose and these positive attributes are worth noting. The idea is to begin focusing on the strengths of the patient, rather than on the problems, and to capitalize on the opportunities presented. Every patient has certain strengths and these should be utilized to facilitate change. This approach is described more fully in the next chapter.

One of the main goals of the assessment is to continue and strengthen the change process by clarifying concerns. Depending on the counsellor's preferred theoretical orientation, this intervention can take many forms. At the very least, the counsellor may sharpen the reflection process while more directive approaches may establish a specific target concern. In each case, however, the general goal will be to help the patient define and prioritize his concerns. Cognitive approaches may attempt to do this through lists, systemic approaches through punctuating beliefs about different relationships, existential models through clarifying questions (Strasser and Strasser, 1997), and psychodynamic approaches through reflection and interpretations. In all cases, the assessment still aims to elucidate and delineate the concerns brought to the session, not just for the counsellor but for the patient as well.

The smallest change in thinking for a patient may spur multiple changes in his life. This is a fundamental belief in brief therapy. Change can happen at any time and can be initiated by the slightest alterations in perception. The assessment is ample opportunity to set such changes in motion. A skilled counsellor will approach the assessment with this in mind. Bloom (1981) reminds counsellors not to ignore stating the obvious. Problems can so completely submerge a patient that he may have difficulty 'seeing the forest through the trees'. Sometimes a simple suggestion or clarification can have the power to relieve the blockage in a system. These types of interventions are a cornerstone in brief therapy. They emphasize the belief that the patient is the agent of change.

Because of this belief, the assessment can also be particularly useful in managing the waiting list at a primary care setting. Long waiting lists seem to be the hallmark of today's health care environment, both in the mental and physical health departments. Depending on the flexibility of setting in which a person works, using one day a week to meet with and assess new patients can be quite beneficial. First, this will help to select patients for brief therapy and refer inappropriate patients to other resources. In this way, a patient will not have to wait 2 months only to be transferred to another waiting list. Secondly, because of the nature of brief therapy assessments, an initial meeting can help patients to further the change process while waiting for more continuous care. Often the brief encounter with a counsellor can help the patient to feel heard and understood. This alone can have great therapeutic value. In addition, the assessment session offers enough time to create small changes which may make the situation more manageable for the patient or even dissipate the situation altogether. A day or few hours set aside each week for assessments means that patients are seen promptly and care given immediately. The value of such service should not be under-estimated.

Assessment outcomes

After the assessment, several issues should be resolved. As noted above, patients will have been selected and referred as appropriate. Good therapy requires referring. No one counsellor can treat all patients and certain patients will be better served by more specialist care. To treat a patient who would receive better care elsewhere borders on unethical practice. As such, brief therapy promotes the use of outside resources. A good counsellor should have a professional know-ledge of the resources available. These will include local and national volunteer services, support groups (including group therapies), paid agencies and specialists within and outside the primary care setting. Educational programmes can also be beneficial: too often a simple lack of information can be at the root of distress. Parenting classes, stress management seminars, and even financial planners are all viable options for many patients.

Length of therapy

Another central issue to be determined by the assessment is the expected length of counselling. This may or may not include a formal contract. Different orientations will require different lengths and also how explicit the counselling contract will be. Moreover, the length of brief therapy can vary considerably depending on the setting and patient. Yet, by the end of the assessment, the patient should have at least a general expectation of how long counselling will last and an understanding that one of the aims of counselling is to be brief. Ideally, the length of treatment should be adjusted according to each patient. Some patients may only require three visits while others may need more. As the counsellor becomes more experienced, she will also become more skilled at judging the length of time necessary for each patient.

Context will also play a role in the length of counselling offered. Some settings may require that each patient should be offered the same amount of time regardless of the presenting problem. In such instances, each patient may be offered a specific number of sessions. This may be the case where patients are highly attuned to receiving 'equal' care and where patients are not familiar with therapeutic practice. The present medical community practices in such a way that treatments often do not vary in length: flu injections take 2 minutes, physical examinations 20 minutes, and broken bones heal over several months. These all generally take the same amount of time for each patient. Thus, patients unfamiliar and still wary of mental health services may incorrectly label themselves or another as 'more disturbed' should the lengths of treatment vary. If a patient had a cousin who was offered three sessions and then is offered 20 sessions by his counsellor, such a patient may become discouraged, believing that he is more 'mentally ill'. In time, a more accepting attitude to counselling may change this perception but at present it is a legitimate reality that will need to be considered.

In such settings, a less formalized contract may help to alleviate the situation. Patients can be given the expectation that counselling will be brief but without a specific number of sessions set. In such cases, a counsellor might approach the issue of time by saying:

> The length of counselling does vary as we try to tailor counselling to each person's needs and pace. However, it usually takes anywhere from 3 to 15 sessions for counselling to have an effect. Some people take less, some people may take two or three sessions more, but this is the general time range that you can expect and to which you will need to make a commitment.

This approach has the advantage of being more flexible but it also curtails the effects of having a specific end date. Counsellors who prefer to work with formal contracts and utilize time limitations as a structural tool may wish to be more specific. In such cases, the counsellor and patient will need to negotiate length and decide on a set number of sessions from the assessment.

Another alternative is the modular scheme proposed by Strasser and Strasser (1997). Patients are offered a 12 week 'module', including two follow-up visits. Counselling is then terminated as agreed. However, if the patient and counsellor still feel that further counselling would be beneficial, then the patient may seek an additional module after a period of separation. This incorporates the structure of a strict ending approach but also recognizes that some patients will benefit from additional care. Instead of compromising the contract set and extending counselling, patients are able to return after several weeks or months. During the interim, patients will need to act independently. It is a time for the patient to test out the changes created by counselling and to focus on areas to be tackled in the next module. As such, patients begin to act as their own therapists – clarifying and testing changes – while time helps to solidify acquired skills. In this way, the approach promotes patient autonomy, incorporates the stringent boundaries, but also remains flexible to accommodate human nature.

An awareness of time helps to bring issues to the surface, reflects the reality of life, and prepares the patient for the end of counselling. As such, a counsellor needs to use time as a therapeutic tool. Instead of avoiding issues of time, such matters can be used to progress the course of counselling. When discussing time issues, the counsellor should always be explicit and professional. Apologies or ambivalence concerning the briefness of counselling will only undermine the therapeutic value of time.

Spacing and length of sessions

Besides contract length and the explicitness of time limits, the counsellor will also need to consider the spacing of sessions and the handling of missed appointments. Sessions are often set up on a once weekly basis, unless a patient is engaged in intense psychotherapy, which will require several meetings per week. Depending on the patient, however, the counsellor may want to vary the spacing of sessions to optimize the benefits for the patient. Later in counselling, counsellor and patient might want to consider spacing the sessions over a fortnight and then monthly. This will allow the patient to test his skills over time. Contracting a specific number of sessions, rather than a specific amount of time, allows for this flexibility. The issue of missed appointments, however, will need to be discussed. The patient will need to know how to cancel appointments and under what circumstances such appointments will be counted towards the sessions contracted (see Chapter 6).

A final time consideration will be the length of each individual session. Traditional sessions are often 50 minutes in length. From a brief therapy perspective, however, this need not be immutable. Time will be maximized through a more flexible approach. Some sessions may require an extended length of time while others may need be only 5 or 10 minutes. If a patient is coping reasonably well and a simple check-up on the progress made is all that is needed then a counsellor is best to shorten the session. Restricting a session to 10 minutes can send the message that a patient is capable and doing well. In this way, time has been used as a tool. It helps to underscore the progress made by the patient. How these extended or condensed sessions will be counted towards the contract will need to be discussed with the patient.

For reasons such as these, however, self-management of one's sched-ule is highly recommended. Every setting will vary on the amount of flexibility offered, but the more one is able to control one's own time schedule, the more efficiently one can make use of time as a tool. Such matters should be addressed with the appropriate people within a setting as highlighting the need for time flexibility will ultimately help others to understand the nature, goals and benefits of one's work.

Working briefly with your client

Flexibility

The successful practice of brief therapy relies on several factors, but perhaps the most important is the counsellor's flexibility. No other characteristic carries as much weight in determining the effectiveness of counselling and the ability to work within restricted time frames. Of course, the traditional emphasis on counsellor warmth, genuineness and empathy remains undisputed but counsellor flexibility plays an equally important role in a brief approach. The flexibility of a counsel-lor often plays a critical role in establishing the aforementioned relationship conditions. The more flexible a counsellor is towards a patient's belief system or lifestyle, the more understanding she will appear to the patient. The more a counsellor is able to adjust the pace of the session to the needs of a patient, the more comfortable the patient will feel with the counselling. Counsellor flexibility is fundamental to sound therapeutic relationships.

Since no two people are exactly the same, no two counselling sessions should ever be identical. No one solution is right for every problem. For instance, a therapist may be familiar with working cognitively for anxiety related issues. Gradual imaginary and then *in vivo* exposure have produced quick and lasting changes in the past. One day, however, a patient presents with a lift phobia. This has been caused by an accident in which the patient was a passenger in a lift which dropped twenty floors. The patient was seriously injured in the incident and has never been able to ride in a lift since the accident. This has caused her great difficulty as she lives on the twentieth floor of her building and works in a company spread over 6 floors of a highrise. She arrives in counselling seeking to overcome her fear. The counsellor begins talking about exposure methods, including imagination exercises. On hearing this, the patient becomes highly distressed: she will not even entertain the thought of imagining herself inside a lift. Although the counsellor tries to calmly explain the rationale behind exposure and the research documenting its effectiveness, the patient only becomes more and more upset.

If the counsellor in this case were to continue to promote the benefits of exposure methods, she would stand a good chance of alienating the patient, who may never return to counselling. Of course, a referral is an option but so too is counsellor flexibility. Instead of becoming stuck in her own pattern of cognitive exposure, the counsellor could attempt to work cognitively but with less of a prescribed approach. For instance, she might first ask the patient to define the problem clearly. She might find that the patient defines the problem in terms of the past saying, 'The problem is that someone should have checked those cables on a more regular basis.' In this situation, the counsellor could begin treatment by having the patient call various lift service companies asking them how often they service lifts and what safety measures they take to safeguard against accidents such as hers. This would both serve to begin exposure to lift-related discussions and to switch the focus away from danger and towards safety aspects of lifts. Alternatively, the counsellor might ask the patient what she expected the counsellor to say or, if she were the counsellor, what she might suggest to the patient to begin treatment. From there, counsellor and patient might be able to negotiate some steps towards change.

In both cases, the counsellor is still able to work from a cognitive framework but is also able to adjust her approach according to the patient. This flexibility allows her to build a therapeutic relationship with the patient while responding to the patient's needs. Indeed, flexibility is not only a tool for the counsellor but part of the philosophy of counselling in general. Most theoretical models aim in one way or another to increase a patient's options. Many aim to help the patient move from rigid, outdated belief systems to more versatile, adjustable patterns. This is flexibility. As a result, flexibility by the counsellor is not just conducive to counselling but also reflective of the work taking place within the therapeutic encounter. To be flexible is to lead by example. It exemplifies the philosophy of counselling and, in particular, of brief counselling. Flexibility with one's approach will also ultimately allow one to use time most efficiently. Instead of applying the same schedule to all patients and problems, flexibility allows the counsellor to condense or lengthen counselling as necessary.

Being flexible, however, does not mean giving up structure or boundaries. These are still important areas which will need to be monitored by the counsellor. Instead, flexibility is about changing according to patient need. It means finding creative approaches, utilizing resources, expanding one's own capabilities, and even adjusting goals so that time and counselling are maximized for each patient. Moreover, this philosophy does not end with each session. It is something that must encompass and filter into every aspect of a brief therapist's work. The counsellor needs to be flexible not only with the patient but also with the working environment. The more versatile a counsellor is with scheduling meetings, offering feedback, working with the GPs and sharing limited resources, the more she will find the setting adapting towards her needs. Flexibility breeds flexibility.

Aims and techniques

The goal of brief therapy is to help a patient with his difficulties within as short a time period as possible. From this perspective, counselling is less concerned with patient 'cure' than patient growth. That growth may be an increase in self-awareness, in coping skills, in problem-solving, or in patience and understanding. Whatever the gains, the aim is to help the patient become more self-reliant in dealing with the emotional difficulties brought to a session. The counsellor seeks to increase the patient's capacity to help himself. Therefore, at one level the brief therapist may be more active in her interventions, but at another level she will be less active in order to encourage the patient's ability to problem-solve independently. The goal is to initiate change. Permanent change is the responsibility of the patient.

Two methods often used to cultivate this ability in brief therapy are (1) the continual reference to future solutions and (2) the continual reference to skills used in the past (Hudson-Allez, 1997). These techniques are used to help focus the patient away from the problem and towards more positive solutions:

Patient: I just can't seem to cope with this situation any more. It's the same thing over and over again. And, I get no help from my family. I do everything for the house on my own. I cook, I clean, I get the kids to and from school, I do all the laundry . . . everything. It's impossible.
Counsellor: It sounds quite difficult and yet it also sounds as if you have managed to do quite a bit of it by yourself for a long time.

P: Well yes – that's what I want to change! It's wearing me out! But I just don't know what to do.
C: How have you managed to do it so far?
P: Many times I've had to make lists just to keep everything straight in my mind and other times things would just not get done for quite a while . . .

In this example, the counsellor helps the patient to discover and focus on the skills that she already has. From here, patient and counsellor might make a list of the various tasks to be done and then prioritize them according to urgency. Hence, the skills that the patient has presented are put to use. Additional time management and assertiveness techniques might be introduced later, but the initial coping strategies are derived from patient experience. This underscores the patient's previous, and thus present, ability to cope. Focus is shifted away from the difficult aspects of the problem and towards effective management.

An alternative shift of focus will be away from the present difficulty and towards future possibilities. Again the patient is encouraged to develop his solutions, as in this example:

Patient: I just don't see how it is going to work. She is so set in her ways. We just don't seem to get along anymore. I don't even find myself attracted to her like I used to be.
Counsellor: Can you think of something that she might do which would give you hope again? How would she have to be?
P: More forgiving. Not nagging me the minute I walk in the door to do this or that, especially since I've been out all day working hard for the two of us.
C: Good. So now we know how you would like her to change. What might you be able to do to help her make this change?

Change is encouraged through the use of future orientation with this patient. Instead of discussing his frustration, the counsellor moves the patient towards thoughts of a better situation. This can be done by asking the patient, 'What needs to change in order to make you happy?' Often, the patient is so focused on the problem that he has not even formulated an acceptable solution. The situation is similar to the familiar cry, 'the build up of nuclear arms is out of control!' This may be true but a more productive stance will be one that begins to address *how* to stop the build up of nuclear arms. A patient's frustration may also be legitimate, but a more time-effective approach will focus on specific examples of what needs to change.

As with all patients, interventions may not work as planned. The scenario might continue:

Patient: I don't know! If I knew I wouldn't be here! I've been trying to get her to stop nagging me for months!
Counsellor: Well, how about when you were young? Did your mother ever nag you to do things?
P: Sure, every mother does. She used to nag me to clean up my room or do my homework all the time.
C: How did you deal with that?
P: Like every child, I screamed and grumbled until I was blue in the face. But I do remember one time when I was supposed to clean up my room and I just didn't have time – I was late for a date. So instead, I scribbled a note to my mom and left it on this huge pile of smelly clothes. It said something like, 'I know I was supposed to do this but I got scared that I might never meet a woman as great as you – so I decided I'd better start looking now'. She wrote back, 'Nice try but you still have to clean this up' . . . but at least she didn't shout at me when I got home.
C: What about now? Seems like you are grumbling until you are blue in the face again. Do you think something similar might work with getting your wife to change?

The example shows how both techniques can be combined to help the patient gain a more positive focus. When an attempt to focus on the future brings more frustration from the patient, the counsellor moves to highlight the patient's effective use of skills in the past. Eventually, these skills are brought back to the present situation and specifically to the solution previously offered by the patient. In each example, the patient remains the agent of change and his abilities, rather than his deficiencies, are highlighted.

However, future solutions and past skill elaboration are two directive methods of brief therapy which may be too active for some orientations. Less directive focusing techniques can also facilitate patient growth and self-reliance. Challenging assumptions made by the patient and exploring value systems are two active existential techniques that can help a patient to focus and produce change. In brief approaches, these techniques are simply refined to catalyse change more rapidly.

Patient: I have wanted to change jobs for quite some time but I just feel like such a failure for not being able to find satisfaction in this job.
Counsellor: However, previously you expressed your dislike for individuals for do not confront problems head on – that such an attitude wastes precious time. How do you think those beliefs fit in with your beliefs about job completion?
P: Well, both attitudes are important to me – I mean, being a fighter and sticking through things, but also being a fighter and facing a problem. I guess I really haven't faced up to what a problem this job has become for

> me and I guess it really is a waste of time to keep pursuing something that
> is so unrewarding for me . . .

Just like the previous techniques, challenges and value comparisons can help a patient to focus on the problem in a more productive manner. Similarly, the punctuation techniques of systemic counselling help to achieve the same goal – a redirection of focus (Bor et al., 1998).

No matter which orientation a counsellor uses, the techniques of that orientation usually help the patient to refocus in a more positive or useful direction. The goal of brief therapy is to maximize this ability within the patient. By enabling the patient to accentuate different aspects of the situation, the patient can develop the ability to examine a problem more productively. Thus, increasing focus promotes self-help – a primary goal of brief therapy.

Themes

The emphasis on self-help engenders the need to consider recurrent themes, rather than specific problems. Although some patients may simply require assistance on a particular difficulty, many patients will present with a problem that reflects a broader dysfunctional pattern in their lives. In order to encourage self-reliance, these patients will need to be made aware of such themes, as in this instance:

> Jeremy entered counselling seeking help with his marriage. He had been drinking one night with some friends when he made a pass at another woman. His wife overheard the remark and, despite Jeremy's pleas for forgiveness, she still felt extremely suspicious of his behaviour. Jeremy sought counselling because he felt he did not know which direction to take. He felt his wife was his best friend, but that he must have made a pass at this woman for a very good reason. As such, he was thinking of pursuing the relationship. The more he thought about the extra-marital possibilities, the more exciting the prospect became to him.
>
> Initially the counsellor and Jeremy worked to help clarify the situation and focused on the advantages and disadvantages of each scenario. However, during the course of these discussions, an underlying theme emerged. Jeremy had difficulties in almost all of his relationships, not just with the present situation with his wife. He believed that he was above the rules of other individuals and did not need to treat others as he would like them to treat him. As a result, counselling moved towards an exploration of this particular attitude and the repeated effects it had on people. By focusing on this theme, rather than any one particular relationship problem, the patient was able to make improvements in several areas of his life. Moreover, the patient was given the template to locate the possible

cause of future difficulties on his own. By discussing the underlying theme to Jeremy's relationship problem, he was able to address other relationships on his own.

Themes are an important aspect of brief therapy. In this way, patients achieve the ability to recognize and treat problems independently of the counsellor. This perspective is instrumental in producing long term change and, hence, in keeping the patient from repeatedly returning for counselling. Brief therapy is about handing over the role of counsellor to the patient. It is passing on the particular tools that each patient will need for future problems. For some, this will simply be the ability to make lists and prioritize, for others it will be increased coping skills, while for many it will be recognizing their own patterns of thoughts and behaviours. Whatever the instrument needed for each patient, brief therapy recognizes the importance of reinforcing such skills. It promotes independence and, just as importantly, it demystifies the process of counselling. When patients are able to become their own counsellors, counselling will no longer be some 'out there', mystical process. Instead, it will be a process that they carry with them into each situation everyday. It will promote prevention of mental health difficulties rather than finding solutions after problems have occurred.

Process

The brief therapist also needs to be aware of the processes taking place in session. These are often a powerful indicator of underlying themes. Process reflects what is happening in a session beyond content. It is about why a patient is responding in a particular way, how the session has strayed from the main problem at hand, or even how the counsellor is reacting to the patient. Process is everything taking place in the therapeutic encounter besides the flow of information and words. Such issues are often indicative of the processes which the patient faces and creates in everyday life. If the patient makes the counsellor feel uncomfortable in session, the patient probably makes others uncomfortable. If the patient reacts harshly to suggestions, this process probably occurs outside the session. These patterns can be very telling clues to the contributing factors maintaining a patient's difficulties. As such, a skilled brief therapist will always pay attention to content and to process.

Claudia was a shy young woman referred to counselling for depression. Although she seemed eager to be in counselling, she hardly made eye contact with the counsellor throughout the assessment. She agreed to meet with the counsellor for an initial six sessions and also agreed to use time in between sessions to supplement the in-session work. The first week Claudia completed her homework assignment and began to discuss her feelings of loneliness with the counsellor. Indeed, she appeared quite affable. However, during the following two sessions, it became evident that Claudia had not completed her between-session work, once citing that she was too busy and the next time saying that she had been in the process of doing the work when she had been distracted. The counsellor commented how it appeared as if the homework was not really all that important to her. Claudia promptly rejected his explanation. However, after some discussion, Claudia admitted that she did not feel she needed to be in counselling. She felt others were the cause of the problem and became quite angry that others were always pestering her to attend certain functions or volunteer her time. When the counsellor commented on her emotion, Claudia quickly reverted back to her quiet and amenable shy self.

From this behaviour, the counsellor began to suspect that Claudia's depression was a result of a passive–aggressive pattern of behaviour. She went to great lengths to create a favourable impression but this left her with little time to enjoy the things that she liked. She would accept unwanted invitations because she did not like to say 'no', and then would become sick at the last moment in order to avoid having to attend what she considered a boring affair. The same pattern had recreated itself in session. Claudia had agreed to do the homework assignment but failed to do any work because she felt it a waste of her time. After a few sessions, the counsellor and Claudia were able to discuss this pattern of behaviour and how it affected her life. Claudia began to recognize that this method of relating to others ultimately added to her depression rather than helping to deflect it. Together they began to identify instances where Claudia was likely to behave in this manner and to explore alternative methods of coping with unwanted requests.

By focusing on the process taking place in this instance, a potential impasse was not only overcome but used as a therapeutic tool. The process of the session helped to highlight a causal element of the patient's depression. Had the counsellor been unaware of the processes taking place, counselling might have served only to recreate and reinforce those patterns.

This example also emphasizes that crises or set backs in session are often critical markers which can be used to the benefit of the patient. For the brief therapist a 'set back' is a 'step forward' – it brings to the forefront unresolved issues which can only help to strengthen the patient's understanding of the problem. Difficulties and set backs are indicators of areas requiring further exploration or reinforcement, and the counsellor should be reminded of another famous adage, 'Adversity is opportunity'. Nowhere is this more true than in the counselling setting. As such, difficulties in session should not be swept aside for fear of losing momentum in the limited time available. Momentum can be gained from a crisis. It is the perfect opportunity to explore emotions, thoughts, patterns and values in session. Instead of impinging on time, it will help to maximize its use.

Likewise, the counselling relationship should never be sacrificed in order to compensate for limited time. As in all therapies, it remains of paramount importance. Limited time does not mean limited empathy. All patients need to be heard and brief counsellors should not under-estimate the power of good listening. As a patient tells his story, the counsellor needs to balance listening with more active interventions: recognizing that true listening can at times be a commanding inter-vention. Trust and a solid working relationship are invaluable, so even in brief therapy a counsellor needs to take the time to build the relation-ship properly. It should never be forfeited in an attempt to move the patient forward. Such efforts will rarely bring about the desired result and, in the end, time will be lost in having to re-establish a working trust.

Homework

Regardless of one's theoretical orientation, between-session work is an important consideration in brief therapy. Life outside the counselling room is full of learning opportunities and practise moments. In brief therapy these are viewed as essential to the patient's development. Therefore, between-session work is often used to help maximize the effects of such incidents. Using the time between sessions is a realistic approach to change. Patients need to learn that counselling is a process that can take place at any moment, not just in the counselling room, and that it is a process which they can effect on their own. In this way, between-session assignments help the patient to gain independence from the counsellor. They are also a way for the patient to try out new behaviours, test new thought patterns, and attempt further reflection in a 'real' environment, not just in the counselling room. The real test of any counselling is how well it prepares the patient for the difficulties encountered in everyday life. As such, between-session work can be seen as a fundamental feedback system which regulates the progress made in session.

A patient is not just in counselling for one hour every few weeks. Counselling is a *process* which suggests that it is something on-going, unfolding and continual. When people talk about seeing a counsellor, they will often use the phrase, 'I'm in counselling'. This reflects the belief that counselling is not just restricted to the time in session, but it is a commitment that encompasses a patient's whole life. In this regard, between-session work is something that takes place regardless of whether or not it has been assigned. Thus, activities set up by patient

and counsellor are a way of making this work more explicit and productive for the patient.

A variety of tasks are suitable for the patient between sessions. Each
counsellor will need to choose which assignment is most appropriate
given the patient, the problem, the work done in session, and the theoretical model being used. For some, homework tasks may be as simple
as, 'During the week, I would like you to think about what we have
done in session today and notice any changes or feelings that are a
result of our work.' For the more directive counsellor, specific assignments are often negotiated. These may include reading material,
writing thoughts or essays on a particular issue, filling out questionnaires, monitoring thoughts and behaviours, engaging in imagery
rehearsal, or performing certain behavioural tasks. The particular
assignment chosen will depend on the task at hand, so the work may
often vary from week to week. However, they will always need to be
tailored to the interests and capabilities of the patient.

The exact work should be negotiated by counsellor and patient
together. 'Assigning' work without discussion will do little to
strengthen the therapeutic relationship while decreasing the likelihood
that the work is completed. Moreover, the patient's involvement in
determining between-session work underscores the patient's role as the
agent of change. It helps the patient to both focus on the problem at
hand and to become more involved in the process of counselling.
Negotiation also facilitates the creation of appropriate and productive
tasks. The patient's input will help the counsellor to judge how much
can be managed, while the counsellor's view will help the patient to
extend his capabilities. Open discussion will also make certain that the
patient understands the task and has the opportunity to ask for clarification if needed. On a final note, if between-session work is set, it
should always be discussed during the following session. Just as a
therapist expects that the work will be done, the patient should also
expect that the work will be discussed. As an important part of the
therapeutic process, it needs to be treated as such: important issues are
never treated lightly or forgotten.

Ending a course of counselling

Ending a course of counselling properly is just as meaningful as the work
conducted during that counselling. It will need to be approached professionally and with careful thought. The end of counselling will be an
ever-present factor in brief counselling; however, this does not mean that
a counsellor can take it lightly. Patients will still need to be sufficiently

prepared for the end of formalized counselling. This will include addressing any fears or apprehensions that the patient may feel about finishing. It may also entail discussing feelings of loss spurred by the impending perceived loss of therapeutic support. Such feelings are a normal part of counselling and should be presented to the patient as such. The patient should also be made aware that difficulties and set backs are likely to be encountered after counselling has been terminated. The counsellor will both need to reassure the patient that such experiences are normal and prepare the patient to cope with these incidents.

The most formidable tool that a patient will have for this is his feelings of independence. Strategies that will help the patient to recognize and believe in his own abilities are critical, particularly towards the end of counselling. At this time, the counsellor should increasingly allow the patient to direct the course of counselling in order to underscore the patient's autonomy and new-found skills. The counsellor should focus attention on the positive changes made and actively address possible obstacles in the future. Indeed, a patient will need to know what to do should a relapse occur. Role-plays where the patient plays the part of the counsellor can be particularly useful towards the end of counselling, or similar activities that increase the patient's ability to think autonomously and therapeutically. The counsellor's role at this point is to contain the patient's fears and to prepare the patient for the future.

The practice's policy on returning to counselling should also be reviewed. Although this may have been discussed at the outset of counselling, patients will often need a reminder. As returning to counselling in a primary care setting is not always possible, follow-up visits as a standard feature of brief therapy are recommended. These may be specifically contracted or may result from strategic tapering of the sessions by counsellor and patient. Follow up visits will also help to encourage feedback from the patient. The more time a patient has to practise the skills, values or behaviours learned with the counsellor, the more accurate will be the feedback given.

As Dryden and Feltham note, 'There is no one right way to terminate counselling . . .' (1992: 171), and, in many instances, a counsellor will not be given the luxury of a formalized closure. However, whenever possible the approach to termination should be in keeping with patient need and the previous style of counselling. Patients may lose confidence towards the end of counselling and request additional sessions. They may even present a crisis at the 'eleventh hour'. Only under the most exceptional circumstances is the extension of counselling advised. The confidence that a counsellor shows in a patient despite the 'new' difficulties presented will only help to foster the patient's belief in his capabilities.

Conclusion

Counsellors need to be well prepared for the rigours and stresses inherent in the practice of brief therapy. This chapter provides only a small sample of the issues that need to be considered. A more in-depth analysis of brief therapy is beyond the scope of the present chapter but essential to any counsellor wishing to practise effective and proficient brief therapy.

Effective brief therapy is practised by choice. The philosophy recognizes the power of the patient and the value of time as a resource and therapeutic tool. The approach offers treatment which promises quick but efficient solutions. It enables the patient to resume and improve his life within a more condensed time period, thus reducing the amount suffered by the patient. It promotes the independence of the patient and increased patient awareness of the therapeutic process. In this regard, brief therapy approaches bestow a dignity and respect for the patient unparalleled by more long term counselling approaches.

Although long term approaches certainly have their benefits and are an essential part of mental health services, brief therapy is also a necessity. From this perspective, today's counsellors have a responsibility in developing the methods proposed here. As a permanent and integral part of mental health services, brief therapy must be approached with the same professionalism and rigour that have helped counselling gain a respected place in the world today.

Key points

- Change begins before the face-to-face assessment meeting.
- The assessment is therapy. Change has begun before the patient enters the counselling room and the therapist's task is to further this positive change during the assessment.
- Flexibility of the therapist is essential for the effective practice of brief therapy.
- Future solutions and past skill use are two effective interventions often used in brief therapy.
- Between-session homework is an important part of the brief therapy approach. It reflects the belief that much change occurs outside the counselling room.
- The termination of therapy should be handled with as much care as the course of therapy.

References

Bloom, B.L. (1981) 'Focused single session therapy: initial development and evaluation', in S.H. Budman (ed.), *Forms of Brief Therapy*. New York: Guilford Press.

Bor, R., Miller, R., Latz, M. and Salt, H. (1998) *Counselling in Health Care Settings*. London: Cassell.

Dryden, W. and Feltham, C. (1992) *Brief Counselling: a Practical Guide for Beginning Practitioners*. Buckingham: Open University Press.

Hoyt, M. (1995) *Brief Therapy and Managed Care*. San Francisco: Jossey-Bass.

Hudson-Allez, G. (1997) *Time Limited Therapy in a General Practice Setting: How to Help Within Six Sessions*. London: Sage.

Strasser, F. and Strasser, A. (1997) *Existential Time-Limited Therapy: the Wheel of Existence*. Chichester: John Wiley.

CHAPTER 10

THE COMPETENT PATIENT

Sheila Gill

There are hundreds of books about great counsellors but few if any works written about great patients. (Miller et al., 1997)

Books about theories of counselling abound. This particular book describes the 'doing' of counselling in the unique context of primary care, largely within the setting of general practice and this chapter concerns itself with looking at 'the patient' in the context of the general practice setting. It explores how the way the patient sees himself, and how the view held of him within this setting by different professionals, influences the therapeutic process. How the patient is viewed is critical to the whole concept of patient care and management because, after all, the world of counselling and the world of general practice would have no existence or meaning without 'the patient'! Indeed it might be frivolous (and profound) to speculate on what might happen to the world of counselling (and medicine) itself were all the patients to get well.

Fruggeri and McNamee pose an interesting question: 'What different scenario would we see if we change the point of view through which (traditionally) we see the patient?' (Fruggeri et al., 1991: 35–46). This chapter addresses the position that assigns competence not only to the professional, that is the doctor and the counsellor, but also to 'the patient', whose identity is not only defined by the problem he has or the distress that he currently endures. To assign competence to the patient is to reframe his self-image and relationships with others. To 'reframe' is to see a situation differently from the commonly held view of it (Watzlawick et al., 1977) and is without question one of the most impactful and affirming skills that counsellors have in their repertoire. Reframing a problem is achieved not by changing any of the 'facts' but by attaching new meaning to the patient's apparent problem. For example, a seemingly overprotective parent could also be viewed as caring, concerned and attentive. To reframe means to offer the patient a broader or different perception consistent with the view of a patient who said: 'I am more than my problems!' The fundamental principle of this perception is based on the view that the patient is competent and capable even in the midst of distress or illness. The implications of working within this framework can be challenging and demanding for the individual counsellor as traditional models of therapy attend to pathology and assign competence only to the counsellor. We are taught in our training as counsellors to focus on and to uncover 'what is wrong with the patient'.

The advantage of reframing the patient as one who is competent is that it broadens the scope of the counselling conversation. The whole of the patient's life becomes relevant to the counsellor and not just the presenting problem. Such an approach attempts to track the patient's path through life's ups and downs as well as sharing the pain and difficulties from more immediate events. It includes his cultural and family origins, as well as all the resources and survival skills he has employed up to the present. The whole constellation of relationships that have contributed to the patient's present circumstances inform the therapeutic conversation. The fact that the patient is viewed as one who is resourceful does not mean that the counsellor ignores the patient's present or past distress. Indeed, the orientation of the counsellor has to be characterized by a warm and positive appreciation of all facets of the patient's life. It is only when the counsellor truly takes on all the dimensions of the patient's pain that it is possible to respond to the patient in a way that validates both the story of his distress and his competence. Such a response can open up the possibility for the patient himself to begin to include in his own self-narrative examples of his resourcefulness as well as his distress. This approach has to be innovative and inventive. It places extra demands on the counsellor trained in the traditional 'error-deficit' approaches to problem formulation and resolution. As the patient begins to see himself differently he can quickly move on to making changes in his present situation. Once he begins to alter his perceptions he cannot easily return to the 'trap and the anguish of a former "view" of reality' (Watzlawick et al., 1977).

Factors that promote patient competence within the context of primary care

Successful outcome to counselling in primary care is usually grounded on a genuinely respectful and collaborative relationship between doctor, patient and counsellor. When a sound relationship between counsellor and doctor exists, there is usually a consensus of meaning about the counselling process. For example, when a patient presents himself as depressed, sick or in crisis it can require effort, skill and experience to see him as one who is also able and responsible. This is especially true when the patient himself may not be seeing himself as anything but 'in need' or in distress. To have the doctor and counsellor working together with a shared view that is respectful of the patient's ability to contribute to his own self-healing can powerfully contribute to a successful outcome for the patient.

The following case example illustrates a successful collaboration between doctor and counsellor.

Pedro, a 32-year-old South American man, had a wife and two children (aged 7 years and 6 months) and came to the GP requesting that their eldest son Vann should be seen by a psychiatrist. Pedro said that he and his wife no longer knew what to do with Vann. Their son was 'running wild'. Each day of the week Vann's teacher complained to Pedro about Vann's latest behaviour problems in the classroom. Pedro had begun to feel that there was something really wrong with their son. When the GP questioned Pedro it appeared that Vann's 'misbehaviour' had begun when they came to the UK, 18 months previously, and had worsened since the birth of his sibling. Prior to these events Vann had been a 'normal' boy in a 'happy' family. The family's command of English was very poor and Vann knew no English before he came to the UK. Appreciating the stressful impact such factors might well have had on Vann and his family, the GP felt that to refer Vann to the psychiatrist might be unnecessary and wished to avoid the stigma attached to such a referral. She suggested instead that the family should first share their concerns with the practice counsellor. This decision was based on the GP's understanding of the counselling process within the general practice, which was based on brief psychotherapeutic principles.

Pedro attended the first counselling session accompanied by his son Vann. Pedro began by describing the aspects of his son's behaviour that were causing him such distress. As he spoke the counsellor noted Vann looked upset. When she asked him what was he thinking of, as his father spoke about him, he replied: 'I did not know that I was causing this upset.'

Eight weeks passed since the time the referral had originally been made and the date of the first session. When asked by the counsellor whether anything had changed in that time, Pedro said that Vann's behaviour had improved a little. When asked what difference was noticed, Pedro said that the teacher complained less often about his son. The counsellor asked Vann what he had been doing that caused his teacher to complain less. Vann replied that because he was learning more English, he now understood instructions from his teacher better and so he was improving at mathematics. As he said this, Vann smiled and added: 'I could even do better at maths!'

What appeared to be dawning on Vann was his own contribution to the evolving circumstances. He had begun to see himself as an agent of change and he was becoming engaged in the therapeutic process. As the discussion developed between father, son and counsellor, an agreement was made that Vann would try 'to be good' [specific behaviours were discussed in detail] from Monday to Friday each week. On Fridays after school and at weekends, Vann would be free of these rules. Pedro promised his son that if he kept to this agreement he would take him to see *Space Jam*, a film Vann much wanted to see. The therapeutic endeavour was gathering its own momentum. The promise made by the father was seen by the counsellor as evidence of the father's returning sense of control in the situation. This was positively reinforced by the counsellor, as representative of the father's involvement with, and thoughtfulness on behalf of his son.

One of the effects of positive reframing is that it can instil hope of the possibility that change can occur. At this point in the conversation, both father and son were visibly more relaxed. They had begun to look at each other and exchanged smiles. To voice such observations, for example, how a person has begun to smile or has stopped clutching at the chair handles etc., can powerfully reinforce the first tentative signs of going in a desired direction.

The counsellor at this point addressed Vann and said that up to now they all had talked a lot about his changing his behaviour, could he now think what he might like his father to do that was different. Vann volunteered that his father occasionally used 'swear words'. It was agreed that the father would use such words at weekends only, the same days during which his son was 'allowed' to be naughty. If the father proved successful in this, Vann would consider accompanying him to the cinema! The idea of setting time boundaries for Vann within which different behaviours were 'allowed' was to encourage him to gain control over his own behaviour. Encouraging him to be free from rules at the weekends was intended to make the whole task 'possible'. The idea of asking Vann to reflect on his father's 'good' and 'bad' behaviour and to impose boundaries on his father, served two purposes. One was to 'upgrade' Vann's position within the family, by asking his advice. This could help to encourage Vann who was aware that his negative behaviour was causing distress. It was also intended to meet Vann at a boy's level – the level of irrepressible humour!

Father and son were seen for only one more session accompanied by mother and younger sibling. Five weeks had elapsed between sessions. At the second meeting father smilingly said that there were 'no more problems'. The family were feeling much happier. Vann's performance at school had improved and the teacher had hardly complained at all. Father and son had developed the habit of going to the cinema together to their great mutual satisfaction. When asked by the counsellor to what did he attribute such change, the father said that he had never thought of rewarding Vann for good behaviour himself. This was a simple and clear example of a patient using the therapeutic process and getting on with its implementation himself – in this instance, a joint effort between father and son.

Certain themes emerge in the above example that contribute to the promotion of patient competence. The GP had positively made the referral to the counsellor as a non-pathologizing option. The counsellor had reinforced this approach by focusing on the effort to change demonstrated by father and son in the first session, whilst at the same time giving precedence to the problem of Vann's disruptive behaviour. The counsellor had also 'trimmed' her intervention, to be brief, to suit the level of motivation manifested by both father and son. At the second session, it seemed to the counsellor that both father and son, indeed the whole family, were 'up and running'. In response to this perception the counsellor suggested that they end counselling sessions with the under-standing made explicit that the patients could return if and when they desired it.

The approach illustrated above could also be seen as illustrative of the essence of brief therapy which is based on the recognition and elic-iting of patient resourcefulness. This approach could be described as the search to 'underscore ... explicitly, the microstrengths within the [patient], strengths that are barely perceptible and that "could fly under the radar" of the [patient's] ability to notice' (Weber and Levine, 1995: 45–72). The focus is on what is already there in the present, and which is rooted in past experience. Sufficient hope was generated in the first session with Pedro and his son to perhaps contribute the energy required to maintain the effort until change itself took on its own momentum. In this case, an important pattern of reinforcement of good behaviour had embedded itself in the life of father and son, that is, going to the cinema together to their mutual satisfaction. The change towards self-agency achieved in the present was not a new entity, but was based on the family's past history of good relationships. The family had become re-united with their history of competence.

The case could also be illustrative of how the period that elapses between the time the referral is made and the time of the first coun-selling session can be utilized within the therapeutic process. On the one hand inevitable NHS waiting lists can be a cause of great anxiety for the hard-working professional counsellor. On the other, it can be useful to include such a waiting time into the counselling process in a positive way. The patient will have tried whatever he could do to alleviate distress during that waiting time. Positively connotating this effort, whether seemingly successful or not, can have a powerful effect on the patient. If the patient has not recovered nor been successful in reducing his distress, the effort involved in surviving in the midst of pain can still be attributed to patient skill and resourcefulness. Viewing the patient through a positive lens allows no effort to be wasted. This may not always be obvious to the patient himself and it can be com-pletely lost if the counselling is drenched in so-called 'problem talk'. It becomes a main counselling task to encourage an awareness of what

has already been achieved, which may include being 'well' or just surviving.

If the patient is encouraged to express his wellness, abilities and
resourcefulness it can powerfully reinforce these very qualities. Creating the context for the patient to be able to bring his abilities into
awareness becomes the counselling task.

Sally, aged 19, was referred to the counsellor with a history of depression,
attempted suicide and abuse of the family by her father 3 months earlier.
The counsellor was struck by the patient's 'easy' demeanour, quite at odds
with the description encased in the referral form. Sally immediately told
the counsellor: 'I've picked myself up and I'm fine.' The counsellor encouraged her to tell the story of how she had 'picked herself up'. The interview
became an account of the past 3 months of Sally's life, including the time
she had taken 50 paracetamol tablets and realized that she actually did not
want to die and how she dragged herself into the Casualty Department of
the local hospital, to the present day. Through the support of members of
her family and her GP she had reached the point where she was enjoying
life, was in a steady relationship and had returned to work. When the counsellor asked Sally if anything said in the interview had been useful to her,
she exclaimed: 'I had picked myself up, but until now I didn't know that I
had!' Such awareness is the result of joint work both by patient and counsellor.

This case illustrates the complementary roles of both patient and
counsellor in the counselling endeavour. The capacity to change lies
with the patient – the role of the counsellor lies in eliciting the patient's
narrative that includes both the story of the distress and the story of
how the patient has coped and grown. Competence, like distress, has a
history. This is the critical point. Current distress can so overwhelm the
patient (and attending professionals) that it can alter recall of past
behaviours/experiences (Hewson, 1991). This in turn reinforces a
patient's current attitude, which may be one of helplessness and a
feeling of incompetence in the present situation. Thus, the importance
of working with the patient to uncover past behaviours that are
examples of the patient's resourcefulness becomes clear. As suggested
earlier, it is only at the moment when the patient includes the story of
both distress and competence in his own self-narrative that he becomes
the agent of change, and this can lead him to new pathways of independent thinking and self-determination. Only in the recounting of her
tale did 19-year-old Sally become aware of her proven ability to survive
and to change.

In primary care, the counsellor has the unique freedom to be in the
position of re-framing the patient as able and competent, even if he is

unwell or distressed. When a fresh perception of the individual is offered by the counsellor to the patient, attention has to be focused too on how the context of the general practice setting may contribute to or detract from the promotion of such an alternative version of self. The following case describes how the counsellor can interact with other members of the multidisciplinary team so that the patient may be viewed more positively within the practice setting, which in turn is encouraging of the patient's competence.

The counsellor's introduction to her patient, Barbara, was dramatic. One of the practice receptionists approached the therapist minutes before the first interview and, in conspiratorial tones, exclaimed: 'I see who you've got this morning!' She raised her eyes and disappeared. Across the referral form the GP had written 'CHALLENGING CASE!'

Barbara, a 53-year-old single woman, had been married twice and had two separate families of three children. The GP diagnosed her as suffering from depression. Barbara had recently begun to demand higher doses of antidepressant medication. The situation was getting out of hand. The GP had worked out a very complicated regime on Barbara's behalf for the dispensing and collection of the medication. It involved the collection of daily prescriptions from the surgery's reception staff by Barbara. Minor mishaps in these daily arrangements were a regular occurrence. This often led to fiery outbursts between Barbara and the reception staff.

Barbara said she was unclear as to why she had been referred for counselling. However she was willing to try anything, as she was feeling so desperate. Early in the first session the counsellor said to Barbara that she was not going to discuss with Barbara her medical care as that was a conversation for Barbara to have with the doctor. Now that Barbara did not need to persuade the counsellor to focus on her medication, she was being invited to begin to talk differently. She then told a story of her survival in the face of tremendous pain and abuse by her first husband. When one of her daughters had disclosed to Barbara that she herself was being abused by Barbara's husband, Barbara decided to act. It took courage on her side to 'throw her husband out' as she had had a strict upbringing. Barbara married a second time, had three further children with her second husband, now aged 7, 9 and 11, and divorced again. Her living accommodation was hopelessly overcrowded. She shared her small bedroom with two of her children.

Having listened carefully to Barbara's story the counsellor said: 'How have you managed to survive as well as you do? Where do you get your strength from?' The use of a questioning technique in counselling is in itself valuable quite outside the content of the question itself, especially when offered in the context of warmth and appreciation of the patient's resourcefulness. In this case such a question affirmed Barbara's formidable coping ability whilst at the same time it validated her pain. Barbara's response to the counsellor's intervention was to dissolve into uncontrollable sobbing. She said she had not cried for years. It is easy for the counsellor to feel overwhelmed when patients show such obvious distress. The counsellor later asked Barbara to think about her priorities and which she most wanted to work on in sessions. Such an intervention is again affirming of Barbara's ability to assess and evaluate her own needs. Barbara had no difficulty in responding. Her priority was to improve her accommodation. She asked the counsellor if she would write to a housing officer on her behalf. Barbara was given a copy of the letter and perhaps for the first time saw herself positively described. This in itself further reinforced the affirming approach begun within the sessions.

The counsellor gave feedback to the GP and conveyed the fact that Barbara was a unique survivor given her past circumstances. None of the details of Barbara's story were revealed to the GP. Nor did the GP ask for them. The GP's interest was immediately alerted by this alternative view of this 'troublesome' patient. One positive description jogged the memory of another positive description. Gradually a more affirming picture of Barbara emerged within the practice setting. The practice administrative staff typed the letters to the housing service and obviously learned something about Barbara's difficulties. It is reasonable to surmise that this itself might have led to a change in attitude among staff members towards Barbara.

The task for the counsellor towards the end of the therapeutic endeavour is to find ways to help embed the new story of competence and resourcefulness into the patient's thinking. One way is to ask the patient to begin to gather the evidence from his own life, that supports the new story, by asking questions such as:

- Who else notices the change in your life?
- Who else has said similar things about how you are managing to the ones we have discussed?

It is evident at times that the changes the patient has made are deep and sustained changes when he begins voluntarily to recount stories that exemplify his skills and competence either in the present time or from his life in the past. In the case of Barbara, it emerged that her pet name in the family was 'The Survivor'. Up to this point, she had never dared to believe this version of herself which was at odds with the way she felt about herself. Barbara recounted too how, through counselling, she felt more comfortable in the practice setting, made easier by the fact that, as time had elapsed, Barbara's need for medication was greatly reduced. There was no further hassle attached to her presence in the practice. The GP's final words on Barbara were: 'She is no longer a problem.'

At times of change and growth, patients need to be supported within the general practice setting and in their own lives. Working in a team can be a real strength in this regard. As patients begin to show signs of recovery, it is important for the GP to be made aware of this so that he can contribute to supporting the patient in the direction of positive growth. This stresses the importance of 'interim reports' or the snatched word in the doctor's room that the patient appears to be doing well. Better still, a fuller discussion in a more secluded setting such as the counsellor's room. The counsellor should ask the patient's permission to recount to the doctor when improvement is noticed, though details of a patient's discourse to a counsellor are never a matter for discussion.

Factors that can inhibit a patient's competence within primary care

The case examples described above illustrate how a shared under-standing of the counselling process that is grounded on a basic recognition of the patient as a competent person, between GP and counsellor, can powerfully contribute to a patient's recovery. Working within time constraints in a general practice the counsellor cannot afford to confine the therapeutic process only to the conversation between counsellor and patient. Besides an awareness of how the practice setting itself can be influential on a patient's recovery and progress, factors such as the wider social/cultural system also need to be taken into account by the counsellor.

The next case example illustrates how factors outside the patient-counsellor relationship need to be addressed by the counsellor in order to promote patient well being and competence.

Diane was a 64-year-old woman suffering from depression and on anti-depressant medication for 10 years. She was referred to the counsellor by the GP. When the counsellor asked the GP what expectations he had of the counselling endeavour, the GP replied: 'She is a hopeless case.' This is not an altogether unusual response from busy and sometimes care-worn doctors, especially when their previous attempts to help patients are thwarted.

If the doctor makes a referral, conveying his sentiments, which nega-tively connotes the patient, the patient will invariably become aware of this. Such negative connotations need to be addressed by the counsellor with the patient and the referrer at some stage in the therapeutic endeav-our. This may pose a professional dilemma for the counsellor, where loyalty to both the patient and to the GP may seem irreconcilable. With Diane, these issues were addressed later rather than earlier in the course of counselling.

At the first interview, the first thing to be noted about Diane was her appearance. She was neat, trim and attractively dressed. Although torment was obvious in her face, her appearance was at odds with the mental picture the counsellor had conjured up following the GP's description of her as a 'hopeless case'.

Diane recounted a story of enormous distress, pain and endurance. She described the despair she felt at the time of her separation from her husband 15 years earlier. She was suddenly deprived of the comforts of a middle class existence and had found herself having to exist on state benefits. Diane's life's work over the years was dedicated to her children's upbringing. She received no financial help from her ex-husband.

Diane's husband had had ongoing affairs with numerous other women and had spent the family's income on his own needs. Diane had endured this, whilst caring for five children, until her youngest child was 15 years old. At that point in her life, Diane said that she had banished her husband from her life. Diane recounted her story as one of self-blame and guilt for ending her marriage.

Her story could be viewed as a story of distress with her as victim, or alternatively as a story of huge effort, dedication and a noble adherence to her own principles of love and commitment. Nuala O'Faolain, an Irish journalist, writes about the childbearing/childcaring years in terms of '. . . that fleeting time in the individual woman's life that has been extended to define womanhood altogether' (O'Faolain, 1996). This quotation in itself reflects popular gender ideas endemic in Western culture, which in themselves powerfully influence people's views of women, including GPs, counsellors and patients. Part of the therapeutic task in this case was to help Diane to unpick such ideas and beliefs about womanhood that had contributed to her guilt for having 'broken up' the family.

Accordingly, the counsellor asked Diane: 'Have you ever considered what might have happened to your children if you had not banished your husband?' This question affirmed Diane's decision to change her situation. At the same time it challenged the thinking on which her guilt was based. Its effect on Diane seemed to release her into a different way of viewing her situation. She replied, 'You know, I've been wanting to ask myself that question for years, but was afraid to do it until you asked it now.' At this point Diane smiled.

Diane wrote to the counsellor in order to change the date of the fourth session, because she was going on holiday abroad with one of her sons, the first holiday she had had in years. She wrote in her letter: 'I'm feeling much stronger.' When Diane came for the fourth session, she looked radiant. She not only had gone on holiday, but she had elected to do so instead of taking care of three grandchildren, which was expected of her in the summer holiday. 'I've earned it,' she said. This was something new and different for Diane. She recounted how she had arranged to go to exercise classes and relaxation classes twice a week.

Somewhere between the fourth and fifth session, which was a four-week period, Diane had begun to feel very low. Diane had also injured her back. She was seen by a doctor, who was not her regular GP. During this consultation, the doctor said that her back problem was related to her emotional problems. Antidepressant medication was subsequently increased. Following this visit, Diane had her fifth session with the counsellor. She said that being told that her problems were the result of emotional difficulties had made her feel worse. Diane felt angry. She had decided that instead of accepting the medical advice offered, she would visit her own GP and discuss a possible reduction in her medication.

As Diane spoke, it was clear that over the past few weeks, even though she had been feeling 'low', she was still resourceful. She had arranged a few days in the countryside as a break and had visited an osteopath who had relieved her back pain. The ability to identify difficulties, and seek and use appropriate help, is in itself an indication of the presence of coping resources. The counselling task at this point was again to affirm Diane's ability, even when she was feeling low, to take control of her situation now, as she had done many times in the past. The fact that for the first time Diane questioned her need for medication was also positive. She had developed new insight that led her to question the medical model that assigned her to the position of being a passive recipient of prescriptions for anti-depressant medication without any re-appraisal of her on-going condition.

If the GP could be encouraged to view Diane as a competent woman who sometimes feels low, but with a significant record of getting back on track, more than a 'hopeless case', it would help to sustain the changes achieved by the counselling process, long after the formal ending of counselling. As part of the normal procedure for giving feedback on completion of a case, the counsellor shared ideas about Diane with the GP. The GP was very open and willing to think differently about Diane and expressed his grate-fulness for receiving such feedback. His attitude changed to one of posi-tive appreciation of Diane and he began to reflect on Diane's dose of medication and the possibility of its reduction. The painstaking sharing of ideas about the meaning of the counselling endeavour, sharing news of progress and the meanings implicit in referrals and their significance for patients should be seen as an essential part of the work of a counsellor in general practice.

Conclusion

Whilst placing much emphasis on recognizing the patient as compe-tent, this chapter has attempted to illustrate how such an approach is successful only if it is embedded in a context in which proven tra-ditional counselling skills of warmth, genuineness and empathy are included. All of these skills help to create the context in which the patient's self-awareness grows so that his self-narrative includes both his pain and his competence. His present distress does not wipe out the memory of his past achievements. The skilled counsellor will also closely track the patient and ensure that feelings of vulnerability and sadness are expressed. As one patient, an author, said in counselling, 'Just because I am able to write books, people forget that I too suffer and am in need of help!' Reassurance was given to this patient that his pain and confusion were appropriate reactions to his loss. It did not mean that he was not competent and able. Indeed, the very fact that he had sought counselling and could express his pain was a measure of his on-going resourcefulness, even in distress.

To approach a patient only as one who is 'in need', is based on a tra-ditional psychotherapeutic and medical model. To view the patient as competent and resourceful, even when in distress, is an important modification of this perspective. This can have many dimensions and implications, both ethically and in terms of the efficient provision of psychological care of patients within a health care setting. One outcome of this approach for the patient may be that the gains derived from a brief therapeutic encounter with the counsellor may endure long after counselling as such has ended. The gain for health care workers is that a spirit of collaboration pervades the practice setting, which benefits everybody. In practical terms such an approach is in line with current medical practice which emphasizes the brief interventionist approach as one that can bring about effective and lasting change.

Key points

- A different view to that embodied by the traditional psychothera-peutic/medical model assigns competence to the patient as well as to the professional.
- Viewing the patient as competent enables the counsellor to work briefly and ethically.
- Such a view recognizes that the identity of the patient is not co-terminous with his problem and that the patient is competent even in distress or illness.
- The emphasis in this approach lies in finding ways to heighten the patient's awareness of his own self-agency and resourcefulness.
- It is possible for the counsellor to work in a collaborative way, with the primary care team, to promote a positive view of the patient that helps to enhance and prolong the beneficial effects of therapy.

References and further reading

Fruggeri, L. and McNamee, S. (1991) 'Burnout as social process: a research study', in L. Fruggeri, U. Telfner, A. Castelluci, M. Marzari and M. Matteeini (eds) New *Systemic Ideas from the Italian Mental Health Movement*. London: Karnac Books.

Hewson, D. (1991) 'From laboratory to therapy room: prediction questions for reconstructing the "new–old" story', *Dulwich Centre Newsletter*, 3: 5–12.

Hoyt, M. (1995) *Brief Therapy and Managed Care*. San Francisco: Jossey–Bass.

Miller, S., Duncan, B. and Hubble, M. (1997) *Escape from Babel*. New York: W.W. Norton.

O'Faolain, N. (1996) *Are You Somebody? The Life and Times of Nuala O'Faolain*. Dublin: New Island Books.

Watzlawick, P., Weakland, J. and Fisch, R. (1977) *Change: Principles of Problem Formation and Problem Resolution*. New York: W.W. Norton.

Weber, T. and Levine, F. (1995) 'Engaging the family', in R. Mikesell, D. Lusterman and S. McDaniel (eds), *Integrating Family Therapy: Handbook of Family Psychology and Systems Theory*. Washington, DC: American Psychological Association.

White, M. (1991) 'Deconstruction and therapy', *Dulwich Centre Newsletter*, 3: 21–40.

CHAPTER 11

COUNSELLING AND THE USE OF PSYCHOTROPIC MEDICATION

Jo Sexton

Counsellors employed in primary health care settings by definition work in a medical environment. They will usually be working alongside medical health practitioners familiar with both pharmaceutical methods of treatment as well as psychotherapeutic models of intervention. It is conceivable that a patient may have concerns regarding the form of treatment offered to him and these may influence his response to a referral for counselling. Patients who have been given psychotropic medication and who are also referred for counselling may decide to talk to the counsellor regarding issues such as side effects and addiction to their drug. Although it is not the counsellor's responsibility directly to advise the patient about medication she will be better placed to understand the effects of medication and related problems such as treatment compliance if she seeks to learn more about prescribed drugs.

When a patient presents to his GP with psychological distress, the GP may respond to the patient's difficulty in one or more of the following ways. He may :

1   Suggest strategies that the patient can use to help himself without any further professional intervention.
2   Refer the patient for counselling or psychotherapy.
3   Prescribe psychotropic medication.
4   Suggest a meeting with other members of the patient's family in order to gain a clearer understanding of the problem and to engage them in support and care.
5   Refer to another specialist, such as a psychiatrist.

The doctor's decision will be based on his experience, expertise and knowledge of the patient and available resources.

Psychological or behavioural problems are sometimes difficult to assess and diagnose accurately in the time-limited context of primary care settings and treatments may therefore be prescribed on the basis of trial and error. For instance, the GP may decide to intervene *medically* by prescribing psychotropic medication, *psychologically* by suggesting a course of counselling or *socially* by addressing lifestyle events and family context. An intervention in one area (biological, psychological or social) will inevitably have a ripple effect on the other two. This is the central principle of the biopsychosocial approach (McDaniel et al., 1992), namely that the biological cannot be treated in isolation from the psychosocial and vice versa.

The form of treatment offered to the patient will depend on

- the nature and severity of his problem;
- his and the GP's beliefs about medication and counselling;
- availability of time;
- relationships with the other professionals involved, such as nurses, specialists and social workers;
- attitudes of others, such as family, friends, employers and colleagues.

The GP may not have gained sufficient insight from one short interview with the patient to ascertain the most appropriate treatment for his distress. By spending more time with the patient the counsellor, possibly in collaboration with other medical practitioners, may have the advantage of being able to make other recommendations such as:

- using medication if it has not already been prescribed;
- referral to another professional;
- involving members of the family.

Any recommendations would be made in collaboration with all parties involved.

It is advantageous for the counsellor to have some knowledge and understanding of the range and effects of psychotropic medication commonly prescribed in a GP practice and their implications for counselling and the counselling relationship. This chapter will consider the following:

- The structure of the central nervous system.
- Types of psychotropic medication.
- Applications of counselling in conjunction with prescribing medication in general practice.
- Possible interactive effects of psychotropic medication and counselling.

The view taken by the author is that available treatments for psychological problems are varied and different approaches and combinations (for example, medication and counselling) can be beneficial.

Figure 11.1   The central nervous system

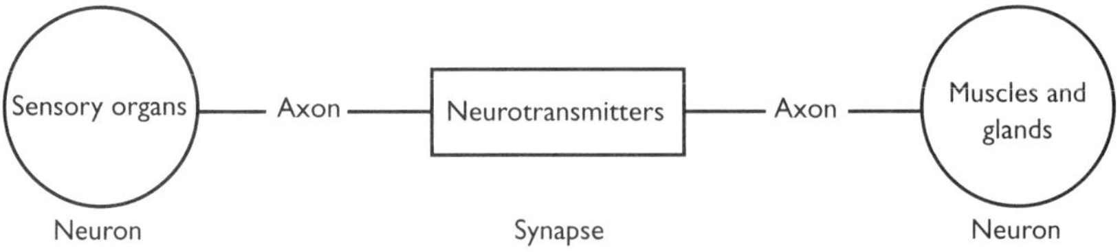

The central nervous system (Figure 11.1)
===

The central nervous system is composed of the brain and spinal cord. Thoughts, emotions and behaviours result from the activity of nerve cells which are called *neurons*. The 'activity' of neurons depends on a complex system of chemical reactions. These reactions are triggered by input messages in the form of nerve impulses from the sensory organs. These are the eyes, ears, taste buds, nose and skin. Output messages from the brain cells are sent to the muscles and glands which react accordingly. These reactions may be desirable, as when messages from the sensory organs result in the body feeling relaxed and at ease. Conversely, when the body feels tense and uncomfortable the changes are undesirable. Messages are transported from one neuron to another along *axons* measuring anything from one micro metre to one metre in length. An axon from one neuron connects with that of another at a point called the *synapse*. It is here that the main activity of the central nervous system takes place. Chemicals known as neurotransmitters are responsible for the transmission of messages between neurons; these include dopamine, serotonin, acetylcholine, gamma amino butyric acid (GABA) and norepinephrine. Each of these chemicals will have its own transmitters and receptors for the sending and receiving of messages in the form of electrical impulses along axons. It is these chemicals, situated in the synapses, that are mostly affected by psychotropic medication.

Psychological distress may occur when the activity between neurons produces unwelcome sensations. These adverse reactions may occur as a result of an internal malfunction of the central nervous system such as with endogenous depression, or to external stimuli that are too much for the system to cope with. Burnout is an example of this, that is, when someone has pushed themselves beyond their capabilities. Symptoms may take the form of mood change, problematic behaviour or physical illness such as irritable bowel syndrome.

Both medication and behaviour can affect brain chemistry. Medication works directly on one or more of the neurotransmitters in the synapse to restore a normal balance. The use of medication alone will not necessarily cure the patient fully from the problem. Medication that acts on brain chemistry can provide relief from symptoms. This in turn may enable the patient to develop and acquire better ways of coping, which may then bring about a more permanent cure. Sometimes symptoms can be so severe that they prevent a counselling intervention from working and drugs are required as a first aid measure before the patient can engage in a psychotherapeutic relationship. Take the following example:

For 6 months following her husband's death Elsie was completely overwhelmed by feelings of grief. She did not go out, hardly ate, and lost all interest in herself and other people. She was prescribed an antidepressant which helped to lift her mood and she was then seen by the counsellor for a total of six sessions spread out over 6 months. Elsie became more active and sociable. Five months after starting the medication Elsie had appeared to come to terms with her loss and was leading a more active life than she had done since before her husband's death. The medication was gradually reduced and Elsie continued to manage well.

The imbalance of the chemicals in the brain brought about by a causative factor and resulting in some form of mental distress may be treated by re-educating the mind without the use of medication. Counselling can facilitate changes to lifestyle by addressing and changing cognitions, emotions and behaviours.

Caroline had been devastated by her redundancy as a business manager. She took the matter personally, even though she was one of many who had been forced to leave their jobs. Apart from the practical concerns connected to her finances, she had lost a lot of self-confidence and self-esteem. She was opposed to taking medication as she felt that she wanted to resolve the issues on her own. This attitude became a starting block in counselling for her to regain the personal qualities that had appeared also to have been made redundant at the time when she lost her job.

There is a role for the counsellor in supporting distressed relatives/carers and also to recognize the signs and symptoms of acute psychological disturbance which require the patient to be urgently referred to a doctor. Psychotic illnesses, such as schizophrenia, can be controlled by medication and therapeutic support, but as yet there is no complete cure that can be offered to the patient with this condition.

Psychotropic medication

Counsellors are taught to assess psychological problems using formulations derived from

- the conceptual framework which they use in practice;
- their own professional training and experience;
- knowledge of biological processes in behaviour;
- observation of behaviour and affect;
- recognitions of patterns of behaviour;
- diagnostic or classification systems used in counselling and medicine.

Since there may be conflicting views about the nature of psychological problems among professionals, it is helpful to familiarize oneself with the Diagnostic Statistical Manual (DSM IV) produced by the American Psychiatric Association, which provides definitions of mental illnesses, as well as an up-to-date textbook of psychiatry (Rees et al., 1997).

Having assessed the patient (which may include a counselling assessment), the physician may decide to prescribe psychoactive medication which he will choose from one of four basic groups. (For drugs in common use, see Appendix.)

Antipsychotics

Psychotic illnesses such as schizophrenia and manic depression are characterized by the patient at times being out of touch with reality. A psychotic person may not see himself as being unwell but may be subjected to altered perceptions such as hallucinations and delusions. An example is someone who is paranoid and convinced that he is being followed though there is no definite evidence of this. Antipsychotic medications bind to the dopamine receptors but their precise mode of action is unclear. Other types of receptors and transmitters may also be involved. These drugs have many side effects and long term use of them can cause brain damage (Lickey and Gordon, 1983). In some cases they are prescribed in smaller doses for non-psychotic problems such as depression, anxiety or psychomotor agitation. The opposite of an antipsychotic is an amphetamine, which increases the release of dopamine and may produce schizophrenic-type symptoms in some individuals.

Antidepressants

Depression is often characterized by a persistently low mood as well as a combination of a range of biological symptoms such as insomnia, eating difficulties, lack of energy and digestive problems. The condition can be brought on by an event such as a relationship breakdown when the depression would be termed *reactive* or by an unaccountable imbalance in brain chemistry when it would be classed as *endogenous.*

The most common groups of antidepressants in use are tricyclics, monoamine oxidase inhibitors (MAOI) and 5HT reuptake inhibitors. The benefits of each are very individual, though some are more likely to treat certain conditions than others.

It is not always clear how these drugs work, but the most likely theory is that they reverse a deficiency of certain neurotransmitters. Antidepressants are not usually addictive, though patients can become dependent on them and so withdrawal should be gradual. They do not cause tolerance, which means that the patient does not have to keep increasing the dose to maintain the benefit. Initially the GP may start a patient on the minimum dose with a view to increasing it once any side effects have been dealt with. Possible side effects include nausea, dry mouth, palpitations, constipation, sweating, rashes, dizziness, headache and changes in sexual interest. These reactions are likely to be worse for the first few days of introducing the drug. Sometimes side effects can be a reason for the patient deciding to stop the medication.

Depending on the type of drug, it can take from 10 days to 3 months for the full benefit to be felt. For this reason, the patient must be counselled not to expect that it will be a 'morning after' pill that has immediate benefits. One advantage of the 5HT reuptake group is that improvement may be noticed sooner than with tricyclics or MAOIs. Patients who notice an immediate improvement after taking an antidepressant are most likely to be reacting to the placebo effect.

Risks to be aware of with antidepressants are:

1   Tricyclics can be fatal if taken in overdose. For the depressed patient this is especially important and it may therefore be preferable to make the patient regularly renew his prescription and to receive counselling rather than to send him away with several weeks' prescription with no provision for monitoring or follow-up.

2   MAOIs can be fatal if certain prohibited foods are eaten. The foods to be avoided are cheese, meat extracts such as oxo, yeast extracts such as marmite, alcohol, pickled herrings, banana skins, broad bean pods, flavoured textured proteins and any food that is not fresh. The combination of any of these foods with an MAOI can cause a massive rise in blood pressure that can prove fatal.

3   5HT reuptake inhibitors can have the effect of making the patient feel over-confident. This can sometimes have undesirable consequences such as when someone suddenly leaves his job or ends a relationship because the situation is not entirely to his liking. It has been known for people with suicidal thoughts to act them out having taken Prozac whereas previously they lacked the courage to do so (Kramer, 1994).

Tranquillizers (anxiolytics/hypnotics)

Tranquillizers are prescribed for anxiety, an irrational fear which may be caused by a phobia or a change in life events making it difficult for the person to relax. They are also used to remedy difficulties in sleeping, as a muscle relaxant and to aid in withdrawal of alcohol. The most commonly used (non-prescribed) tranquillizer and the one that has been in use the longest is alcohol.

Benzodiazepines were considered to be a major breakthrough in the early 1960s. The main danger with them is that they can be addictive. Prolonged use can cause side effects such as drowsiness, low blood pressure, skin complaints, confusion, urinary retention, changes in libido and light headedness. They work by potentiating the actions of GABA, an inhibitory transmitter. From the onset of treatment the brain works very hard to overcome the inhibition and the initial improved feeling of well being soon begins to fade. An increase in the dose of benzodiazepine can bring back the better feeling and greater dependence on the medication. Production of adrenaline is also affected and may cause quite frightening symptoms, especially during withdrawal (Armstrong, 1992).

For the reasons stated above, long term use of a benzodiazepine is to be avoided. Some antihistamines are used for insomnia but may cause daytime drowsiness. Some tranquillizers and hypnotics can irritate the stomach, cause dependence or react dangerously with alcohol.

Lithium

Lithium is prescribed for manic depression (bipolar affective disorder), a condition where episodes of elevated mood alternate with depression. An antipsychotic or antidepressant is sometimes included in the treatment (Lickey and Gordon, 1983).

Unpleasant side effects with some mind-altering medication can sometimes cause more problems than the illness itself and withdrawal can be difficult (Lickey and Gordon, 1983). A patient may lose any sense of personal motivation to resolve problems since he sees the illness as a medical problem beyond his control and assumes that he is at the mercy of the pills (Hammersley and Beeley, 1992).

Past experiences and family beliefs (Burnham, 1986) may determine the willingness of a patient to use medication.

Shirley was a middle-aged woman who was extremely depressed as a result of her life appearing to be 'a total mess'. She had become agoraphobic, obsessed with cleanliness and had physical problems which included skin complaints, stomach cramps and excessive perspiration. The counsellor felt it would be appropriate for Shirley to be prescribed medication in order for her to be more amenable to the psychotherapeutic process. When this was suggested Shirley indicated that she was strongly opposed to the idea. Upon further exploration of her feelings, it was discovered that since she was a child her mother had been very depressed and had become dependent on various medications. On more than one occasion she attempted suicide by taking an overdose of prescribed medication. Since Shirley first became depressed members of her family had impressed upon her the fact that she would end up like her mother if she started on psychotropic medication. The counsellor explained to Shirley the difference between the tranquillizers that her mother took and modern day antidepressant drugs that could help her to feel better and on which she would not become addicted.

The full range of available psychotropic drugs is listed in *Mimms* the catalogue of medical specialities issued to doctors, and the *British National Formulary*, issued regularly by the British Medical Association. Both are usually available in GP practices.

Applications of counselling in combination with medication in general practice

Each counsellor will have her own preferred way of working. Some may prefer to stay strictly within one discipline or to encompass different approaches. Aspects drawn from different orientations will be considered in working with patients referred by their GP.

Transference and countertransference

The relationship between the patient and doctor can have a profound effect on how the former accepts any help from the latter. If the relationship is such that the patient is able to put his trust in the doctor, he is more likely to accept help that is offered. This kind of a relationship would mean that there is a positive transference for the patient with his doctor. If the patient is amenable to what the doctor advises, his countertransference for the patient is likely also to be positive, creating a more conducive relationship for a successful outcome of treatment. Within this scenario, prescribing medication and/ or referral for counselling may be taken as being an extension of himself, something good and to be trusted.

Sometimes the positive transference can get in the way of successful treatment. The patient may not want to disappoint the doctor by admitting that medication or referral to another specialist is not helping. He may want to hang on to his problems in order not to lose the support of the doctor. If the patient's transference is negative, not only is the doctor's help likely to be rejected but anxiety and depression will possibly be heightened. This may in turn affect the doctor's countertransference of wanting to be of help to his patient .

Splitting

When two professionals are involved with a patient the temptation to split may result. Jacobs (1992), for instance, describes how a patient may use a defence mechanism of splitting object images of the two therapists, idealizing one and devaluing the other, and/or telling different things to each. The patient may decide to take the prescribed medication and reject the counselling or vice versa. In order to minimize the effects of splitting, open communication between the three parties is encouraged .

Collaboration

An example from the author's own work will demonstrate how collaboration between doctor and counsellor can benefit the patient. In this example the counsellor had not been given full details of the patient's medication.

Paul was initially seen for counselling a year ago in response to extreme anxiety. It was agreed that he would receive 12 sessions of counselling. At the end of these he felt better able to cope with his anxiety although it was still a problem to him. He would have liked to continue counselling on a private basis but limited finances did not permit him to do so. One year later Paul was re-referred for further counselling. On the second of these occasions he mentioned his lack of sleep despite using sleeping pills. Although the counsellor always made a point of checking with patients whether they were on medication, in this case the patient had not previously mentioned his sleeping pills, thinking this was not significant. When the counsellor found out that the pills were a benzodiazepine and that the patient had been taking them for over 25 years she realized they could be exacerbating the patient's symptoms. The counsellor mentioned this to the doctor who agreed to help with a withdrawal programme.

Collaboration helps everyone involved with a patient to acquire a fuller picture and to work together to provide a more beneficial treatment programme. It avoids the patient being given conflicting advice, and including the patient in the collaboration process gives him a sense of personal empowerment (Hammersley and Beeley, 1992).

Drug dependency

Patients who have become dependent on tranquillizers can be assisted by counselling as part of a withdrawal programme. Guidelines on the use of medication during withdrawal can be obtained from the Council for Involuntary Tranquillizer Addiction (Armstrong, 1992). During withdrawal, symptoms for which the medication was originally prescribed may return with a vengeance. Support from a counsellor can prove invaluable by offering guidance, reassurance, understanding and advice on diet, exercise and relaxation.

Within the therapeutic relationship, the counsellor may come up against the feeling of 'being stuck'. This feeling may be a reflection of the patient's sense of being stuck on medication and as such may need exploring (Hammersley and Beeley, 1992). Collaboration between the doctor and counsellor should enable an effective withdrawal programme for the patient.

Withdrawal from psychotropic medication that does not cause dependency, such as antidepressants, should be undertaken gradually. Although the patient is not addicted to the drug he may miss the beneficial effect if it is withdrawn too quickly. 5HT reuptake inhibitors such as Prozac can have the effect of making someone feel better than they could normally expect to, and so without the drug normality can feel like a disappointment (Kramer, 1994).

Behaviour

The counsellor who adopts a more directive approach may find that patients are helped by processes such as cognitive behavioural tasks, relaxation and visualization techniques. There is a plethora of material available in the form of self-help audio tapes and manuals available from bookshops to assist with these.

Problems such as anxiety and panic attacks seem to respond particularly well to more directive approaches, especially if linked to psychodynamic principles. By teaching the patient how to manage his symptoms he will be helped to resume normal activities. Examining the factors leading to the development of the problem will reduce the like-lihood of the problem resurfacing in the same way or indeed in some other guise. The author has found that patients have shown greater control over anxiety attacks by learning correct breathing techniques than by taking prescribed beta blockers.

Suicide

The counsellor, by spending more time with the patient and having a greater psychological understanding of him, may sometimes be in a better position than the doctor to know when there is a risk of poten-tial suicide. Tricyclic antidepressants can be fatal in overdose due to the increase in heart rate that they produce (Armstrong, 1992) and there-fore they should only be prescribed in small quantities if there is any risk of suicide. 5HT reuptake inhibitor drugs are less likely to cause death with overdose but may make the patient more inclined to try to attempt suicide due to the increased sense of confidence that they can produce (Kramer, 1994).

It is not uncommon for suicidal ruminations to be acted upon at a point in time when a depressed person begins to recover. This phenom-enon is due to extreme depression, often rendering the sufferer un-motivated to help himself even to the point of ending his own life when that might be seen as the only way out of his despair.

Possible interactive effects of psychotropic medication and counselling

Counselling and drug treatment are each effective ways of helping dis-tressed patients. Sometimes one method will have an advantage over the other. Counselling alone is likely to benefit those with a transfer-ence neurosis, personality disorder and various forms of depression. Medication on its own can help to relieve symptoms of mania, depres-sion, insomnia, anxiety and schizophrenia. For most problems a combi-nation of both kinds of treatment may prove to be beneficial.

Due to the time taken for referral and an appointment being offered, some time may have elapsed between the patient seeing the doctor and then the counsellor. Depending on whether or not the doctor prescribed medication as well as counselling the patient may or may not keep the appointment with the counsellor. Figure 11.2 depicts what may happen as a result of being offered counselling either with or without medi-cation. From the diagram it can be seen that the patient can opt to

Figure 11.2   Options for a patient referred for counselling by a doctor

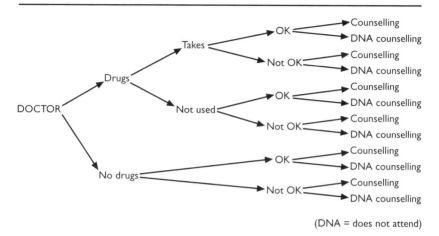

(DNA = does not attend)

respond in various ways as to whether the doctor prescribes drugs as well as counselling. These intermediate experiences can affect the dynamics of counselling (Lickey and Gordon, 1983).

A patient who is offered medication for his psychological distress may see it as a 'quick fix cure'. For some, this might be the desired treatment while for others they may feel 'fobbed off' since the focus is only on the symptom and not on any possible underlying cause. If a doctor is able to let the patient talk over his problem this on its own can sometimes be all that is required. Other patients may need more time to talk about their distress and benefit from the support of a trained counsellor.

If the patient has been prescribed medication as well as counselling, the counsellor should be aware of this and of the patient's attitude towards the medication. The patient may have concerns about becoming addicted to medication, especially if he has had experience of someone who is or has been drug dependent. He may have started taking the medication and have had unwelcome side effects. If the counsellor has some knowledge of the effects of psychotropic medication she can help to reassure where appropriate. It will often be the case that patients who have opted for counselling often want to help themselves without pharmacological assistance. The following transcript illustrates how a counsellor talked to a patient who was depressed and lacking in confidence about her reluctance to use medication.

Counsellor: Was it your idea to come for counselling?
Patient: The doctor suggested I should see you. He also gave me a prescription for Prozac but I don't want to take pills.

Counsellor: You don't?
Patient: I prefer to sort things out myself.
Counsellor: You prefer to manage on your own?
Patient: I've always been independent.
Counsellor: Always! Can you remember when you were first aware of being independent?
P: [*after some thought*] Since I was a teenager, when I was about 15. [*After further thought*] When I was very young and I used to fall over I was told off by my mum for making a lot of fuss. My sister was never any trouble and people used to say that I should be good like her.
C: So what did your mum say to you when you used to fall over?
P: She used to say that I should learn to look after myself and to not make a fuss.
C: And it was when you were about 15 that you changed.
P: Well that was when my periods started and I used to have really bad stomach aches. I persuaded my mum to buy me some Feminax but whenever I took them she used to pull a face. I knew she thought I ought to just put up with the pain.
C: What was that like for you?
P: I felt a failure.

The counsellor was able to guide the patient to see that her sense of being a failure if she used medication was connected with her mother's strong beliefs against it. The possible effects of medication on her depression were explained. She was also helped to see how if she felt better about herself and her situation as a result of taking medication this would positively impact on other aspects of her life.

Other concerns about medication that patients may express:

- 'I will become addicted.'
- 'I won't be able to drink/drive.'
- 'I might put on weight.'
- 'What will people think?'
- 'I've heard it can affect my sex life.'
- 'I don't want to be a zombie.'

In some cases, depending on the medication, these concerns may be justified. The counsellor can assist the patient in finding the best way to come to terms with any side effects and to minimize their impact on his life. If the counsellor feels that the patient is being detrimentally affected by attitudes to medication from other people it might be appropriate to address these in a session with the parties involved.

The counsellor may have a concern that a doctor prescribes psychotropic medication too freely and sometimes unnecessarily. It may be that the doctor is unaware of the efficacy of counselling alone or that he assumes patients like to be given a prescription to take away with them. Conversely, the counsellor may feel that medication is sometimes not prescribed when it could be beneficial. Talking through such concerns with the doctor could improve collaboration and care.

The counsellor should, in relation to medication, be aware of her own thoughts on the combining of drug treatment with counselling. The counsellor may have had personal experience of using psychotropic medication herself or have known other people who have. Experiences such as these may bias her one way or the other. She could have been influenced by attitudes conveyed in her training, approaches to counselling or other sources of information. A counsellor not familiar with the Biopsychosocial Approach is more likely than not to see herself and the GP as working separately and there might even be competitive aspects to their relationship. Such a situation could encourage the counsellor to see the pharmacological intervention as interfering with her own treatment approach. To have the counsellor and the GP leading the patient in different directions is undoubtedly not conducive to a good therapeutic experience for the patient and consequently is unlikely to produce a positive outcome in terms of treatment.

In a situation where a patient is both taking medication and also receiving counselling it is harder to determine whether a change in symptoms is the result of medication or of counselling. When there is an improvement in symptoms it may be appropriate for the GP to suggest a reduction or cessation in medication while the counselling continues to ensure that any underlying issues have been dealt with. If symptoms persist or worsen it is wise to question the suitability of the medication or counselling since one or other may be indicated in the deterioration. An example would be someone who has been anxious and is becoming depressed. Anxiety can sometimes be a defence against depression which in turn can be an avoidance of anger (Clarkson, 1995). For repressed anger to be resolved it is often necessary to work through the anxiety and depression. The counsellor, possibly in collaboration with the doctor, will need to discern the most likely reason for an apparent downturn in recovery and will need to consider the most appropriate support for the patient.

The following vignettes illustrate how medication can hinder or enhance the treatment of a patient who is also having counselling.

Nick had been seeing the counsellor for 3 months because of obsessive compulsive behaviour. He was not taking any medication. There had been a gradual improvement in his symptoms. One week he reported that his ritual checking of locks, switches etc. that had been his main difficulty had all but stopped. However, he had now for no apparent reason begun to feel depressed. He discussed with the counsellor the issues involved and wondered whether he should see his doctor for some antidepressant medication. The counsellor explained that the depression could be a necessary stage for him to go through as part of his recovery (see above). Nick decided not to ask for drug treatment. Two weeks later he expressed a lot of anger, which he had previously not allowed himself to do. This was the final stage in what turned out to be a successful outcome of counselling. Had Nick taken antidepressants when he felt in need of them it is possible that his treatment could have been impeded.

Margaret also had a problem of obsessive compulsive behaviour which in her case was manifested in ritual hand washing associated with a fear of contracting HIV. After several weeks of counselling her problem showed no signs of abating and she was becoming increasingly depressed as her symptoms began to affect her day-to-day living. It was agreed that the counsellor would talk to Margaret's doctor. The doctor suggested a course of Prozac which Margaret was willing to try. The medication appeared to be effective, her mood lifted and she could see a way forward with her new life.

In the counselling sessions she seemed more willing to open up about constraints put upon her by her family. Margaret was observed to change from being a shy, timid individual to a more confident young woman. The Prozac was later withdrawn and the frequency of her hand washing ritual was significantly reduced.

Conclusion

Psychotropic medication and counselling both affect the chemistry of the central nervous system. They can be used separately or together as treatment for psychological impairment. The benefits of using one or both forms of therapy will depend on the patient's problem, his relationship with the practitioners and his personal preference for treatment.

The physician will use his knowledge of medicine to determine the most suitable medication for his patient. To some extent his choice of drug will be a case of trial and error within a particular group. When counselling is used instead of or as well as medication the counsellor will aim to help the patient to deal with his problems from a psychological standpoint. Counselling addresses underlying causes of distress, relationship difficulties and changes of behaviour whereas medication works specifically on symptom relief.

When medication and counselling are used in conjunction with each other good collaboration between the doctor and counsellor is imperative. If one practitioner works in isolation from the other 'splitting treatment can be like one person steering a car with another using the throttle with no communication between them' (Ostow, 1993: 166). In some cases a patient may need counselling in order to benefit from medication and/or may need medication to benefit from counselling.

Finally, spontaneous recovery may happen without the assistance of any kind of professional help.

Key points

- Input messages from the sensory organs activate neurons in the central nervous system which determine thoughts, feelings and behaviours.
- Psychotropic medication affects the chemistry of the central nervous system allowing changes to thoughts, feelings and behaviours.
- Counselling can change thoughts, feelings and behaviours which can affect the chemistry of the central nervous system.
- Transference issues between the patient and doctor can affect the former's decision about using medication and having counselling.
- The system of which the patient is a part will affect attitudes to counselling and medication.
- Some conditions will benefit more from a combination of medication and counselling.
- Good collaboration between the mental health care professionals will help to determine the best form of treatment.
- Recovery can sometimes be hindered by using a combination of treatments.

References

Armstrong, P. (1992) *Back to Life*. Liverpool: Print Origination Ltd.

British National Formulary (1996) London: British Medical Association.

Burnham, J. (1986) *Family Therapy*. London: Tavistock.

Clarkson, P. (1995) *The Therapeutic Relationship*. London: Whurr.

Hammersley, D. and Beeley, L. (1992) 'The effects of medication on counselling', *Counselling Journal*, August: 162–4.

Hoyt, M.F. (1995) *Brief Therapy and Managed Care*. San Francisco: Jossey–Bass.

Jacobs, M. (1992) *The Presenting Past*. Buckingham: Open University Press.

Kramer, P.D. (1994) *Listening to Prozac*. London: Fourth Estate.

Lickey, M.E. and Gordon, B. (1983) *Drugs for Mental Illness*. New York: W.H. Freeman.

McDaniel, S., Hepworth, J. and Doherty, W.J. (1992) *Medical Family Therapy: a Biopsychosocial Approach to Families with Health Problems*. New York: Basic Books.

Mimms Monthly Index of Medical Specialities. London: Haymarket Publishing Services.

Ostow, M. (1993) in M. Schachter (ed.) *Psychotherapy and Medication*. New Jersey: Jason Aronson.

Rees, L., Lipsedge, M. and Ball, C. (1997) *Textbook of Psychiatry*. London: Arnold.

Appendix: Psychotropic medication in common use

Generic name	Trade name
Antipsychotics	
Phenothiazines	
chlorpromazine	Choractil, Largactil, Thorazine
prochlorperazine	Buccastem, Stemetil, Vertigon
trifluoperazine	Stelazine
Antidepressants	
Monoamine oxidase inhibitors	
isocarboxazid	Marplan
phenelzine	Nardil
tranycypromine	Parnate
Tricyclics	
dothiepin	Prothiaden
lofepramine	Gamanil
amitriptyline	Tryptizol, Domical, Amitril
5HT selective reuptake inhibitors	
fluoxetine	Prozac
paroxetine	Seroxat
sertraline	Lustral
Tranquillizers	
Benzodiazepines	
diazepam	Valium
chlordiazepoxide	Librium, Tropium
lorazepam	Ativan
Hypnotic	
zimovane	Zopiclone
Lithium	
lithium carbonate	Priadel, Lithonate

CHAPTER 12

TRAINING IN COUNSELLING IN PRIMARY HEALTH CARE

Gilly Pembroke

Until recently, it has been possible for just about anyone to call them-selves a counsellor, and to set themselves up in practice with perhaps only the most basic of counselling skills training. It was also relatively easy to offer counselling to an agency or in private practice where coun-selling was in demand. It is true that some people can be helped by the provision of a sympathetic listener (such as that given by a relative or friend), but it is also possible that although this may give transient relief, many may simply find their problem aired, but unresolved. Of greater concern is the inadequately trained counsellor making an in-correct assessment, perhaps failing to detect severe psychological dis-turbance such as psychotic disorder or personality problems, and who subsequently may intervene in a way which exacerbates the situation. Poorly trained 'colleagues' may at best be ineffective, but at worst be dangerous, and are largely responsible for the poor light in which coun-selling is sometimes regarded.

Since the 1950s, under the influence of Balint and others, GPs have attempted to incorporate various forms of formal psychotherapy into their consultation techniques with limited results. Demands on time, underdeveloped skills and training, and the inadequacy of the psycho-therapy method itself were the most commonly quoted reasons for lack of success. In addition, the introduction of psychotherapy into the complex doctor/patient relationship was seen to destabilize that special bond.

The 1970s saw the introduction of clinical psychologists into health care and some GPs referred patients to them. However, the service was at best patchy and under-resourced and it soon became clear that if such therapy was to be more widely available in primary care, it would have to be offered by other members of the team (France and Robson, 1986). Long waiting lists, inadequate funding, and in some areas no option for onward referral compounded the problem and led to GPs turning to lay counsellors for help in the early 1980s. For some time, help of a sort had been undertaken in surgeries by do-gooders, friends or relations or even the spouse of a GP, though demands for higher levels of professionalism increased.

Counsellors have proved a valuable resource in working with patients in GP practices (Bor et al., 1998; Pembroke and O'Sullivan, 1994), and there is now well-documented research to demonstrate the effectiveness of counsellors' work across a wide range of problems. With the demand for increased professionalism and the requirement that counsellors demonstrate they have received adequate training and are in on-going supervision, it is reasonable to suggest that in the new millennium counselling will become a recognized profession.

To date, however, health authorities have not been uniform in their individual recognition of counsellors as an integral part of the primary care team and funding of such a service has at times been non-existent, while at others inadequate. In order to cope with the complex needs of patients, counsellors have been recruited by GPs, but a lack of nationally recognized training criteria has resulted in wide variation in standards of practice and efficacy of treatment and care. Further complications arise from the wide range of courses available, from certification after only one week of training to Postgraduate Diploma or even Masters level taken over three to four years. This makes selection of counsellors very difficult as potential employers may be unable to determine the level and breadth of their training.

It is a welcome relief that with the growing pressure from voluntary and professional bodies such as BAC (British Association for Counselling), BPS (British Psychological Society) and UKCP (United Kingdom Council for Psychotherapy) regulation is now being introduced into training and practice. A need to bring the UK into line with the European Community regulations has also provided an impetus for professionalization. Although there is still no statutory body which regulates training, qualification and registration, a voluntary register of suitably qualified independent counsellors has just been established in the UK. This Register is only accessible to accredited members of BAC or COSCA (Confederation of Scottish Counselling Agencies) or on a temporary basis to counsellors who are sponsored through a Registered Sponsoring Organization (RSO), but only for the duration of their contract with such an organization. This is an important step in the move towards statutory registration.

Such regulation not only serves to protect patients from incompetence, but also addresses such issues as accountability and codes of ethics, both of which serve to enhance good practice. On-going professional training is not only in the best interest of the patient, but also serves to increase effectiveness and confidence in the counsellor. It enables counsellors to exchange ideas with colleagues, provides a context for supervision, the opportunity to share skills, and stimulates personal growth and development. On-going training also gives the counsellor further credibility, broadens her experience and widens her knowledge base. As a result, she can collaborate far more effectively with her colleagues and other professionals at all levels.

This chapter examines some of the issues relating to the training of counsellors and provides some pointers towards the additional specialist training that is required to work effectively in a primary health care setting.

The personal qualities required

A primary care health counsellor will need to have good knowledge of psychological problems and excellent therapeutic skills. In addition, administrative skills are required to keep records and compile reports for her colleagues when required. She must be honest and reliable, able to work under pressure and to manage waiting lists efficiently. She will also need to be in good health so that she can, with the best of intention, be regularly and consistently available for her patients. She needs to be able to communicate effectively with patients and colleagues, and a basic understanding of medical jargon is certainly an advantage.

Warm and empathic, a general practice counsellor needs to be able to work with patients where problems are neither immediately apparent nor clearly defined. She must survive amidst uncertainty and unclear direction, and within the muddle and confusion that can exist in multi-disciplinary teams. She will need to be adept in problem-solving without necessarily having a strong urge to take responsibility for others' problems and implementing appropriate solutions.

A primary care counsellor needs to understand that entering into this specialty carries with it enormous commitment, not only to her practice and the patients within it, but also in relation to time and discipline to maintain and continue supervision, personal therapy and on-going professional development. She will also need to be able to manage her own stress levels. She therefore must be able to balance the composition of her life between work and relaxation, and above all she needs a readily available and generous sense of humour.

Training courses are mindful that some prospective counsellors enrol on courses to provide them with a therapeutic arena in which their own problems can be explored. In such cases, training should be deferred until the trainee has undergone her own personal therapy, and at least to the point where personal issues no longer interfere with practice.

Networking

Not only will the counsellor need to be able to collaborate successfully with the GPs, she will also have to be competent in networking with all members of the community mental health team. Each professional group (for example, psychiatrists, psychologists, CPNs) may have a different perspective on problems and professional roles. This requires a working knowledge of their respective roles and functions, and of when it is appropriate to enlist their help.

Knowledge of a wide range of approaches

Because of the diversity of presenting difficulties that are likely to be referred, the counsellor will be more effective if she is able to draw on a number of therapeutic approaches. Though evidence from research has been established, it has been shown that different conditions respond better or more quickly to different therapeutic approaches. No one approach is considered adequate for all problems, patients and situations. Clinical realities have come to demand a more flexible, if not integrative, perspective (Beutler, 1983). More than 400 different counselling approaches and orientations have now been described, but only the more conventional and better documented ones are referred to in this chapter. It is perfectly acceptable for a counsellor to begin her training in any of the approaches given below. Training courses will teach their own favoured theory, but usually incorporate thinking and practice in most, if not all, of the following approaches:

Psychodynamic

Based on the theories of Freud, this approach is based on the belief that it is our early experiences which influence our present attitudes and behaviour. Through interpretation, and the making of links between past and present, a patient can be helped to let go inappropriate thoughts and behaviour. For further information on this approach the reader is referred to *Psychodynamic Counselling in Action* by Michael Jacobs (1991).

Person-centred counselling

Carl Rogers described this approach in the 1930s and 1940s which is based on a belief that if certain core conditions (congruence, unconditional positive regard and deep empathic understanding) are provided in a therapeutic context, the vast resource for growth and change which is possessed by every person can be activated. Since the counsellor works with what the patient presents, and examines issues in the context of present functioning, there is less chance of destabilizing a vulnerable patient through the exploration of too painful earlier events. Low self-esteem, which may lead to feelings of depression, is especially amenable to this approach. For further information the reader is referred to *Person-Centred Counselling in Action* by Mearns and Thorne (1988).

Cognitive-behavioural therapy

This approach, which is used widely in NHS settings by psychologists, was modified by Beck in 1976. Sessions are structured and usually include goal-setting and homework assignments. This approach has been shown to be particularly effective in the treatment of phobias and obsessive–compulsive disorders, depression and anxiety. For further reading, consult Beck et al. (1979) *Cognitive Therapy of Depression* and France and Robson (1986), *Behavioural Therapy in Primary Care*.

Family systems theory

The importance of learning a family systems approach when working within the context of a general practice cannot be overstated. Problems are viewed in the context of relationship dynamics, which in turn are organized around a series of beliefs. Specialist training in family and couple counselling is required as the dynamics are far more complex than when working with individuals. The reader is referred to *Medical Family Therapy* by McDaniel et al. (1992) and *Family Systems and Chronic Illness* by Rolland (1988).

Solution-focused therapy

Described by Steve de Shazer in 1985, this approach emphasizes the patient's strengths and resources without the need to focus on their pathology, their history or the cause of the problem. Since significant change can frequently be produced in a very short time, brief therapy has much to recommend it in a busy GP practice where time is of the essence or the number of sessions is limited. However, careful assessment is required since not all patients are suitable for such an approach. More information is available in *Clues – Investigating Solutions in Brief Therapy* by Steve de Shazer (1988), and also in Chapter 8.

Knowing which approach to adopt for any particular patient and problem, and having an extensive 'toolbag' from which to choose, is going to be useful, if not essential. It is worth bearing in mind, however, that it is possible to work successfully using an integrative or eclectic approach (Dryden and Norcross, 1989) provided that the counsellor has first received a thorough training in one particular theory. This is necessary in order to prevent confusion in the mind of the counsellor and ultimately within the therapeutic relationship. The counsellor should always be able to explain at any given time which approach she is using and why.

Counsellor training

The training of a primary health care counsellor can be considered in two parts:

1   Basic training.
2   Additional specialist training in primary health care counselling.

The possible training routes are summarized in Figure 12.1.

Basic training

Qualifications

It is now widely recognized that for a general counsellor to be adequately qualified, she needs to have undertaken a minimum of 450 hours of counselling training which includes 200 hours of skills development and 250 hours of theory. In addition, she needs to have the experience of 450 face-to-face supervised counselling hours. At this level, she is eligible for BAC Accreditation and subsequent inclusion on to the United Kingdom Register of Counsellors. Such courses normally require part-time attendance over the course of 3 years. A large number of institutions offer counselling training at this level and it is helpful to contact the BAC, BPS or UKCP for lists of approved courses. In addition to the regulation of counsellors, there also exists a move to regulate training centres which can apply for BAC recognition.

Figure 12.1   Possible route options for qualified primary health care counselling

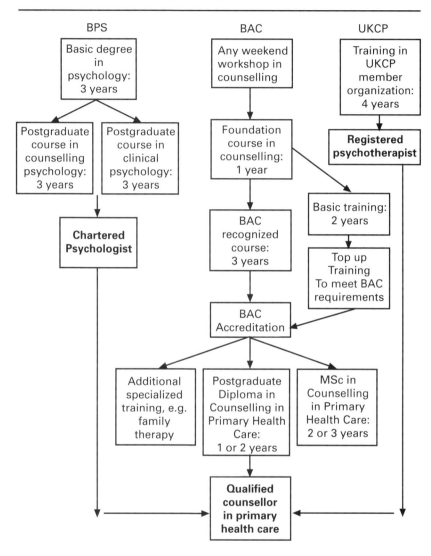

For anyone who has not yet undertaken any training, it is preferable to choose one of the recognized courses as the route to accreditation is likely to be more straightforward. However, for those who have completed another training but which falls short of the necessary criteria, it is possible to undertake a top-up training providing that it can be shown that the core training is sufficiently comprehensive. Short courses and weekend workshops are not usually regarded as sufficient as the professional bodies increasingly look for depth and consistency in training.

If you are planning to seek professional registration, it is important to discuss the content of the course with the course tutor to ascertain which professional body and code of ethics they adhere to, and to satisfy yourself of the standards of teaching qualifications and experience offered. Often, the course to which you apply may be one which is geographically the nearest, and therefore the trainee must accept whichever theoretical approach is presented on that course. If a student wishes to follow a particular theory, it may mean travelling further afield, which could add to the overall training cost.

Obtaining practical experience

Another aspect to be considered is how each course enables students to gain practical experience. Some students find that they have completed an intensive 3-year course of skills and theory, but emerge with little actual practical experience. Certain courses now insist that students gain at least 100 hours of supervised practice before receiving certification – though many students find it difficult to find patients at this stage. It is a chicken and egg situation which has yet to be resolved. Placements may be available under the supervision of a fully trained counsellor but they are usually in short supply and it is worth investigating their availability before enrolling on a course.

Some training courses provide clients for trainees. At Relate, for example, a fully qualified counsellor undertakes a Reception Interview and screens the clients to determine their suitability for work with a trainee. After an initial induction period, Relate students can begin client work. Each session is closely monitored by a tutor, and supervision can gradually be spaced out as the trainee widens her expertise. This means that practical counselling experience can be gained concurrently with skills and theory training, whilst continuing to safeguard the client, which is an efficient method of teaching. Many centres provide the training free, in return for the counselling given by trainees. The Metanoia Institute in London also helps trainees gain practical experience. Metanoia offers a low cost counselling service to the public – the counselling undertaken by their trainees, which allows students to receive on-going clients during the course of their training.

Placements

Where help with practical experience is not offered by a training centre, it is left to the student to make their own enquiries to agencies, such as a drug or alcohol rehabilitation centre, a bereavement centre, or organizations such as Shelter for the possibility of counselling some of their clients. Counsellors lacking the necessary practical experience have sometimes offered their services to GPs at low cost or even free, and with shortage of funding, surgeries have been tempted to accept this cheap though inexperienced labour. Such contracts are now actively discouraged and recent Guidelines to the Employment of Counsellors in Primary Care by the Counselling in Primary Care Trust and Derbyshire Health Authority have helped to educate GPs in understanding the need for counsellors to have gained adequate supervised practice. Readers who require further help with placements should read *Handbook for Trainee Counsellors, Psychotherapists and Counselling Psychologists* (Bor and Watts, 1998).

Some placements are available at local hospitals. There may be a demand for cancer counselling in the Oncology Department or counselling in an HIV/AIDS unit. Students who already have the experience of a medical setting, perhaps from their families or previous work such as nursing, should find it much easier to integrate. Even working as a receptionist in the local Family Planning Clinic or other medical context will give valuable insight into ways of working that will ultimately help the general practice counsellor.

Reference has already been made to the temptation faced by GPs to employ cheap trainee labour where placements are available in some GP surgeries. However, it is now recognized that a trainee primary health care counsellor is comparable to a doctor doing his pre-registration year. Both require close monitoring, supervision and support. It is recommended that newly fledged counsellors do not work alone in primary health care. They should be employed in surgeries where a fully qualified general practice counsellor is already *in situ*, and from whom they can learn. Referrals can then be screened and the trainee can proceed more safely.

Self-awareness

Many training courses require students to first do a one-year Foundation Course before embarking on a diploma course. This is an excellent idea for it gives the student a taste of what might be expected of a counsellor and provides an introduction to the theory and skills required. Some trainees have little idea of the amount of personal commitment that is required. They expect to help their clients in some way, but are unprepared for the training in self-awareness that is essential if a counsellor's own personal difficulties and prejudices are not to unconsciously 'block' communication with the patient. Such discovery of self-awareness is sometimes unsettling and may stir up painful issues for the counsellor during her training. It is therefore essential that adequate support is offered, and one reason why weekly therapy for the trainee counsellor is required on many training courses. Counsellors also need to be aware that such training can upset the balance of their own relationships.

The British Association for Counselling offers an Information Guide to Training and Careers in Counselling. They can also supply the very comprehensive *Directory of Training in Counselling and Psychotherapy* which lists all courses in the UK from 'tasters' to PhD level plus more advanced and specialized training for counsellors.

Additional specialist training for primary health care counsellors

Having completed a basic core training in counselling, the counsellor who wishes to specialize in primary health care may consider which specialist training route she will take. Although the majority of counselling courses probably do not adequately equip a counsellor to work in general practice, until recently there have been few specific training courses for primary health care counsellors on offer. In 1991, the South Derbyshire and North Derbyshire Health Authorities received funding to develop general practice counselling within their area. As a result, the Derbyshire Counselling Scheme was set up and became the pioneer for advancement in this field. It was followed by the founding of the Counselling in Primary Care Trust. Under the Directorship of Dr Graham Curtis Jenkins, the Trust aims to support, promote and develop counselling and psychotherapy and the use of counselling skills in primary care. It is an invaluable source of information about all aspects of primary care counselling and holds a comprehensive database of counsellors working in general practice.

At the time of writing (1998), specialist postgraduate training in primary care counselling is offered at Bristol University, Stockton Psychotherapy Training Institute, the University of Strathclyde, Bilston Community College, Wolverhampton, the University of Keele, and the University of Newcastle Upon Tyne. Entry requirements include the completion of a Diploma in Counselling, which is equivalent to BAC Accreditation, that is, 400 training hours and counselling experience of 200 client hours over a 2-year period. Students should be working in a health care setting or undertake a placement for the duration of the course. The Counselling in Primary Care Trust can supply further details on request.

Other health authorities in addition to Derbyshire have started to recognize the importance of integral health care, and it is worth enquiring locally to see what is on offer. In Hampshire, for example, the Southampton and SW Hampshire Health Commission and the Southampton Pastoral Counselling Service are joint sponsors of a 3-month post-qualifying general practice course. In addition to addressing all the usual relevant issues, it also includes 5 hours observation and discussion at the Department of Psychiatry, Royal South Hants Hospital. This is arranged in the Psychiatric outpatient clinic, and/or an inpatient ward, and/or in the Psychological Therapies Service and aims to increase the understanding of how general practice counselling fits in with the psychiatric services. Such an important dimension of training is rarely on offer, and is to be envied.

The number of specialist general practice counselling courses is still inadequate and the counsellor may be required to pursue a more generic route. She has the option of pursuing further training and this might involve, for example, the completion of a family therapy course. The Institute of Family Therapy in London offers a range of courses in family therapy and also has short courses in primary care issues.

Cost of training

Counselling training can be very expensive. It may be possible to obtain limited funding for course fees through bursaries, sponsorships, or from the counsellor's own GP practice. The Counselling in Primary Care Trust supply useful information about funding for mature students. In addition to tuition fees, additional expenses include course books and relevant reading, regular supervision and probably weekly personal therapy. Counsellors need to allow between £25 and £40 for therapy sessions, depending on the person's qualifications and location. It is worth 'shopping around', not only for compatibility, but because some therapists are more sympathetic to the plight of trainees and offer therapy at a reduced fee. Lastly, provision must be allowed for personal growth and professional on-going development.

On-going professional development

There are numerous short courses, workshops, seminars, training days, lectures and conferences on a wide range of relevant topics. Many of these are advertised in the British Association for Counselling Journal and by their Counselling in Medical Settings division. Information will also be posted on relevant notice-boards at training centres. The Conference Unit at St George's Hospital Medical School also runs excellent one- and two-day multidisciplinary seminars on topics very relevant to primary health care counselling, as do the Priory Group of Hospitals and the Henderson Group of hospitals respectively. Training days are also run by the BAC Counselling in Medical Settings (CMS) division, Derbyshire Health Authority and many other organizations.

Conclusion

The role of a primary health care counsellor is unique and requires specialist training which is not normally included in the curriculum of basic training courses. The counsellor needs to be taught the biopsychosocial perspective, integration, collaboration, networking and flexibility that comes from working within a multidisciplinary team. She needs an adequate knowledge of abnormal psychology, psychotropic medication, routes for onward referral and a sound understanding of her own limitations. As yet, opportunities for ongoing specialist training are limited and counsellors will need to be resourceful in selecting an appropriate package for their continued personal growth and professional development that is commensurate with counselling in primary health care.

Key points

- Primary health care counselling is unique and specialist training is required.
- The majority of formal counselling training courses do not adequately equip a counsellor to work in primary health care.
- Basic training is first required up to BAC Accreditation level.
- On-going training can be specific, generic or through placements.
- Current options for specialist training are limited.

References

Beck, A., Shaw, A., Bush, B. and Emery, G. (1979) *Cognitive Therapy of Depression*. Chichester: John Wiley.

Beutler, L. (1983) *Eclectic Psychotherapy: a Systemic Approach*. New York: Pergamon.

Bor, R. and Watts, M. (eds) (1998) *Handbook for Trainee Counsellors, Psychotherapists and Counselling Psychologists*. London: Sage.

Bor, R., Miller, R., Latz, M. and Salt, H. (1998) *Counselling in Health Care Settings*. London: Cassell.

Dryden, W. and Norcross, J. (1989) *Eclecticism and Integration in Counselling and Psychotherapy.* Essex: Gale Centre Publications.

France, R. and Robson, M. (1986) *Behavioural Therapy in Primary Care: a Practical Guide.* London: Croom Helm.

Jacobs, M. (1991) *Psychodynamic Counselling in Action.* London: Sage.

McDaniel, S., Hepworth, J. and Doherty, W. (1992) *Medical Family Therapy: a Biopsychosocial Approach to Families with Health Problems.* New York: Basic Books.

Mearns, D. and Thorne, B. (1988) *Person-Centred Counselling in Action.* London: Sage.

Pembroke, G. and O'Sullivan, J. (1994) Audit of Counselling in Twyford Surgery 1990–1994. Unpublished report for Hampshire Medical Audit and Advisory Group.

Rolland, J. (1988) 'Family systems and chronic illness. A typological model', in F. Walsh and C. Anderson (eds), *Chronic Disorders and the Family.* New York: Haworth Press.

de Shazer, S. (1985) *Keys to Solution in Brief Therapy.* New York: W.W. Norton.

de Shazer, S. (1988) *Clues – Investigating Solutions in Brief Therapy.* New York: W.W. Norton.

Appendix: List of useful addresses

The following names and addresses may be useful. Many more can be obtained from the *Counselling and Psychotherapy Resources Year Directory*, available from the British Association for Counselling.

British Association for Counselling, 1 Regent Place, Rugby, CV21 2PJ.
Telephone: 01788 550899

The British Psychological Society, St Andrews House, 48 Princess Road East, Leicester, LE1 7DR.
Telephone: 0116 254 9568

UK Council for Psychotherapy, 167–169 Great Portland Street, London, W1N 5FB
Telephone: 0171 436 3002

Counselling in Primary Care Trust, First Floor, Majestic House, High Street, Staines, TW18 4DG.
Telephone: 01784 441782

The Metanoia Institute, 13 North Common Road, Ealing, London, W5 2QB
Telephone: 0181 579 2505

Relate Marriage Guidance, Herbert Grey College, Little Church Street, Rugby, CV21 3AP
Telephone: 01788 573241 (See also your local telephone directory)

Tavistock Clinic (Institute for Human Relations), 120 Belsize Lane, London NW3 5BA
Telephone: 0171 435 7111

Tavistock Institute of Marital Studies, 120 Belsize Lane, London NW3 5BA
Telephone: 0171 435 7111

CHAPTER 13

SUPERVISION IN PRIMARY CARE COUNSELLING

Damian McCann

Supervision has been variously described as 'the cornerstone of counselling' (Williams, 1996: 440), 'a profession in its own right' (Carroll, 1996: 28) and 'a process ostensibly intended to safeguard standards of practice' (Smith, 1996: 427). From these descriptions, there is no doubting the importance of supervision and it is precisely because of this that there is a requirement for all counsellors (trainees, qualified practitioners and supervisors alike) that they receive regular supervision as part of their professional role.

This chapter explores the supervision of counsellors working in the context of primary health care. It examines the contribution supervision makes to the counsellor on a day-to-day basis, as well as the larger developmental trajectory. Given the diversity and high turnover of patients, it is not surprising that more traditional supervisory practices, geared as they are to smaller case loads in less complex settings, may need some revision if they are to have relevance to counsellors working in primary health care. This chapter is therefore concerned with developing effective and ethical supervisory practices in this context. Three contrasting supervisory models are used to highlight considerations relevant to the setting.

Implicit in the discussion that follows is the importance of sound training leading to effective practice. Supervisors are greatly assisted in their task by the adequate preparation of counsellors for the complex and, at times, demanding roles they will be required to undertake during the course of their work. It is possible that particular issues and dilemmas counsellors bring for supervision may be less a reflection of their own lack of experience with regard to complex clinical work and more a matter of inadequate training. For this reason, it is suggested that this chapter be read in conjunction with the one on training (see Chapter 12).

Defining supervision

Supervision is a formal professional arrangement between a supervisor and counsellor (or counsellors if the supervisor is working with a group) whose purpose, according to the British Association for Counselling, is to ensure the efficacy of the counsellor/client relationship. Additionally, supervision is also concerned with offering support and development to the counsellor working in primary health care. Irrespective of their model, most supervisors incorporate three essential functions into their practice: educative, supportive and administrative.

1 The *educative function* is that part of supervision which provides on-going training for the counsellor in her professional role and development. This should not, however, be confused with didactic teaching, although there may be times when such input is required by a counsellor. Supervision provides a context in which primary care counsellors are facilitated in an evaluation of their work within an environment in which there is an openness to new learning.
2 The *supportive function* relates to the counsellor's need for a space to reflect on the counselling task within a safe and trusting supervisory relationship. The interface, however, between the personal and professional role raises some challenging issues for the supervisory endeavour. Some supervisors draw a clear line between the two whilst others provide a measure of support in both the personal and professional domains.
3 The *administrative function* is concerned with assisting the counsellor to work within and manage the demands of the agency setting, adhering to ethical standards of practice and addressing practice issues and dilemmas as they arise.

The supervisory arrangements should also reflect the counsellor's stage of training and development, as this will enable the supervisor and counsellor to work well together.

Effective supervision

As with any relationship, there is no automatic guarantee of a successful partnership. Those that work usually have a commonality of purpose, a high degree of commitment and collaboration and an interest in the contribution that each of the participants has to offer. Clarity about one's needs also goes a long way towards defining the type of supervisory relationship a counsellor requires, as well as determining whether a supervisor is in a position to meet those needs.

The relationship between supervisors and trainees has been studied (Carroll, 1994) and it was found that trainees do not have clear expectations of their supervisors from which they can negotiate a partnership. The level of passivity and lack of agency, which is congruent with the power imbalance, often results in supervisees being 'prepared to fall in with the supervisor's ways of setting up and engaging in supervision' (Carroll,1996: 92). Although this may have less relevance to qualified counsellors, the point concerning the need for agency is well made. Counsellors should think carefully about their supervisory needs. Listed below are a number of questions which counsellors would be well advised to consider in finding a suitable supervisor.

- What are my supervisory needs?
- Can my supervisory needs be met through one-to-one supervision or do I need to think of other alternatives, for example, dual supervision, or group supervision?
- Would I work better with a male or female supervisor?
- Do I need to be supervised within a particular theoretical orientation and if so, has the supervisor experience of this model?
- Is the supervisor available to the extent that I may need him or her to be available?
- Where does the supervisor stand in relation to gender, power, ethnicity and sexuality?
- Is the supervisor familiar with adult learning objectives and have I made him or her aware of my learning needs and how these can best be met?
- How will my developmental needs be assessed?
- Am I clear what will happen if difficulties arise within the supervisory relationship, for instance, if I do not agree with the supervisor's point of view, or if the supervisor feels that I am unfit to practice?
- Can I afford the time, cost and effort required to make supervision work for me?

Supervisors should also be clear on the following:

- Am I qualified and in a position to offer on-going supervision to counsellors in primary health care?
- Do I have enough of an awareness of the context of primary health care and an understanding of the particular issues inherent in working in such a setting?

- Have I clarified my relationship and level of responsibility with regard to the counsellor's work?
- Do I have the necessary training in the particular model(s) that the counsellor uses in her work with patients?
- Is my approach and style of supervision a good enough fit for the counsellor?

Although some of the questions raised may seem alarmist, many counsellors and supervisors have found themselves in deep water because they have not properly considered the nature of the supervisory contract.

Lindsay, a newly qualified counsellor in primary care, found herself an independent female supervisor who agreed to meet with her once a week to support her professional practice within the surgery. The supervisor in question assumed that, because Lindsay was a qualified practitioner, she was more experienced than she actually was. Within her first month, Lindsay was struggling to meet the demands placed on her within the surgery. To ensure that she kept up to date with her administration, Lindsay was taking work home. She would often arrive for supervision unprepared and the supervisor began to worry about Lindsay's capacity to cope. Attempts to address Lindsay's difficulty in coping were met with hostility in which Lindsay would accuse her supervisor of not understanding what was happening in the surgery, that is, that she was in a new post and, as such, the demand for her services was justifiably high. Lindsay was sure that the pressures on her would ease in time but her supervisor was not so sure.

The supervisor worked with Lindsay towards limiting her work load and encouraged her to communicate the need for this to others. The situation did not improve, however, and the supervisor felt that she had no option but to directly express her concerns regarding Lindsay's tendency to take on too much and her general level of disorganization. Only at this point did Lindsay admit to her struggle and her supervisor began to be of some value to her and her work.

The supervisory contract

Assuming that the counsellor and supervisor have addressed some of the above-mentioned questions, the supervisory contract usually incorporates the answers to these questions and this in turn frames the supervisory relationship. The supervisory contract is essentially a mutually agreed statement incorporating the aims and objectives of the supervisory endeavour.

Contracts usually outline the roles and responsibilities of each of the parties involved and also cover the practical aspects of supervision, namely the frequency and duration, the costs, arrangements in the event of the supervisor not being available, and so on. They may incorporate more elaborate aspects of supervision, for example, specific learning objectives, developmental reviews, and regular discussions about the effectiveness or otherwise of the supervisory relationship itself.

Some counsellors and supervisors may be reluctant to draft a formal supervisory or consultative contract. There may be a number of reasons for this resistance. First, there may be a tacit agreement that supervisory contracts are more appropriate for trainees than for qualified practitioners. The maxim that 'we are both mature and responsible adults who know what is expected of us' may suffice. Secondly, the parties involved may feel that such a document interferes with the emerging relationship, particularly if the model of supervision is one in which there is a high degree of uncertainty, curiosity and collaboration. Thirdly, contracts, by their very nature, make the power dynamics within the supervisory relationship overt, and there may be a wish to avoid this.

Supervisory contracts by their very existence imply a need for some definition of the supervisory relationship. The challenge of such contracts is that of creating a meaningful working document that provides a framework for practice. It goes without saying that the document itself does not equal an effective supervisory relationship, but without it, supervisor and counsellor may find themselves struggling to define the nature of what it is they are doing.

Peter, an experienced counsellor, found himself a new job in a new area and had to change supervisors. He had developed a good working relationship with his previous supervisor and, although reluctant to change, was pleased with the outcome of the discussion he had had with his new supervisor. The discussion had been wide ranging and there was an agreement to have three supervisory sessions which would be used as a basis for helping them decide whether they could work together in the future.

During the three sessions, Peter found himself feeling irritated with his supervisor's style of questioning. The supervisor would question Peter closely on a decision to follow a particular direction with a patient, when Peter's main priority at this point was to say how the client was making him feel – this being consistent with his previous supervisor's approach. The mismatch between Peter's need and his supervisor's input offered them an opportunity to consider their differences and decide together how they would manage these. The acceptance of the need for a contract as a basis for supervision forced them to address the issue and reach some agreement. What they discovered was a real incompatibility between their respective approaches and Peter decided to find himself an alternative supervisor.

Although this may seem an unsatisfactory outcome, it did at least prevent Peter and his supervisor entering into a dysfunctional supervisory relationship in which supervisor and counsellor struggle for an illusory meeting point. Some practitioners may argue that such a struggle is of itself the very essence of supervision, but as with couple relationships where conflict interferes with the capacity to think and reflect, the union soon founders as the battles escalate. This is not, however, to argue that supervision or consultation should be a bland mix of polite conversation and consensus, but the balance between containment and discomfort, as a basis for development, needs to be carefully assessed by both parties to ensure a sufficient degree of fit between a counsellor and her supervisor or consultant. This does of course beg the question of what constitutes 'good enough supervision' within primary health care and the remainder of this chapter will be devoted to addressing this issue.

Models of supervision

Three models of supervision relevant to the supervision of counsellors in primary health care are advanced. These are termed:

1   The supervisor-centred model.
2   The supervisee-centred model.
3   The consultative model.

Although they are presented separately, they should be viewed as part of a continuum in which a supervisor adopts a particular level of responsibility with regard to a counsellor's work, as well as the proximal relationship a supervisor has with regard to the setting in which the counsellor undertakes that work. This can be conceptualized using a model that employs two axes.

The supervisor-centred model

A supervisor operating within this model is often engaged in a process whereby she will assume an active and pragmatic role in relation to the counsellor's therapeutic practice. This may involve offering advice to the counsellor, suggesting particular diagnoses in relation to the counsellor's clinical presentations and, to some extent, managing the counsellor's development (Smith, 1996). At issue here is the supervisor's motivation for adopting such a stance. For some counsellors, that is,

Figure 13.1   Framework for supervision and consultation

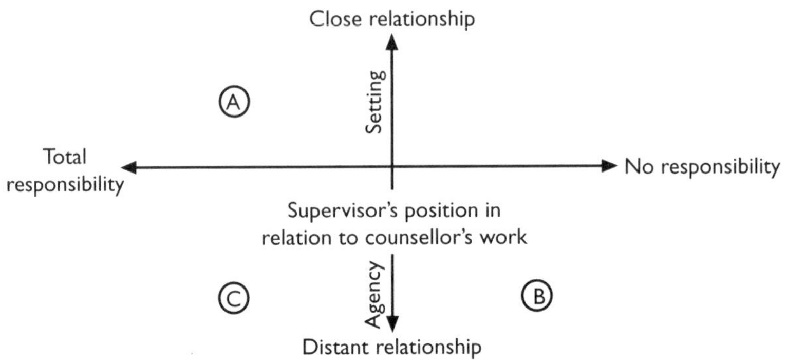

```
                          Close relationship
                                 ▲
                                 │
                               ᵍⁿⁱᵗᵗᵉˢ  Setting
              Ⓐ
   Total                         │
  ────────────────────────────────────────────────────▶  No responsibility
 responsibility      │
                  Supervisor's position in
                  relation to counsellor's work
                                 │
                             Agency
              Ⓒ                  │              Ⓑ
                                 ▼
                        Distant relationship
```

Three positions are outlined: these should not be viewed as exhaustive

Position A: A supervisor with a high degree of responsibility in relation to a counsellor's work and who has a close relationship to the agency setting in which the counsellor undertakes that work. The supervision may be supervisor- or supervisee-led

Position B: A supervisor removed from the counsellor's setting and who has little or no direct responsibility for that counsellor's clinical work. This approximates more to the consultation model

Position C: A problematic position for any supervisor to occupy. In theory, the supervisor has clinical responsibility for the counsellor's work, but in practice has little or no direct relationship to the setting in which that work is undertaken

---

those still in training or just newly qualified, or those in which their supervisor is also their line manager, this master/apprenticeship model may be just what is required. However, when it is related more to the supervisor's own style of supervision than to the needs of the counsellor, problems can arise. For instance, if a counsellor lacks confidence, she may be drawn to a supervisor who, rather than overseeing the clinical work, actually takes responsibility for it and becomes increasingly directive in relation to what she thinks should be happening with that counsellor's clients. Carroll (1996) terms this phenomenon 'vicarious counselling', and if left unchallenged it can be very detrimental to a counsellor's development. This is not to deny that some counsellors may need a high level of supervisory input for a period of time, and that supervisors may need to protect the counsellor and client from too much exposure, but a supervisor will usually have a developmental framework in mind so that the counsellor will be encouraged towards an increasing degree of autonomy over time and the supervision will be working towards that end.

The supervisor-centred model can be utilized in a range of supervisory practices, namely one-to-one, dual and group supervision. In essence, the counsellor will be offered support, both in terms of her clinical work and also in relation to her professional development. This may take the form of regular one-to-one meetings where the counsellor brings for discussion her work with her clients and her professional relationships with colleagues both within and outside of the primary care setting. The effectiveness of this approach rests on the counsellor articulating a model of practice so that the supervisor can determine whether she is able to supervise within this model. Other relevant considerations concern how the counsellor's practice will be discussed, the methods used and the nature of the feedback.

Jackie was a newly qualified counsellor working in a GP practice who contracted to meet with her supervisor once a week for one hour. The supervisor was not actually employed in the surgery where Jackie worked, but she had in the past been a member of staff at the surgery and so was familiar with the working of the practice. In addition, her 8 years of experience enabled her to speak with authority about the work that Jackie was undertaking and the setting in which she was seeing her patients.

The pattern was quickly set, whereby Jackie would bring her most pressing concerns for discussion and her supervisor would offer her some expert observations and direction with this work. This supervisory input was actually quite limited, the observations being more a reflection of the supervisor's restricted framework for thinking and words such as 'very depressed', 'quite disturbed', or 'very resistant patient', often structured the discussions.

In her second year of practice, Jackie began to challenge the recurring themes and remarks. This was consistent with her own developing ideas and increased competence. Her supervisor was unable to accept these challenges and dealt with Jackie's attempts to expand the frame of reference by falling back on her own expert stance, suggesting that Jackie was trying to run before she could walk. The power battle that was beginning to emerge was totally ignored by the supervisor and Jackie began to talk about her frustrations outside of the setting with other counsellors and supervisors. Through these conversations she was able to formulate a plan of action and began to talk more openly in the supervisory setting about her frustrations with the supervisor's expert stance and her own one-down position within the relationship. Together, they were able to construct a new supervisory relationship based more on principles of reciprocity rather than complementarity.

This emerging developmental schema was respectful of both participants, but the struggle between supervisor and counsellor was a necessary part of the developing supervisory narrative and experience. Had it continued to be denied or ignored, both parties would have lost a valuable opportunity to lift the supervision to a new and more appropriate level.

The close attention to detail which the supervisor-centred model offers is particularly helpful to those counsellors who are still in the process of developing sound frameworks for thinking and practice, and those who continue to need assistance in gaining a clear understanding of the primary care setting and the opportunities that it affords.

Doug arrived for supervision with a particular difficulty he was experiencing with a referral from a GP in the practice where he worked. The referral involved 24-year-old Jenny who, according to the GP, was in urgent need of help for depression and loneliness. During the initial consultation, Jenny explained that she had for some time developed an attraction for her GP and had finally confided these feelings to him during her last consultation. According to Jenny, her GP became very angry and punitive towards her, suggesting she were mad and recommended immediate counselling with the practice counsellor. Jenny was very clear in her own mind that her GP was equally attracted to her, but felt that he was worried about his position, particularly if he acted on his feelings. Doug spent the best part of an hour exploring the situation with Jenny and found himself feeling confused and out of his depth. Following the consultation, he decided to speak to the GP in question and told him what Jenny had said. The GP was uncharacteristically annoyed and agitated with Doug, suggesting that he did not have the time to waste on such nonsense and that Jenny was always accusing men of fancying her. He restated his belief that Jenny is a very disturbed woman and suggested that Doug use his time to help her confront her relationship difficulties. Doug realized that he needed to prolong the discussion with the GP but felt unable to explore the situation further given the GP's insistence that he address the issues where they really belonged, namely with Jenny.

In advance of his second session with Jenny, Doug arrived for supervision feeling anxious and agitated. His supervisor had not seen him like this before and used the early part of the session to elicit the causes for his obvious distress. Doug recounted details of the referral and of his initial meeting with Jenny and his fraught conversation with the GP. During the conversation, Doug's supervisor took charge of the situation and began to suggest clear objectives for taking the work forward. She suggested that Doug was caught in a no-win situation in that he could not begin to make sense of the referral until he had access to more background information. She suggested that he needed to arrange a time for him and the GP to meet and discuss the situation properly, both from the point of view of Jenny's past medical history and relationship with the practice and the GP's own emotional reaction to the situation. She also helped Doug to reflect on the potential complications of working with Jenny given his gender and the possibility that she may need to be referred to adult psychiatry. By the end of supervision, Doug felt much clearer about the next step and felt more empowered in tackling the GP.

Although Doug's supervisor did not have direct responsibility for his clinical practice, and in that sense, could be seen more as a consultant to his work, Doug's reliance on her expertise and experience, consistent with his own level of development, meant that he and his supervisor were operating from a supervisor-centred model of supervision.

The supervisee-centred model

Supervisors comfortable with a 'supervisee-centred model', where instructive interaction cuts little ice, will in contrast to the supervisor-centred model engage with the counsellor's own ideas and style of interaction. Essentially, the complementary relationship outlined in the previous model is replaced in the supervisee-centred model with a more reciprocal relationship. In essence, the conversation between the supervisor and counsellor is part of an open and on-going exploration of new meanings and understandings.

A supervisee-centred approach is essentially a competency based model in which the counsellor receiving supervision is seen as the chief architect of personal learning goals and is also believed to have her own solutions to the problems and dilemmas that are brought for supervision (Anderson and Swim, 1995). The supervisor joins with the counsellor in a mutual search for explanations, meanings and indeed solutions. This does of course raise particular issues with regard to the theoretical approach employed by both supervisor and counsellor in the supervisory endeavour.

Counsellors in primary care, like counsellors in other settings, have a range of options when it comes to choosing a supervisor. At the very least, the supervisor should be familiar with the primary care counsellor's setting and the work she is undertaking. This has particular relevance when the counsellor is working with time-limited contracts and is using brief therapeutic approaches. Although a supervisor with a psychoanalytic training may have something to contribute, tensions may arise if the supervisor is used to working over a longer period of time with clients and is dubious about short-term approaches. Similarly, a supervisor using a behavioural approach, although ideally placed to assist a counsellor in specific pieces of clinical work, may lack the necessary systemic understanding to help the counsellor with the larger trajectory of her work. It is therefore important that the primary care counsellor, if she is invested in a supervisee-centred model of supervision, gives some thought to the theoretical dimension of the supervision she requires to assist her in her clinical and personal/professional development.

A solution-focused approach to supervision, concerned as it is with the identification and acknowledgement of a supervisee's strengths, successful interventions and behaviours (Traintafillou, 1997), may be the most appropriate method available to a counsellor in search of a competency based model of supervision. It is also the case that solution-focused approaches emphasize the importance of short-term pieces of intervention and this makes it an attractive model for primary care counselling where the demand for a counsellor's service often outstrips supply. Most counsellors have responded to this challenge by means of short-term contracts, and a solution-focused approach, searching for strengths and resources rather than deficits and problems, lends itself well to both patients and counsellors alike.

A supervisor using a solution-focused approach will help the counsellor define her supervisory goals, which will also incorporate her clients' conceptualizations of problems, goals and outcomes. The focus in this model is very much on the counsellor's interventions and the client's response to these. Any positive changes in the work with the patient are amplified and applauded by the supervisor and together supervisor and counsellor will clarify the next useful step in the work. Exceptions to the rules are also sought, as these provide important markers on the road to change. The approach is more concerned with the exchange of ideas during supervision than with confrontations between a supervisor who, for example, attempts to instruct a somewhat resistant counsellor to implement a particular intervention.

Some supervisors using this approach have, together with the counsellor, devised ways in which a counsellor monitors her own progress and development through the use of self-supervision or self-observation. For instance, the counsellor may select a goal of helping a patient identify exceptions to the rule, that is, times when he is not so depressed, and will bring examples from her practice for mutual discussion and exploration with her supervisor. The supervisor and counsellor can together assess the degree to which the counsellor is progressing in her work and devise possible solutions if she is failing to attain her goal.

Problems can arise in the supervisee-centred model if a supervisor is not honest about, or does not accept, the level of responsibility she has for a counsellor's work. Her conduct in the supervision sessions may, at times, be more reminiscent of a consultant than a supervisor. This has the potential to create uncertainty for the counsellor, who may be looking to her supervisor for direct help or who, alternatively, assumes more responsibility for the work than her level of knowledge and experience allow.

At the same time, it is still possible to develop a collaborative supervisory relationship even when a supervisor does have direct responsibility for a counsellor's clinical work, although a supervisor who places collaboration above instruction may have to rethink this position when there is a need to act and the counsellor fails to do so.

Jason and his supervisor were working well together over a number of weeks. Jason had recently joined the practice and his supervisor was also his line manager. He especially liked the way he and his supervisor could discuss clinical dilemmas and he felt very empowered when his supervisor would, from his point of view, leave him in charge of the direction that a particular piece of clinical work with a patient should take.

During one supervision session, Jason's supervisor began to worry about a decision Jason had taken with a patient he had been seeing over four sessions. Jason had informed his supervisor that the patient in question did not wish to continue seeing him as he felt there was no point in going on. Jason had taken the patient's wishes at face value but his supervisor had recalled that during a previous session the patient had expressed suicidal thoughts. She therefore, in line with the supervisee-centred approach, quizzed Jason about the possible reasons for the patient deciding to terminate therapy. When Jason failed to acknowledge the previous suicidal ideas his supervisor stepped in to remind him of this and emphasized the need for Jason to speak to the patient's GP and for Jason to arrange a follow-up to monitor the situation. Jason thought this was unnecessary and suggested that his supervisor was over-reacting. His supervisor disagreed and directed him to arrange a follow-up. Jason felt very undermined and was left feeling unclear of his true position within the supervisory relationship.

The consultative model

The consultative model envisages that the supervisor will be someone who is independent of the counsellor and whose main role is to facilitate the counsellor's self-monitoring without actually taking direct responsibility for the counsellor's work with her patients. It has been suggested (Bond, 1996) that this is an effective supervisory relationship for independent practitioners, for practitioners where, for example, the line manger is not actually a clinician, or where the line manager is an experienced counsellor but there would be a blurring of roles if she were to take on supervisory responsibilities. For instance, the practitioner may feel inhibited in using the supervisory relationship to discuss insecurities fearing that this would expose her in the eyes of her line manger and possibly affect her promotional chances. This would essentially compromise the collaborative aspects that are necessary for the consultative relationship to work well. The consultative model may only be appropriate, however, for counsellors who have the experience and competence to assume the level of responsibility demanded by those consulting to their practice. There may also be occasions when a counsellor in such a relationship requires more direct input than a supervisor consulting to practice is prepared to give, for instance, when a counsellor encounters a novel situation about which the consultant has some expert knowledge. It is therefore imperative that a counsellor be clear about the nature of the supervisory relationship into which she has entered, otherwise she may find herself struggling not only in her practice but also within the context of supervision.

Consultants may work with counsellors in a variety of ways. For instance, the consultant may be asked by a counsellor to consult on an individual basis, or in the context of a group. A consultant may also be employed by a multidisciplinary health care team in order to consult to them on aspects of their practice or to assist with team dynamics. The consultant will usually be an experienced clinician or manager who is skilled in maintaining appropriate boundaries in relation to the task at hand. In other words, the consultant will not assume responsibility for the work, but will offer observations, suggestions and possible directions in the knowledge that the counsellor will utilize these as she feels fit. This usually frees the consultant to think at a number of different levels whilst respecting the counsellor's own autonomy and expertise. For consultants to be effective, they must also acquire a knowledge and understanding of the setting in which the counsellor(s) work and the constraints and opportunities this affords.

Anne, an experienced counsellor working in general practice, approached Jim seeking consultation in relation to her clinical practice. Jim, after lengthy conversations in which he clarified the nature of the request and the context of the setting in which Anne was working, agreed to meet with her. What Jim could not have anticipated was the extent to which Anne had a major difficulty with regard to authority and the extent to which she would reject any suggestions he might proffer in relation to her work. Jim became increasingly embroiled in a battle with Anne, who accused him of being over-critical of her work and on one occasion she stormed out of the consultation session. Jim felt very provoked and more than a little anxious about what he was seeing and hearing about Anne's work. He tried to address this directly with her but it only added fuel to the fire. Jim, mindful of his ethical responsibilities, sought external advice. Jim was advised to continue discussing his concerns openly with Anne, but if this failed to effect positive change, then he would have no option but to suggest that

Anne find herself an alternative consultant to her practice. It was also agreed that if Jim was worried about Anne's practice to the extent that he felt she was placing her patients at risk, then he would have an ethical duty to report her to the appropriate professional organization responsible for her registration.

A final area of consideration with regard to consultation is that of peer group supervision and its status within the profession. Peer group supervision usually involves three or more counsellors sharing the responsibility for providing supervision to each other within the context of a group. More often than not, they will be of equal status and will have a commonality of purpose and clinical experience. The advantage of such a group is that it offers the participants a setting in which they can exchange ideas and address clinical issues and dilemmas. On the other hand, it should not be viewed as having equal status with supervision or consultation, in that, unless the group has a very definite member who occupies either of these two positions, it functions more as a forum for mutual support and will usually fail to satisfy the requirements of the BAC or BPS in relation to hours of supervised practice.

Conclusion

Given the pressures and demands on counsellors working in primary health care settings, it seems imperative that they have time to reflect on their work and that they receive support. Supervision is designed to meet these needs but, like any dynamic relationship, in order to make it work counsellors must carefully consider what it is they actually want from supervision as a basis for deciding whether a particular super-visor is right for them. The trials and tribulations inherent in any supervisory relationship may be related as much to the difficult dynamics of the work undertaken by counsellors and the complex settings in which they conduct this work, as to the personalities of the supervisor and counsellor themselves. Supervisors must have a clear understanding of primary health care settings and the complex relationships of the various professionals therein if they are to be of any real assistance to counsellors in these settings. A distinction has been drawn between supervisors who have a clear responsibility for the counsellor's practice and those who have not. Again, it is important that this is clarified before entering into a supervisory or consultative contract. Effective supervision is a two-way process, and if it works well, counsellors will be greatly assisted in their challenging roles within health care settings.

Key points

- Supervision is a formal professional arrangement between a supervisor and counsellor.
- Supervisors offer support and development to counsellors working in primary health care.
- Most supervisors incorporate three essential functions: educative, supportive and administative.
- Clarity about a counsellor's supervisory needs goes a long way towards defining the type of supervisory relationship a counsellor requires and the extent to which a supervisor is in a position to meet those needs.
- The supervisory contract is essentially a mutually agreed statement incorporating the aims and objectives of the supervisory endeavour.
- Three models of supervision relevant to the supervision of counsellors in primary health care are advanced. Practice dilemmas and tensions inherent in all three models are explored.
- Supervisors need to clarify the level of responsibility they have with regard to the counsellor's work and the setting in which the counsellor is undertaking that work.
- A distinction is made between supervision and consultation.

References

Anderson, H. and Swim, S. (1995) 'Supervision as collaborative conversation: The voices of supervisor and supervisee', *Journal of Systemic Therapies*, 14(2): 1–13.

Bond, T. (1996) 'Counselling-supervision – ethical issues', in S. Palmer, S. Dainow and P. Milner (eds), *Counselling. The BAC Counselling Reader*. London: Sage. pp. 430–9.

Carroll, M. (1994) 'The generic tasks of supervision: an analysis of supervisee expectations, supervisor interviews and supervisory audio-taped sessions'. PhD thesis, University of Guildford.

Carroll, M. (1996) *Counselling Supervision: Theory, Skills and Practice*. London: Cassell.

Smith, D.L. (1996) 'The communicative approach to supervision', in S. Palmer, S. Dainow and P. Milner (eds), *Counselling. The BAC Counselling Reader*. London: Sage. pp. 426–9.

Triantafillou, N. (1997) 'A solution-focused approach to mental health supervision', *Journal of Systemic Therapies*, 16(4): 305–28.

Williams, D.I. (1996) 'Supervision: a new word is desperately needed', in S. Palmer, S. Dainow and P. Milner (eds), *Counselling. The BAC Counselling Reader*. London: Sage. pp. 440–6.

CHAPTER 14

EVALUATING COUNSELLING IN PRIMARY HEALTH CARE

Peter du Plessis and Robert Bor

Many counsellors have mixed views about undertaking a systematic evaluation of their service. That may be because they lack confidence or skills in undertaking an audit or research, or feel annoyed at having to obtain feedback from counselling service users by using methods that appear to fail to tap into what really happens in counselling. It may also be because of demands on their time which leave little space to conduct an audit. Yet, with appropriate knowledge and a positive approach, few aspects of counselling practice could be as rewarding as an evaluation that leads to an objective measure which demonstrates good and effective counselling practice. Evaluation of counselling practice is also increasingly requested by both practice managers and general practitioners in an era of evidence-based practice.

We are now routinely asked to justify counselling in terms of cost and outcome. Questions frequently asked of us relate to what counselling is, what it does, who should do it, how much it costs, whether it works and for how long it should go on (Booth et al., 1997). Rather than viewing evaluation as an external task imposed on the counsellor, we hope that the ideas in this chapter will encourage counsellors proactively to set up their own evaluation projects which could then be used to justify and support their service, and the practice of counselling as a whole (Tolley and Rowlands, 1995). Before looking at how to proceed with evaluating counselling in primary health care, we first examine some of the deterrents that may be experienced when conducting service outcome and evaluation research.

Factors that may deter counsellors from evaluating their practice

There are several reasons why counsellors working in primary health care settings may be disinclined to initiate an evaluation of the counselling service. An emphasis in our training on the *practice* of counselling may make it seem irrelevant to some counsellors to evaluate what they do. It is often viewed as potentially intrusive to counselling to conduct an evaluation while simultaneously developing a therapeutic relationship with a patient (McLeod, 1994). Some counsellors may have received little or no training in audit and particularly in using quantitative research methods. Furthermore, a knowledge of single case ($n = 1$) experimental design, traditionally used in medicine or in behavioural psychology, requires extensive training. Where larger samples or case loads are involved, a knowledge of how to analyse and interpret data is required (Barlow and Hersen, 1994). Research can also be lonely for the counsellor especially where there is minimal collaboration with other colleagues. Lastly, one cannot ignore the fact that some of the negative findings from a primary health care counselling service evaluation may be unwelcome for the counsellor. Counsellors may therefore choose to avoid research and focus instead on the therapeutic process.

Compelling reasons for evaluating a counselling service

The internal market, increasing competition and the need to ration some health services may threaten counselling services in primary health care. Furthermore, by avoiding a systematic study of primary care counselling, the inadequacies of practice may be maintained. Any evaluation project can take time away from counselling activity. In busy counselling settings this may prove problematic as the counsellor struggles to maintain a balance between carrying out the evaluation and providing a cost-effective counselling service. A service evaluation which does not directly address the quality of counselling but instead focuses on activity may prove personally unrewarding for the counsellor.

Counsellors working in primary health care should evaluate their service for two reasons. First, increasingly *fund holders demand this*. As primary health care services change and the demand on finite resources increases, there is a need to justify the service to funders. It is unlikely that new or extended contracts for a counselling service will be agreed in the absence of evidence supporting the need for that service. The systematic gathering and evaluation of data makes it easier to make a case for funding. There are also situations where different health services compete for the same funds, and those services which offer a more rigorous assessment of their service are more likely to increase their share of available funds. This could have implications for the continued funding of counselling services in primary health care.

Secondly, it is *good counselling practice*. As professionals, it is good practice to reflect on how our service grows and develops. Evaluating our counselling service has some educational value because our practice appears different when we look at it systematically and more objectively. Evaluation in counselling also helps to challenge the perception that counselling is a 'soft' activity carried out by 'do-gooders' who do not have a head for figures and do not understand qualitative research methods. Counselling research can also help to challenge the mystique of what happens behind the closed door of the counselling room by clarifying the role, task and activity of counsellors. Data collected in the course of an evaluation can also provide material for publication in professional journals, particularly in new areas and specialties of counselling. It is noteworthy that almost every paper evaluating primary care counselling published in peer review journals over the past 10 years was authored by medically qualified doctors rather than by counsellors.

Publication leads to wider exposure of the profession and may be a selling point for a service to fellow professionals, management and those who fund the service. Examples of recent publications of health service based counselling services are listed in Table 14.1 and readers may want to examine the scope and methods of these counselling service evaluations in order to inform their own ideas and practice.

Evaluation can assist in the planning and development of a counselling service. It may also assist the counsellor in putting a case for additional funding to provide a higher quality counselling service. Lastly, the act of developing a small research project could improve collaboration between the counsellor and other colleagues in the practice who take a role in the project.

Types of evaluation questions in a primary health care counselling service

When evaluating a counselling service, both *quantitative* (aspects of the practice that can be measured in numbers or size) and *qualitative* (aspects that relate to quality) information are of value. A combination of the two provides the most comprehensive picture of the counselling service. It is important to note that service related research takes place in a counselling setting, and not under laboratory or experimental conditions, and therefore our methods have to be adapted accordingly. The study may

Table 14.1 Counselling and service use activity: examples of published research

Du Plessis P., Bor R., Slack D., Swash E. and Cobell D. (1995) 'Assessment of HIV counselling and social care services in a London hospital', *British Journal of Guidance and Counselling*, 23: 45–51.

Bor, R., Lipman, M., Elford, J., Murray, D., Miller, R., Griffiths, P., Janossy, G. and Johnson, M. (1994) 'HIV seroprevalence in a London same day testing clinic', *AIDS*, 8: 697–700.

Bor, R., Elford, J., Murray, D., Salt, H., Tilling, J., Miller, R. and Johnson, M. (1992) 'Patient satisfaction with HIV social care services at a London teaching hospital: an evaluation', *Genitourinary Medicine*, 68: 382–5.

Bor, R., Elford, J., Richey, L., Murray, D., Salt, H., Tilling, J., Miller, R. and Johnson, M. (1992) 'Increasing workload of an HIV/AIDS counselling service in a London teaching hospital', *International Journal of STD and AIDS*, 3: 125–7.

Bor, R., Elford, J., Miller, R. and Salt, H. (1991) 'Update of activity in a district AIDS counselling service: 1988–1990', *Genitourinary Medicine*, 67: 235–8.

Squire, B., Elford, J., Bor, R. et al. (1991) 'Open access clinic providing HIV-1 antibody results on the day of testing: the first twelve months', *British Medical Journal*, 302: 1383–6.

Bor, R., Miller, R. and Salt, H. (1991) 'Uptake of HIV testing following counselling', *Sexual and Marital Therapy*, 6: 25–8.

Bor, R., Elford, J., Perry, L., Salt, H., Miller, R. and Johnson, M. (1990) 'New initiative in a district AIDS counselling unit, 1988–89', *International Journal of STD and AIDS*, 1 (2): 110–13.

Bor, R., Elford, J., Perry, L. and Miller, R. (1989) 'The workload of a new district AIDS counselling unit, April 1987–March 1988', *Genitourinary Medicine*, 65: 113–16.

be retrospective or prospective. The data can be used to give a 'slice of action' or to examine trends over time. The emphasis is on frequencies and therefore the need for complex statistics is largely eliminated. It is helpful to identify which aspects of the survey or study are best answered by qualitative and quantitative methods.

Evaluating case load

In evaluating case load we look at those factors which are more closely and directly related to the patient.

Routine information

Routine information refers to the minimum data or information that counsellors need to collect in order to describe activity. It is advisable to agree the criteria for routine information at an early stage with managers and fund holders, and gather the information as part of day-to-day practice. Most counselling services are required to produce some information about patients who use the service. The requirement is usually about *how* the service is being used and relates to indicators of workload, such as demographic details, the nature of the problems patients present with and the frequency of sessions. This information is mainly quantitative. It may also include information about the time between referral and first appointment, uptake rate of first appointment, total number of sessions offered over a fixed period of time, average number of sessions offered to individual patients, and number of sessions not attended or cancelled.

Non-routine evaluation projects

Certain aspects of a counselling practice do not require on-going evaluation. Instead, a one-off, cross-sectional study should suffice. Non-routine projects of this kind usually arise from:

1   Questions about trends that are observed in a service and for which more systematic information is required to answer *why* the trend appears to exist at a particular time.
2   The need to ensure that a particular agreed standard of practice is maintained. For example, an audit of patient notes to assess whether the agreed level of communication with referrers is maintained could be undertaken.
3   A requirement to check whether changes and recommendations made on the basis of previous evaluation projects have been maintained.

Other non-routine evaluation projects may seek to explore how two or more aspects of a counselling service relate to one another. For example, a counsellor may want to establish why patients fail to attend sessions. The study could examine a number of factors relating to attendance, including some of the following:

- Time waited for the first appointment.
- Who referred the patient.
- Gender of the counsellor.
- The choice of therapeutic approaches offered.

Non-routine evaluations could also explore qualitative aspects of the service. An example would be to study the relationship between the referrer's reason for referring a patient and that patient's own definition of their problem. This may reflect the level of understanding that the particular referrer has of the counselling service.

Evaluating counselling service issues

The evaluation of service issues refers to the *effectiveness* of a service and mainly relates to administrative and practical concerns. These may include a measure of patient satisfaction of administrative issues such as:

- The actual *time waited* for an initial appointment since the referral was made: Are the criteria for waiting times fulfilled? Do the patients feel they were given sufficient information about the reason for the delay in being seen?
- *Reception staff* and *the waiting area*: Are patients welcomed by staff when arriving for an appointment? Is the waiting room comfortable? Is it adequately heated? Do patients feel that messages left for the counsellor are passed on and are their calls returned?
- *Location*: Were there adequate directions provided by the counselling service?
- *Counsellor characteristics*: Did the patient feel comfortable with the counsellor allocated? Was the counsellor punctual?

Many practical and administrative aspects of the counselling can be studied, but to investigate too many at the same time can be confusing and unnecessary. It is therefore prudent to list the essential factors that need to be evaluated and then rotate these so that only one or two aspects are looked at in a particular study.

The following are examples of studies that examine the practical aspects of the service.

Access to service

Most counselling services are required to have a fair and equitable access. A service may appear to have fair access, but experience has shown that disadvantaged and minority groups are seldom represented in the same proportion to the catchment area population (McPherson and Murphy, 1997). Unequal access may be as a result of a service not being appropriately advertised. For example, promotional literature may assume that all patients can read and understand English. Unequal access may also result from selection bias in the mind of the referrer. For example, patients with relationship problems may be referred directly by their GP to outside agencies because the GP is unfamiliar with the counsellor's proficiency as a marital or family therapist.

Effectiveness of the service as viewed by referrers

An important concern when setting up a study of referrers' views is how the counselling service can be improved or changed from their perspective without compromising the standards and ethics of general counselling. Most general practices are a hub of activity and feedback about both practical and therapeutic issues is often neglected. An evaluation of the methods and frequency of communication between colleagues, the structure of counselling referral forms and the nature of confidentiality may shed light on what areas of the practice might be improved.

Evaluating referral trends

Evaluating referral trends could help to clarify the extent to which different referrers' knowledge of counselling and their perceptions of what happens in sessions affect referral rates. A study may examine the range of psychological problems that a particular referrer identifies and how these relate to the profile of those referred in terms of gender, race and social background. Findings could explain how gender, race and age influence the way that some GPs interpret a patient's psychological symptoms. Information could also be gathered on what referrers tell their patients about the counselling service and process, if anything at all.

Patient satisfaction

Patient satisfaction surveys are probably the most difficult to conduct. The Griffiths Report (Griffiths, 1983) recommended obtaining service users' opinions to monitor professional standards and this was subsequently endorsed by the White Paper *Working for Patients* (Department of Health, 1989). Some would argue that it introduces the patient's subjective response to counselling, which may be difficult to measure or compare. Patients' answers are often influenced by a sense of loyalty, duty and/or appreciation of their carer (Jenkins and Jakes, 1991). Some attempts to measure patient satisfaction have therefore been of dubious validity (Corrie, 1996). Although NHS patient satisfaction evaluations consistently seem to demonstrate high levels of satisfaction, averaging between 75% and 80%, patients are prone to complain about the perceived lack of involvement in establishing goals for counselling, lack of choice of treatments received and the time delay between the referral and initial appointment (Brant, 1992). It is essential to include items about those aspects of the service that patients feel could be improved. Valuable opportunities may be lost if patients feel that their opinions and experiences are not sought and acted upon. It is important to consider a range of methodologies when designing a patient satisfaction evaluation. There should also be a sensitivity to a patient group's ability to express themselves, their level of understanding and the diverse interpretations of what a positive outcome is.

Although all these issues are important to consider when preparing a patient satisfaction study, the questionnaire in Figure 14.1 illustrates a very basic evaluation instrument that can be used. The sections of the questionnaire are as follows:

A   Biographical information. This section solicits information on the profile of the patient.
B   Referral process. The answers to these questions provide information about the referral procedures.
C   Practical issues. This section provides information about the counselling environment and reception staff. Questions should be limited to those aspects which can be changed or improved.
D   Process of treatment. This provides information about the subjective experience of the counselling process.
E   Outcome. Information gathered reflects the subjective impression of whether the patient felt helped by the course of counselling.
F   Overall impression. This provides an opportunity for the patient to give feedback about the service and experience without being confined to leading questions.

Remember to keep the questionnaire reasonably short. It is off-putting to the patient to have to complete a long survey. Also ensure that it is checked for spelling, accuracy and readability before giving it to patients to complete.

Assessing the value of counselling

An area of evaluation that counsellors sometimes avoid is that of assessing the effectiveness of their therapeutic work. The questions that counsellors need to be asked are about outcome: *Who* should judge the outcome, *when* in the therapeutic process should it take place and *what*

Figure 14.1   Patient satisfaction questionnaire

What do you think of the counselling service?

The counselling service is committed to providing the best possible service. Sometimes we fall short of our aim. We would like your honest impressions of the quality of service you receive. We would like to take your opinions into account for the future planning of the counselling service.

A. Referral Process

✔ Were you aware that you had been referred to the counselling service?

YES	NO

✔ Did you receive any information about the service from the person who referred you?

YES	NO

✔ If YES, do you feel the information was sufficient?

Very Sufficient	Sufficient	Insufficient	Very Insufficient

✔ Was the time between when you were referred to when you had your first appointment satisfactory?

Very Satisfied	Satisfied	Dissatisfied	Very Dissatisfied

B. Practical Issues

✎ Were you satisfied with the distance from your home to the location where you were seen?

Very Satisfied	Satisfied	Dissatisfied	Very Dissatisfied

✔ How satisfied were you with the waiting area?

Very Satisfied	Satisfied	Dissatisfied	Very Dissatisfied

✔ Did you feel satisfied with the reception when you arrived for your appointments?

Very Satisfied	Satisfied	Dissatisfied	Very Dissatisfied

✔ How satisfied were you with the counselling room you were seen in?

Very Satisfied	Satisfied	Dissatisfied	Very Dissatisfied

✔ Were you offered appointments at convenient times?

Very Convenient	Convenient	Inconvenient	Very Inconvenient

C. Process of Treatment

✔ Did you feel UNDERSTOOD by the Counsellor?

Very Understood	Understood	Not Understood	Misunderstood

✔ Did you feel RESPECTED by the Counsellor?

Very Respected	Respected	Disrespected	Very Disrespected

✔ Do you feel that the counselling you received was useful?

Very Useful	Useful	Not Useful	Unhelpful or Wrong

✔ Were you satisfied with the DURATION or LENGTH of the counselling?

Very Satisfied	Satisfied	Dissatisfied	Very Dissatisfied

D. Outcomes

✔ Has counselling helped you deal with the problem that led to your referral?

Very Helpful	Helpful	Unhelpful	Very Unhelpful

✔ Has the problem improved?

Yes	No	Slightly	Don't know

✎ In the space below please write something about how you feel the problem has improved, stayed the same or worsened and what part counselling has played in that. Add any other comments.

_____

_____

_____

_____

E. Overall Satisfaction

✎ Overall, how satisfied are you with the QUALITY OF SERVICE you received from the Counselling service. Circle a number between *100 (High Quality)* and *0 (Low Quality)* to indicate your level of satisfaction.

HIGH QUALITY   **LOW QUALITY**

100 |-|-|-| 90 |-|-|-| 80 |-|-|-| 70 |-|-|-| 60 |-|-|-| 50 |-|-|-| 40 |-|-|-| 30 |-|-|-| 20 |-|-|-| 10 |-|-|-| 0

Thank you for taking the time to share your views

are the criteria for high standards of counselling work? The following questions may help in preparing this type of evaluation:

- Should the counsellor, the carer or the patient judge the outcome and standard of counselling?
- Should the evaluation take place during the counselling process, at discharge or at follow-up?
- Should the goals that are set in the counselling sessions be used to assess the standard of counselling, and if so, do the counsellor and patient need to agree on the goal?

It is desirable to link outcome of counselling to factors such as the presenting problem and the length of counselling involvement (Hewson, 1994). It is also helpful to go back to the main evaluation question from time to time when deciding which of these factors should be included and which ones excluded in a particular project. The outcome of counselling needs to be studied in relation to a broad range of measures in order to fully assess the impact (McLeod, 1995). Measures such as psychological distress, social functioning and the impact of counselling on a patient's use of services and medication are suggested. Noting what other researchers have done and incorporating their ideas into your study can help to save valuable time (see Table 14.2).

A method of measuring outcome is through the Goal Attainment Scale (GAS), used by Kiresuk and Choate (1994) and more recently by Booth et al. (1997). In contrast to standardized scales which assess patients on the same dimensions, the GAS allows change in individual patients to be measured in relation to specific symptoms or problems that are targeted in the intervention. The application of this in general practice counselling clearly illustrates the value of this approach. Goal-setting is an individual measure, a way of making the expectations of individual patients more explicit, which then allows for qualitative comparisons as opposed to quantitative measures between individuals on the same scale. It further allows for the individual perspective and requirements of the patient to be incorporated into the study. Simply but concisely: before counselling the patient is asked 'What do you want?' and after the counselling, 'Did you get it?' (Booth et al., 1997).

Steps in setting up an evaluation of counselling in primary health care

It is important to take charge of the evaluation process at an early stage to avoid the danger of other stake holders imposing their own questions

Table 14.2 Examples of studies and papers on patient satisfaction and outcome

Publication	Themes of evaluation and outcome
Booth et al. (1997) 'Process and outcome of counselling in general practice', *Clinical Psychology Forum*, 101: 32–40	Questionnaires Evaluating: • GP consultations • Referrals to other mental health services • Quality of life • Problem resolution • Goal attainment • Goal setting
Clarke et al. (1994) 'The development of an outcome audit programme for five therapy professions: evaluating the evaluators', *Clinical Psychology Forum*, 70: 26–31	• Interviews • Facilitating the therapist-led audit • Evaluating outcome audit programme • Future of audit projects
Halstead, J. (1996) 'Psychotherapy outcome audit: what is not going on?' *Clinical Psychology Forum*, 90: 5–7	• Fear of not detecting change • Post-therapy measures • Equation of outcome audit with power • Fear that outcome will show psychotherapy to be ineffective • Problems of dissemination
Neilson, J. (1994) 'Therapist–patient concordance on therapy process and outcome and its implications for service evaluation', *Clinical Psychology Forum*, 73: 5–7	• Therapist/patient evaluations • Helpful versus unhelpful aspects of therapy • Patient satisfaction • Different perspectives, values and degrees of importance attached to events occurring in therapy

and emphasis on the research. This could reflect what is meaningful for them rather than address what is appropriate for the counsellor. The following sequence of steps could be followed in setting up and undertaking research.

Step 1   Establish what *information* is needed to increase your knowledge of the counselling practice that would confirm certain aspects of the practice or that may lead to changes.

Step 2   Establish what *questions* need to be answered. Decide whether these questions could be broken up into smaller or less complicated questions. Take care not to ask too many questions; further aspects could be studied at a later stage.

Step 3   Explore *further ideas* by reading through published literature for similar and related studies. This may also be instructive in relation to methods used. Valuable time can be saved by using or modifying existing measures. Remember always to acknowledge the original author of a questionnaire. Many registered and standardized published questionnaires can only be used if the counsellor is registered with the relevant test publishing company.

Step 4   *Methods*. Decide which existing measures could be used to answer the evaluation questions. Questionnaires such as the Beck Anxiety Inventory (BAI), Beck Depression Inventory (BDI), Beck Hopelessness Scale (BHS) and the General Health Questionnaire (GHQ) are some standardized questionnaires that are used in primary care settings, either on their own or in

Table 14.3 Examples of existing instruments for use in primary health care evaluations

Measure	What it does
Beck Anxiety Inventory (BAI)	Measures the severity of anxiety. It evaluates both the physiological and cognitive symptoms of anxiety. 21 items, takes 5–10 minutes to complete
Beck Depression Inventory (BDI)	Designed to assess the severity of depression. Also used as a screening instrument for detecting depressive symptoms. 21 items, takes 5–10 minutes to complete
Beck Hopelessness Scale (BHS)	Measures the extent of negative attitudes about the future (pessimism), loss of motivation and expectation. 20 items, takes 10 minutes to complete
Therapy Evaluation Questionnaire (TEQ) (developed from the Session Evaluation Questionnaire, Stiles, 1980)	Assesses whether therapy is valuable/worthless on a 7-point scale
Helpful Aspects of Therapy Questionnaire (Neilson, 1994)	17 items, helpful or unhelpful aspects of therapy
General Health Questionnaire (GHQ)	Designed to be a self-administered screening test aimed at detecting psychiatric disorders, particularly psychological components of ill health
The Cross Cultural Inventory Scale – Revised (CCI–R)	Assesses counsellor's ability to work effectively with diverse racial/ethnic groups. Three areas are assessed: • cultural awareness and beliefs • cultural knowledge • cross-cultural skills
Goal Attainment Scale (GAS) (Booth et al., 1997)	Assists patients in establishing 1 to 3 goals, and rating each goal

Although most tests can be administered under supervision, tests should only be interpreted by professionals with appropriate clinical training and experience according to the guidelines of the registering and issuing bodies.

combination with your own locally developed questionnaire (see Table 14.3). If the standardized questionnaires do not answer all the questions, develop your own questionnaire which is specific to the questions and your particular practice. Ideally, questionnaires should be standardized. Ask an experienced researcher to help you with this. Make sure that a small sample of clients are used to pilot your questionnaire so that obvious mistakes and ambiguities can be eliminated.

Step 5   Write up a *preliminary* proposal to help provide a structure and procedure for carrying out the study. This also provides evidence that the counsellor will endeavour to approach the task systematically and has anticipated stages and problems involved in the process of evaluation.

Step 6   Negotiate and encourage *participation* with colleagues in the practice, prior to and during the planning of the study. The discussions should include the use of clinic and counselling facilities, equipment, availability and use of a database or files and time allocation for the study. It is essential to first consult with managers to gain access to non-routine clinic facilities and patient records, and to involve colleagues at an early stage of the evaluation process so that their ideas can be taken into account. This may also reduce resistance to a project. It is also important to ask other colleagues in the practice whether they want to include any questions. Remember to deal with issues of authorship from the outset if a paper is likely to be produced. Failure to do so can contaminate relationships with professional colleagues and lead to an unwillingness or resistance to participate in future projects.

Step 7   Now write up the *final proposal*, taking into account what you have gained in the previous steps. The following headings could be used in writing up the evaluation proposal:

* Background to the proposal.
* The research questions.
* Sampling.
* Methods: what measuring tools will be used to gather information?
* Analysis of information: this section should include how the information will be analysed, by whom and which statistical methods will be used.
* Feedback methods: this may include plans for publication.

Step 8   *Sampling.* It is important to decide what criteria will be used to select participants in the evaluation. This is usually based on what will best answer the questions that are of interest to the counsellor. You will need to decide whether all patients attending the practice over a particular time period will be approached or whether the questionnaire will be given to a sample of those attending.

Step 9   *Gathering data.* Once everyone has been consulted and the study has the support of all the relevant people, data collection can begin. Different methods of data gathering may be used, each ideally chosen to suit the specific project. For example, structured interviews, semi-structured interviews or question-naires are typically used. Each has its advantages and dis-advantages (see Barker et al., 1994). Data can, of course, also be collected from a number of different sources. Some of this can be done without the direct involvement of patients and may entail looking at general practice patient records, counselling service files or consulting a patient database. Structured ques-tionnaires can also be sent to previous clinic attendees, although this may raise questions about protocol and ethics if those who have been discharged are contacted without being forewarned at the time of attending the counselling service.

Step 10   *Analysis of the data.* Consider the cost of data collection, both in relation to time and resources. It may be more cost-effective for administrative staff to add up lists of numbers (frequencies) manually, whilst the counsellor concentrates more on data and the analyses.

Step 11   *Feedback* to patients and colleagues. An important part of a study is concise and clear feedback to service users and colleagues. Patient feedback could be in the form of a poster in the waiting room or a copy of a shortened version of the full report. For GPs, both a written report and short presentation may be of value. Oral presentations facilitate discussion about the meaning and outcomes of the evaluation and consequent action plans.

Conclusion

Service-related research is a means of reflecting on the whole thera-peutic process while at the same time satisfying the needs of pur-chasers, patients and referrers. It also opens up possibilities for collaborative research with colleagues. Counsellors working in primary care settings are under increasing pressure to respond to demands for evidence-based practice. Most counsellors share the view that the efficacy of counselling cannot be evaluated in a reductionistic way, similar to the double-blind placebo-controlled trials carried out in medicine. To dismiss studies of counselling activity and process, however, is both naive and self-defeating. Indeed, the development of primary care based counselling depends on research. Numerous studies are now under way in the United Kingdom, the results of which will help us to understand what happens in primary care counselling and what makes it effective. Outcome research conducted across a range of settings as well as more modest counsellor-led in-house audit initiatives can both add to our understanding of these issues. This chapter serves to introduce counsellors to service-related research, and to the pleasures (and challenges) associated with this.

References

Barker, C., Pistrang, N. and Elliot, R. (1994) *Research Methods in Clinical and Counselling Psychology.* Chichester: John Wiley.

Barlow, D. and Hersen, M. (1994) *Single Case Experimental Design.* New York: Pergamon.

Booth, H., Goodwin, I., Newnes, C. and Dawson, O. (1997) 'Process and outcome of counselling in general practice', *Clinical Psychology Forum*, 101: 32–40.

Brant, S. (1992) 'Hearing the patient's story', *International Journal of Health Care Quality Assurance*, 5: 5–7.

Clarke, N., Elliott, S., Hodgson, C. and Robbins, S. (1994) 'The development of an outcome audit programme for five therapy professions. Evaluating the evaluators', *Clinical Psychology Forum*, 70: 26–31.

Corrie, S. (1996) 'An audit of patient satisfaction within a District psychology service: analysis, valuation and recommendations for future developments', *Psychology Research*, 6: 2–23.

Department of Health (1989) *Working for Patients.* London: HMSO.

Griffiths, R. (1983) *NHS Management Enquiry (The Griffiths Report).* London: HMSO.

Halstead, J. (1996) 'Psychotherapy outcome audit: what is not going on?', *Clinical Psychology Journal*, 90: 5–7.

Hewson, S. (1994) 'Clinicians' role in measuring outcomes', *Clinical Psychology Forum*, 74: 31–2.

Jenkins, K. and Jakes, S. (1991) 'Evaluation and quality assurance by telephone in a district psychology department', *Clinical Psychology Forum*, 36: 34–6.

Kiresuk, T.J. and Choate, R.O. (1994) 'Applications of goal attainment scaling', in T.J. Kiresuk, A. Smith and J.E. Cardillo (eds), *Goal Attainment Scaling: Applications, Theory and Measurement.* Hillsdale, NJ: Lawrence Erlbaum.

McLeod, J. (1994) *Doing Counselling Research.* London: Sage.

McLeod, J. (1995) 'Evaluating the effectiveness of counselling: what we don't know', *Changes: an International Journal of Psychology and Psychotherapy*, 13 (3): 192–200.

McPherson, F.M. and Murphy, S. (1997) 'Deprivation and health: an audit of equity of access to a clinical psychology service', *Clinical Psychology Forum*, 104: 16–18.

Neilson, J. (1994) 'Therapist–patient concordance on therapy process and outcome and its implications for service evaluation', *Clinical Psychology Forum*, 73: 5–7.

Stiles, W.B. (1980) 'Measurement of the impact of psychotherapy session', *Journal of Consulting and Clinical Psychology*, 48 (2): 176–85.

Tolley, K. and Rowlands, N. (1995) *Evaluating the Cost-Effectiveness of Counselling in Health Care.* London: Routledge.

INDEX

Page numbers in italics refer to figures and forms, those in bold print indicate major references.